Working with People

WORKING WITH PEOPLE

Clinical Uses of Personal Construct Psychology

Edited by
GAVIN DUNNETT

Consultant Psychiatrist
The Redcliffe
Centre for Community Psychiatry
Wellingborough

ROUTLEDGE
London and New York

First published in 1988 by
Routledge
11 New Fetter Lane, London EC4P 4EE

Published in the USA by
Routledge, in association with
Routledge, Chapman & Hall Inc.
29 West 35th Street, New York, NY 10001

Set in 10/12pt Palatino
by Input Typesetting Ltd
and printed in Great Britain
by T. J. Press (Padstow) Ltd,
Padstow, Cornwall

Library of Congress Cataloging in Publication Data

Working with people.

   Bibliography: p.
   Includes index.
   1. Clinical psychology.   2. Personal construct
theory.   I. Dunnett, Gavin.   [DNLM: 1. Psychology,
Clinical.   2. Psychotherapy.   WM 420 W926]
RC467.W67   1988   158'.3   87–26398

British Library CIP Data also available
ISBN 0–415–00262–1 (c)
       0–415–00263–X (p)

Contents

Preface

Of many books already published relating to Personal Construct Psychology, none have started from the perspective of examining how PCP is used in different clinical disciplines. The feeling that this was a major gap in the literature crystallised during the sixth International Congress on Personal Construct Psychology held in Cambridge in 1985. Many people to whom I spoke then felt that such an approach would be valuable and refreshing especially to those who had heard of PCP but had neither studied it for itself, nor knew anyone personally who had used it extensively themselves.

Each of the contributors to the book is, or has been recently, an active practitioner in the discipline about which they have written. Each was asked to write clearly with a minimum of jargon to explain how *they* used PCP. They were specifically asked not to be prescriptive, but to write from their personal experience and knowledge. In that sense, there are no pretensions that this is a traditional 'academic' book where authors as individuals are rigorously excluded. Rather to the contrary, it was (and remains) my belief that people trying to see how to use PCP themselves would find other people's personal experience valuable, not to tell them how to use it, but how it can and has been used.

If this book encourages interest in PCP and stimulates new ways of using it beyond those described in the ensuing pages, then it may have succeeded in its intention. If nothing else, I believe it reveals the breadth and scope of activities across a group of interconnected disciplines spawned by Personal Construct Psychology. As such it is an encouraging demonstration of the effectiveness of this approach in causing questions to be asked and innovative solutions essayed.

Gavin Dunnett
Kettering, 1987

Acknowledgments

I would like to offer thanks to David Alexander, Miller Mair and Oscar Hill for their influence and encouragement over the years to further my involvement with Personal Construct Psychology; to the late Don Bannister for his unfailing support and attitude of 'why not?' to my endeavours; and to Fay Fransella for the structure and discipline to achieve some of them. I would particularly like to thank Peggy Dalton for her comments and advice, Wendy Buckby for her invaluable and uncomplaining secretarial assistance, and Mike Gill for putting up with it all.

List of contributors

HILDA BROWNING, Harpenden, Herts, England

PETER CUMMINS, Bexley District Psychology Service, Bexley Hospital, Kent, England

PEGGY DALTON, Centre for Personal Construct Psychology, 132 Warwick Road, London SW1V 4JD, England

GAVIN DUNNETT, Redcliffe Centre for Community Psychiatry, Hatton Park Road, Wellingborough, Northants NN8 3AH, England

STEPHANIE HARTER, Department of Psychology, Memphis State University, Memphis, TN 38152, USA

HELEN JONES, York, England

VINCENT KENNY, Institute of Constructivist Psychotherapy, 21 Summerhill, Dun Laoghaire, Dublin, Eire

SUE LLEWELYN, Department of Psychology, University of Nottingham, University Park, Nottingham NG7 2RD, England

BOB NEIMEYER, Department of Psychology, Memphis State University, Memphis, TN 38152, USA

TOM RAVENETTE, London Borough of Newham, Education Offices, 379–383 High Street, Stratford E15 4RD, England

GINA SELBY, Ashford, Kent, England

DAVID WINTER, Napsbury Hospital, London Colney, Nr St Albans, Herts AL2 1AA, England

1 · Myths, methods and technique

GAVIN DUNNETT

There is no doubt that in any book on the practical uses of a particular approach the question of what techniques are used and how has to be addressed. Increasingly, different theories are identified by their techniques, rather like a signature, often leading to one or both of two equally unwished for consequences. Either the technique takes on a life of its own, increasingly divorced from the theory which gave it birth, or a particular technique is seen as being a sine qua non of a specific theoretical approach. The former problem leads to work being done in the field out of context with the theoretical underpinning of the subject, a process which almost inevitably leads to sloppy research at best or disaster at worst. Most people would accept that it is stupid to meddle with your house wiring without knowing something about how electricity works – simply attaching wires and screwing up plugs is not enough. The *context* in which the wire attaching and plug screwing is taking place is just as important in getting the job done correctly as the practical techniques inherent in it. The second problem leads to a different difficulty. Where a particular technique is seen as *always* having to be employed when working with a particular model, and vice versa incidentally, it produces a narrowness of vision and action on one hand, and a tendency to use the techniques automatically without proper thought on the other. Neither result seems helpful in the vastly varied field of working with people.

This may seem a long-winded introduction to a chapter on techniques used in PCP but I hope the reason for it will become evident. Part of the reason lies in the hope that you will realise that the Psychology of Personal Constructs is not a technique-based approach. In other words, the theory was not devised to make sense of a technique, rather the techniques that have emerged have been developed as a result of using the theory. And given that that is the case, the natural next step is to say clearly that the techniques that have been developed *so far* are precisely only that. Many more ways of using the theory in practice await discovery by individuals or groups wrestling with the problems facing them, and prepared to elaborate new approaches rather than always rely on what has gone before. Indeed the theme of this book is to show you how various authors have elaborated techniques in their respective fields in order to encourage you to do the same.

The repeatedly asked question: What do you *do* when using PCP? has no single answer, and indeed the question's emphasis is almost always in the wrong place. Hopefully this book answers the question for ten people: What do *you* do when using PCP? After all, where the approach insists on the individual unique!y *personal* approach for the patient/client/whatever; and claims to apply to the psychological processes of the therapist/counsellor as much as to the patient/clients, then it has to be accepted that the therapist/counsellor will also have an individual uniquely personal approach, similar perhaps to others to a greater or lesser extent, but different also. There is thus no right way to use PCP nor a wrong way. There are of course ways which will help the client more than others, and these are the ones which hopefully will be chosen. But different ways may work for different clients in the hands of different workers. There is no law that says that an individual is only working in a PCP way when using technique X or one that says if using technique Y he cannot possibly be working in a PCP way.

Now this is not as confusing as it sounds, nor is it a licence to do whatever you want and ignore the consequences. PCP provides the *context* in which the work with people is carried out. That context has characteristics of its own which differ from other contexts, and which therefore encourages some kinds of approach rather than others.

It is therefore important to look at the characteristics of that context before embarking on descriptions of some of the techniques you will come across in the following pages. There are three areas that map out the context: the philosophy of constructive alternativism, reflexivity and the process of construing.

It may seem a little daunting to begin with a philosophy, particularly when its name is such a mouthful. It is also not the intention to begin a philosophical debate here – that has been done and continues else-where. As Kelly (1955) writes in his opening paragraph, 'Constructive alternativism not only underlines our theory, but it is also an explicit and recurrent theme throughout our later discussion of psychotherapeutic techniques.'

Essentially what CA states is that although there is a 'real' world, each one of us makes sense of it in our own unique, individual, *personal* way. There is, therefore, an infinity of different ways of making sense of the same reality, none of them any more right or wrong than anyone else's. As Kelly wrote (1955, p. 15), 'all our present interpretations of the universe are subject to revision or replacement' and he continues 'there are always some alternative constructions available to choose among in dealing with the world. No one needs to paint himself into a corner; no one needs to be the victim of his biography.' Thus the philosophy allows us to say that there are *always* alternative ways of construing our situation or that around us. We may choose not to see them; or not to act upon them when we do, but that does not prevent the alternatives being around, to be explored, discovered and experimented with. It is an essentially hopeful and liberating philosophy which encourages individuals to consider change not just possible but advisable. The way they go about making sense of their worlds is what the theory is about, and the way others can see what sense an individual makes of his/her world, and how to help him/her change is what the techniques are about.

The second item on the contextual map is reflexivity. This is explored in much more depth in the following chapter 'Working with Oneself' but it needs at least a mention here. The notion of reflexivity means that the philosophy of constructive alternativism, the theory of personal constructs, the psychological processes described and the techniques used for exploration and to assist change apply just as much to you or me as to our clients, patients or anybody else. The processes which produce your actions, thoughts and emotions produce everybody else's also. The methods are the same; it's how they are used, and the unique *personal* content that makes people different. Thus the psychology of personal constructs is not about illness, or disorder, or distress; or, for that matter, about the traditional separate psychological trilogy of cognition, conation and emotion. It is about how individuals on a personal basis function psychologically as individuals. Comprehensively. It is as simple, and as complex, as that.

So now we have an underlying philosophy allowing and promoting change leading to a theory that each individual human being operates psychologically by using similar methods. The next questions clearly are what are the methods, and how do people use them differently and gain their own personal interpretation of the world. This huge chunk is what I called earlier the process of construing. To construe is defined in the *Shorter Oxford English Dictionary* as, *inter alia*, 'to interpret, put a construction on (actions, things or persons)'. This is what the theory describes. However, Kelly outlines his theory very specifically, precisely and at length; beginning with a Fundamental Postulate, continuing with eleven corollaries and elaborating on from there. There is no way in this chapter that all that could be described, even if it were appropriate. What is appropriate is to attempt a thumb nail sketch which hopefully will be enough to enable you to understand what follows and/or to encourage you to read further into this fascinating theory.

Kelly postulated that individuals were in the business of anticipating events; that they wished to make sense of their world in order to better anticipate events occurring in it; and that they operated metaphorically like a scientist in doing this. In other words, they set up a hypothesis, tested it out and then incorporated it or rejected it depending on the results of the experiment. The process thus looked something like Figure 1.1. What is immediately clear about this diagram is that the

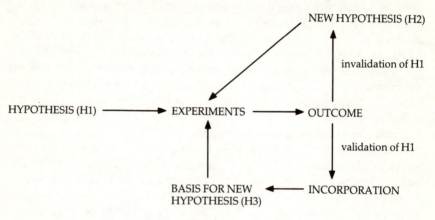

Figure 1.1

process is continuous, inevitable and relentless. We are always testing out our predictions and having them confirmed or invalidated; making up new hypotheses (predictions) to replace ones which have failed, or which are needed to deal with new situations, and trying those out. Every moving, thinking, feeling second is filled psychologically by this process. It is as inevitable to psychological life as breathing is to physical life, and generally occurs at the same level of awareness.

The way an individual sets up his/her hypothesis is by discriminating between things. In order to anticipate, something will be considered to have a particular characteristic (A) which discriminates it from other things which have characteristic (B). The basis of this hypothesis is therefore the construct of A v. B. Constructs are therefore *personal* discriminations and are *contrasts* used by the individual as the basis of hypotheses upon which to found experiments. Constructs are not *opposites*, at least not necessarily, and sometimes can appear quite bizarre to another person. But a discrimination of, for example, *clever* v. *attractive* may make a lot of sense to one individual, and none whatsoever to another.

Individuals then build up these discriminations into a system (construing system) which enables them to anticipate most of what they think they are likely to have to deal with, and with enough flexibility and ingenuity to produce new hypotheses for events they have not encountered before. The corollaries and remainder of the theory charts the way in which such systems are put together; how constructs can relate to one another, how they can be used individually or together and what can happen when things go wrong.

An attempt to put the whole of the above together might look something like Figure 1.2, but remember this is a gross simplification.

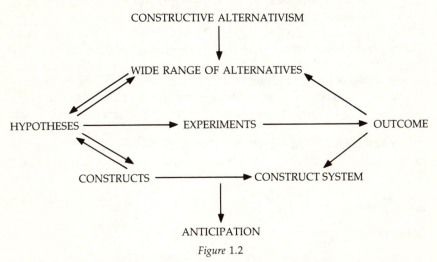

Figure 1.2

At this juncture, two points need emphasising. First, that what has been written so far is but one author's interpretation personally of Kelly's work. Hopefully it is not less valid or useful for that but it is important to remember that reflexivity applies to the theory itself. Indeed Kelly himself indicated that his approach might be helpful until somebody came up with a better one. The second point, is to remind you that we have not even begun yet to discuss techniques. This re-emphasises the original statement that this is *not* a technique based approach to people. It is an approach to help us see how an individual *personally* makes sense of his/her world as though we could see it through *their* psychological eyes. The theory is attempting to help explain the individual's personal theories, and as such it is sometimes called a meta-theory. It is, of course, an individual's own theory originally itself (that of George Kelly) – a fact which is apt to confuse people hopelessly who have not grasped or do not accept the reflexivity notion.

What has been dealt with so far is *context*. This is often harder to get hold of than technique but all the more valuable when you do. The most important part of the context of the psychology of personal constructs is that it is *personal*. This may seem an obvious statement, but it is an important final point before delving into practical techniques. All too often nowadays one seems to see things written about 'Construct Theory'. The 'Personal' often gets dropped. Of course, 'Personal Construct Theory' or 'Psychology' is quite a mouthful and people wish to abbreviate it. Yet it is significant that it is never abbreviated to 'Personal Theory' or 'Personal Psychology'. This may be to do with the feeling in academic circles that introspection is not a valid way of proceeding or that being personal somehow is not suitably scientific, even in the object being studied. But being personal is exactly what this approach is about; it is its great strength and value and appeal. It is also its greatest challenge.

This seems a reasonable point to move from the theoretical and philosophical discussion to the more practical one of techniques. The paragraphs that follow outline some of the more commonly used techniques devised by practitioners of Personal Construct Psychology, or formulated by Kelly himself in his original work. Of necessity they are brief descriptions, and examples of their usage will generally be found in the chapters which follow, as well as more specialist books and papers. However, before even embarking on these, let me reverse the usual order of events and start with a heading which usually ends a chapter such as this.

1 Others

It is all too easy to read a series of descriptions of techniques and think that these are what are important and nothing else matters. So far as PCP is concerned, this could not be further from the truth. What follows are descriptions of techniques which those working in the field have had the wit and inventiveness to come up with *so far*! They are not exhaustive and may yet be proved not to be the best. When you are faced with a particular problem you are trying to understand, don't just use what you have read about, think about it from the standpoint of the theory and see if you can come up with anything that may be more specifically or individually helpful. Which is not to say you should not know about what follows but merely to remind you that you too can experiment with new ideas.

The second statement to be made under this heading is that you do not have to throw away all the techniques from other approaches you have learnt so far. They may be helpful to you if translated to the new context. For example, using a free association approach may be very helpful in eliciting one end (pole) of a construct; a behavioural technique may make sense to a client and allow change to occur. We have to remember our clients may not have the same theoretical bases as ourselves: if we are trying to promote change, using their structures may be more useful sometimes than trying to teach them the one we are using to understand their problem. This is not, as some people have thought, an argument for chaotic eclecticism, but an argument to use the theory to give yourself the widest possible options in trying to help your client, patient or whatever (and yourself!).

2 Elicitation of constructs

There are innumerable different ways of eliciting constructs ranging from the formal triadic method outlined by Kelly to a totally informal approach of picking them out of a conversation. All methods have one aspect in common: one attribute is found first (the emergent pole) and the contrasting attribute (contrast pole) is found by asking the individual what the contrast to the emergent pole is! This may sound long winded but is an important principle to remember. You must not assume that because you know one end of a construct that *you* can tell the contrast, even when it looks obvious. Check it out! It may well not be as obvious as it seems; it frequently will not be the 'opposite'; and as it is the fundamental brick in the system which gives it its unique personal meaning it is trifled with only at great peril of undermining the whole approach.

There probably is no perfect way of eliciting constructs and each individual tends to have his/her own form of words to enquire for contrast poles. For those just embarking on this kind of activity, Kelly's triadic approach as outlined in his chapter on the repertory test (1955, p. 222) is the most straightforward. If your client has three separate people to consider (assuming that your investigation relates to how people are being construed), Kelly suggests that you begin by asking the subject to tell you something about these three people. 'In what *important way* are two of them alike but different from the third?' The response is recorded as the emergent pole of the construct. Once the subject has indicated which two people share this characteristic, you can ask about the odd one out. 'How is this person different?' This response then becomes the contrast pole of the construct. When conducting a repertory test (see below) a range of different people (or activities, things or whatever is the focus of study) will have been collected, and the procedure repeated with different groups of three until a range of constructs have been built up.

It is clear that what is happening is that you are getting hold of the personal discriminations of your client in whatever field you are studying with him/her. You do not have to be intending to proceed to a repertory test at this stage since this may only be a preliminary to laddering or pyramiding individual constructs or investigating their implications (see below). It is important to remember to ask for differences not opposites (an easy error) as a request for an opposite usually leads to a grammatical opposite which may not be the same as a personal discrimination.

Once you have become experienced in identifying and eliciting constructs in this way, then identifying emergent poles from pieces of writing (e.g. self-characterisations), behaviour (role-play) and so forth may become possible always remembering to identify the contrast pole by asking for a difference with somebody or something else.

Two other points may help reduce some confusion at this point. First, remember that constructs each have a 'range of convenience', that is to say they apply to some things and not others. It is difficult for most of us to consider a pair of curtains either male or female for example, or a car to be round or smooth. Each of these constructs, male v. female, and round v. smooth, has a range of objects that I, not my system, feel it appropriate to apply them to. The range is the range of convenience of a particular construct in a particular system, while the items or objects it applies to are known as *elements*.

The second point is that constructs are only represented by words. Round v. smooth is a verbal label for a construct we know when we see it. Many constructs may not have readily accessible verbal labels such as types of behaviour or feelings. Words need not be the only symbols used for constructs therefore; art or drawing, music, actions and so forth, may all be used provided it makes sense to the person holding the construct. In passing this can be extremely challenging to a therapist used to representing constructs verbally but working with a client who prefers to represent them in a different medium.

3 Techniques based on individual constructs

In this section there are three main techniques devised to explore an individual's construct system starting with an individual construct. These are laddering (devised by Hinkle, 1965), pyramiding (devised by Landfield, 1971), and the ABC model (devised by Tschudi, 1977).

(a) Laddering

Constructs do not all have the same predictional impact within a system, and are connected to one another. The difference between constructs like easy-going v. up-tight, and makes good relationships v. difficulty making relationships is one of abstraction. The first construct is more concrete than the latter, although it is clear that there could be a connection between them. In this case the connection is hierarchical; the latter construct is superordinate to the former; or the former is subordinate to the latter. The technique of laddering enables you to find out more superordinate (abstract) constructs in the system connected hierarchically to a *relatively* subordinate (concrete) construct. The process of enquiry in this example might have gone as follows!

Investigator: You see things as easy going as opposed to up-tight?
Subject: Yes.
I: Do you have a preference between seeing things as easy-going or up-tight?
S: Yes – I prefer easy-going.
I: Why is it important for you to see people as easy-going?
S: Because easy-going people are more approachable.
I: And what would people be if not more approachable?
S: Less inclined to share their feelings.
I: And do you have a preference between seeing people as more approachable or less inclined to share their feelings?
S: Oh, more approachable, of course!
I: Why is it important for you to see people as more approachable?
S: Because it lets me make good relationships.
I: And how would you contrast making good relationships?
S: Having difficulty making relationships.

Thus a ladder develops:

easy-going v. up-tight
↓
more approachable v. less inclined to share their feelings
↓
make good relationships v. have difficulty making relationships

By this process, the meaning of a construct is explored by discovering the more general or abstract connections. This may be helpful both to the investigator in understanding the subject's construct which may not make much sense to him; in confirming the sense he has already made of it; in exploring ways which change could be promoted more generally; or in discovering why change is so difficult for a particular person.

(b) Pyramiding

This is a technique enabling exploration in the opposite direction to that of laddering, i.e. from a relatively superordinate (abstract) construct to more concrete subordinate ones. To take the same example as in laddering, but starting from the opposite perspective, the investigator might ask how the subject makes good relationships or what enables people to have good relationships. This brings the response being more approachable. The contrast pole is gained as before and then the process is repeated by asking how or what the subject sees as being 'more approachable', provoking the response 'easy-going'.

The pyramid develops as shown in Figure 1.3.

In this system, it is of course possible to pyramid the contrast poles also, building up a broad and more complete picture.

The essential difference between laddering and pyramiding is that when laddering, the investigator is asking the question 'why', while in pyramiding the questions are 'what' or 'how'!

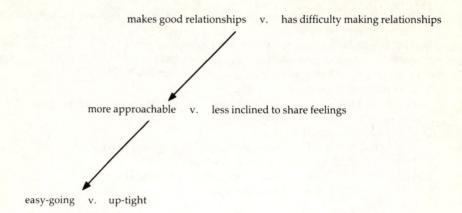

makes good relationships   v.   has difficulty making relationships

more approachable   v.   less inclined to share feelings

easy-going   v.   up-tight

Figure 1.3

(c) ABC model

This technique is designed to investigate the implicative dilemmas inherent in moving from one pole of a construct to the contrast pole. For example, a client may see himself as 'weedy' but may wish to become 'strong'. However, nothing seems to be changing. Why not?

In this model, A is the construct along which change is apparently desired (A_1 being emergent pole and A_2 its contrast or desired end), B_1 and C_1 are the disadvantages of each pole, while B_2 and C_2 are the advantages. In this example, the resulting information can be presented as:

A_1 being weedy	A_2 being strong
B_1 often picked on	B_2 able to stand up for myself
doesn't get girls	get a girl-friend
often feels unwell	be looked up to
C_2 looked after by mother	C_1 have to look after myself
not expected to fight battles	have to leave home

It is now much more understandable why movement has been so slow!!

3 Techniques using systems of constructs

These techniques involve several constructs, or a whole sub-system and are therefore considerably more complex and difficult to do justice to briefly. I shall give three areas of work, although the amount of variety in each is extensive.

(a) Self-characterisation

I make no apology for beginning with this technique which I consider the most useful and underrated technique in the psychotherapist's armoury. The information it can yield is enormous; its flexibility is immense; it is easily administered and it is not complicated to examine by both therapist and client. Yet somehow it seems to come off worse when techniques are written about. Perhaps it is because it is the most subjective technique over which the investigator has least control that makes it seem less scientific and therefore less academically acceptable. Whatever the reason, for the relative novice to the world of personal construct psychology it remains an easily acquired and powerful tool.

Kelly repeatedly makes the point that an investigator/therapist must be credulous which he exemplified with the dictum 'if you do not know what is wrong with a person, ask him; he may tell you'. One simple way of helping them to tell you is to ask them to write a character sketch of themselves. Kelly's (1955, p. 325) example of the instruction is as follows:

> I want you to write a character sketch of Harry Brown, just as if he were the principal character in a play. Write it as if it might be written by a friend who knew him very *intimately* and very *sympathetically*, perhaps better than anyone ever really could know him. Be sure to write it in the third person. For example, start out by saying, 'Harry Brown is . . .'

As in most other areas of his writing, Kelly chose his words with great care to emphasise a whole picture from an external point of view with a minimum of anxiety and threat. There is a deliberate omission of an outline and care has to be taken to guard against being trapped into providing one. Questions such as how long, how detailed, to start where, what should I include and so forth are often raised. My own solution to this is to add to Kelly's own instruction that there are no rights and wrongs about this exercise; it can be as long or as short as the person feels comfortable with; and that he can present it in any form he chooses. I also tend to add that, having written it, sharing it with me remains his choice as we can discuss aspects of it even without my seeing it. These additions have had some unexpected results although only once has a client totally refused to ever let me see what he had written. Apart from prose sketches varying from three lines to 6,000 words, I have received poetry, selections of music (on one occasion composed by the client) and on one memorable occasion, mime. Paintings and drawings have also often appeared at least in part. While these alternative submissions may be extremely taxing to a verbally oriented therapist, they were the chosen medium of the clients and held just as much meaning for them. In PCP, the hard work has to be done by the therapist understanding the client's language rather than the more often opposite experience!

Kelly devotes the best part of a chapter to the analysis of a self-characterisation the scope of which is far beyond this chapter and, indeed, beyond the time most practitioners have available. There are a number of brief points which can be made however. The first line or sentence often indicates the most powerful feeling the writer has about themselves and may be a clear signpost to follow. 'Harry Brown is 47 and a shopkeeper' conveys quite a different initial picture to 'Harry Brown is tall, slim, handsome and is always dressed meticulously.' Similarly, the final paragraph or sentence may be significant, rather in the same way that a client may proffer a vital piece of information at the end of a session when it is safe to assume it cannot be questioned! The body of the sketch gives a clear indication of what the client considers their problems to be; various themes about their life; and often many emergent poles of constructs to be explored individually as above.

Signs of change, hope of movement (or ominously the lack of it) can give indications of what areas might be most productive to start work on. The way it has been written itself is valuable: is it rushed; are there breaks in it; does the handwriting change? What ideas seem to lead on to other ones? Obvious absences can also be interesting.

Finally there is the professional subsuming of personal constructs. This really applies to all work with PCP but it fits here nicely for a first mention. The point of this exercise is to begin to see your client's world *through his eyes*. But this doesn't help you sort out his problems or even understand them on its own. You have to refer back to your own knowledge of the way these psychological processes work to understand *what* he is doing. You have to examine the way he orders and anticipates against your professional knowledge of how it can be done – not, I hasten to add, so that you can tell him how to do it better, but to begin to enable him to see alternatives, try different experiments, create new constructs and dislodge himself from a position in which he may have got stuck.

This, however, is just one form a self-characterisation can take. There are several variations on the theme, such as asking for one written as though some time into the future. This can then be compared with the one written in the present to see the directions of movement considered possible or desired by the writer. Other kinds of approach, such as ones based on Mair's community of selves metaphor, may be tried (Mair, 1977). In this example, a client may feel that there are several parts of himself vying for control. He can be encouraged to give each of these a name, and then write a character sketch of himself as each one in turn. The opportunities are endless, fascinating and illuminating. However, one word of caution. Character sketches are very personal and private communications and should always be treated with dignity and respect however they are couched and whatever their content.

They are not an end in themselves; only part of the route you take to help someone learn about themselves, and thereby, hopefully, learn to be able to change.

(b) Enactment

The techniques surrounding enactment are more to do with 'doing' and 'feeling' than with thinking and writing. It is important to remember that it is not the intention of PCP to be merely a cognitive theory: one where individuals think about how to do things differently. Cognition is important certainly, but not to the exclusion of other psychological activity and the theory makes no distinction between cognition, conation and emotion suggesting that these are just different ways of construing different kinds of constructs. Enactment of different kinds, role-play and fixed role therapy are ways of working directly with behaviour and feeling, although the results may again often be mediated with words.

Many people find the idea of enactment difficult both to understand the significance of, or to carry out themselves. Some therapists, particularly I suspect occupational therapists, are much better trained in this field than others and find it easier and more natural to use. Body posture, repetitive movements, irritating habits, all have been the subject of specific therapies and approaches, and all can be seen as non-verbal symbols of constructs about the person, his view of his environment or a particular activity he is engaged in. Enactment in its broadest form is thus any activity which encourages a person to reconstrue as a result of being encouraged to try behaving differently, and being prepared genuinely to conduct the experiment. Initially enactments are carried out within the safety of the therapy room where acting out of a particular fantasy or role does not have the immediate consequences that may be anticipated elsewhere. Kelly (1955, p.1145) wrote:

> The function of enactment procedures is to provide for elaboration of the client's personal construct system, to provide for experimentation within the laboratory of the interview room, to protect the client from involving core structures before he is ready to consider abandoning them, to free the client from pre-emptive constructions too tightly tied to actual events and to persons, and to enable the client to see himself and problems in perspective.

Enactment can be derived from the therapy situation itself, by encouraging a client to look at himself from the perspective of the therapist. Indeed in any enactment, reversing the roles can be valuable to elaborate constructs and broaden perspective. Character sketches can be a valuable starting point for enactments often mapping out specific roles played by the client. The exploration of self as a community of different selves, along with a group of character-sketches, may lead to a series of valuable enactments. It is however important that the therapist should also be comfortable with this approach as clients often seem to need reassurance and encouragement to embark on enactment.

One specific form of enactment put forward by Kelly is that of fixed-role therapy. This also starts from the point of the client writing a self-characterisation. The therapist (or therapists since it can be a complicated task) then writes a second self-characterisation for the client which is designed to be neither totally similar to nor totally opposite from the client's own description. The aim is to provide the client with some alternative ways of construing the problems outlined in their own sketch. The client is then given the sketch and once they feel they understand or can make sense of the person described therein (and this may involve some negotiation between therapist and client), the client is asked to act as though he/she was the person in the role-sketch. In other words, behave, eat, dress as though. . . . During this time, easy access to the therapist is usually arranged. This process, or some more modified form of it, allows the client to actively try out a different way of approaching their life. Following the experiment, some more permanent changes may result. Some other experiments may become obvious and new alternatives may have become apparent. Clearly this is a potentially more dramatic form of enactment, yet many of us often set up similar kinds of experiments for ourselves. Smaller versions may be easier to develop in practice.

(c) *Repertory grids*

Repertory grid technique has, in my view, become a technique often used without reference to its origins of context and is also often seen as a tool without which Personal Construct Psychology cannot function. Neither of these extremes is justified. Grids sometimes seem to be developing a life of their own, and it is not insignificant that 95 per cent of PCP research papers are based to some extent on repertory grid methodology. This situation has led to two unfortunate side-effects. First, as grids have tended to swamp the literature, so people have become pro- or anti-grid, and arguments have raged on this basis. The second side-effect, equally deplorable, is that for many people first coming into contact with PCP the repertory grid appears paramount, and if they do not see its usefulness immediately, or are put off by its apparent mathematical complexity or its computer-technology, tend to avoid any further contact with PCP at all. So it is without denying the use and value of the myriad forms of repertory grid that I would argue that PCP can be used extensively and effectively without ever having to use repertory grids at all. Having said that, however, it is also worth adding that it is still better to know something about them before discarding their use. If they do seem difficult or irrelevant initially, do not let that put you off using PCP. Repertory grids and PCP are not synonymous.

For many, repertory grids are the scientific face of Personal Construct Psychology. They enable analysis of an individual's construing and provide a mathematical map of their psychological space. The range of uses, the variety of types and the analytic methods are innumerable. For an excellent introduction to this field read Fransella and Bannister (1977) and then Beail (1985).

It is worth emphasising that even for those without a mathematical or computer software orientation, repertory grids can be helpful. A grid, after all, is simply a matrix of constructs applied to elements within their range of convenience. In the field of inter-personal relations, this usually takes the form of a selection of constructs elicited using the triadic method derived from a group of people known to the client. In Kelly's original repertory test, clients were given specific role titles and asked to think of people they knew to whom the title seemed to fit. No individual could appear twice, thus giving a range of different kinds of people.

The constructs elicited were then applied to the people concerned producing a cross-hatched matrix (constructs usually horizontally and elements (people) vertically). In fact, such a simple system can be useful on its own with no statistical analysis as therapist and client can review the results together – the former perhaps to confirm his predictions and the latter to see how he sees people as similar or different to one another. A major advance was the rated grid, where the client is asked to rate (on a scale of 1 – 7, or 1 – 9 usually) the individual people on each construct. This matrix is more complex to deal with 'cold', and so a statistical analysis by computer is often employed. Originally, Slater's Ingrid programme was most commonly used, but recently a whole variety of programmes and packages have been made available. One of the simplest and easiest to use on an available micro is the GAB programme written by Bannister and Higginbotham.

As the range of uses of the repertory grid became wider, so greater variants upon the original format were devised. Various types of implication grids have been developed. Here, the implications for the person of one pole of a construct are explored by looking for links in meaning with the poles of other constructs elicited. Resistance to change grids, dyadic grids and many, many others have appeared. Books, conferences and courses are devoted to this particular field. New types are continuously being devised for new research and clinical applications. It is an exciting and rapidly growing area, well beyond the scope of this chapter to analyse. Suffice to say in conclusion that if you are interested in PCP you should know something about how to construct and use a simple repertory grid; but if your interest is primarily in grids initially, you must take time to learn about the theory behind them.

Conclusion

This is a very brief introduction to some of the more important aspects of PCP and the techniques often used with it. The aim has been to make what follows easier to understand and follow. It is not a substitute for serious study of Kelly's original work or many of the major contributors to the field since then. I hope that some of my own enthusiasm for the approach has come through, and that this will carry you forward through the personal accounts which follow.

2 · *Working with oneself*

GAVIN DUNNETT

Writing about using Personal Construct Psychology on or around oneself seems to be an exceedingly difficult task. In a book devoted to the personal uses different authors have made of the theory as applied to their different disciplines, it seemed essential that a chapter be written about using it personally. When I, as an editor, rather tentatively put this forward, everyone I spoke to agreed that it was essential and interesting. No one, however, would write it!

This is not a complaint; simply a statement. The reasons were excellent and convincing. Nonetheless the impression overwhelmingly was of it being a stimulating idea but where would one begin? In some desperation, and because I had felt it was important, I agreed to write it myself. Over several months I sat and stared at a blank sheet of paper, beginning a number of times only to discard the few resulting paragraphs as trite or academic or simply rubbish. Increasingly I wondered why it was that I was having such difficulty. What was it about writing a chapter such as this that left me with the literary equivalent of being tongue-tied?

The answer, of course, is obvious. It is *because* this chapter is personal. Not, as elsewhere, personal about how to go about a particular task or problem set out by work or clients or patients or whatever. In these situations, the personal part is once removed from the text: the point of reference is narrow and directed towards solving problems 'out there'. *This* chapter is about how I use this theory in my life, for me. What are its values and benefits and disadvantages and problems – for me. It is the crunch point at which all the theorising about PCP being a reflexive approach comes home to roost.

There is no doubt that two major sets of constructs were both at work in me making it difficult to write. First there was a large area which was about 'being professional'. I certainly seem to have been taught or at least imbibed a notion that to be personal was not consonent with being professional. Maintaining objectivity, keeping a distance, separating work from the rest of your life, and other similar injunctions ring in my ears. I have long felt, certainly in the field of psychiatry, that clinical detachment did not always allow a full understanding of some of the people with whom I worked. Which is not to say that the contrast pole, of throwing oneself personally into their lives, would be any more helpful to themselves or us. The idea that some of my personal experience, knowledge and understanding of my world might be useful if it could be practically incorporated seemed to be rejected from the outset. A professional role with a client was almost defined as *not* being a personal one. So intending to write about being personal immediately threatened my view of myself as a responsible professional. Since Personal Construct Psychology demands the personal as central to the whole enterprise: and the personal applies to both 'therapist' and 'client' roles, it follows that to espouse this approach encourages a re-evaluation of what being professional means, and how these apparently incompatible systems can be reconciled.

The second major set of constructs that gave me pause for thought were those centred on vulnerability. Whereas the first group had to do with my core constructs as a professional, and in my case, as a psychiatrist, these had more to do with the sensation of opening up for discussion core ideas about what makes me tick as a human being. Why is being personal important for me?

The answers lie amongst words like honesty, genuineness, dignity, and more abstract notions such as it being a true base for inter-personal relationships. Even as I write, I am struck by wondering how other people will read this. I feel I want to apologise for it, agree that it sounds 'goody goody' and beat a rapid retreat behind a smokescreen composed of anything but being personal. Perhaps being personal is about admitting vulnerability; opening yourself up to criticism, or praise, or derision, or any number of other possible reactions. It is something we ask of our clients daily, yet I suspect we are all resistant to doing it much ourselves.

What I hope has become clear from what I have written is not only the content of why I have found it difficult to write this chapter, but also be beginnings of how I have used PCP to help me sort out the reasons for myself. The methods used to understand someone else's world through their eyes can just as easily be used to make sense of our own. Faced with a problem such as writing this chapter, I began to explore my constructs about writing, about professionalism, and about vulnerability. I know I must have constructs about what constitutes professionalism, for example, but I am not particularly aware of them. Most of the time I just take them for granted. But if I am faced with the feeling that somehow I am about to compromise my sense of professionalism, I can explore what that construct means for me. What is its contrast pole? Why is it important for me to be 'professional'? How do I go about being 'professional'? Once I have explored this myself, I can then choose whether or not to retain the structure as before, or experiment with a modification. In this context, I can say to myself that I am continuing to be 'professional' by using an accepted and highly regarded psychological theory, and that that theory itself requires me to be personal. So long as I am working under the auspices of the theory, and aware of its philosophy and assumptions, I can take on board the idea that being personal is allowable. The next step along this path, of course, is to test out whether my new system works for me, and in part at least, this chapter can be seen as my personal experiment.

I think it important to state here that reflexivity and disclosure are not one and the same. Applying PCP to myself and using it to explore my own approach to life and living does not demand I broadcast the process or results of those explorations. Equally, the emphasis on the personal in Personal Construct Psychology does not demand that I spread my personal attitudes around willy nilly. Reflexivity and the personal refer to a sense of awareness within the individual that this psychology works for him too, and the mechanisms he may use professionally are as personal to him as they are to the clients/patients he works with.

There is an analogy I sometimes use when trying to explain this phenomenon to students or trainees, which I call the 'air' analogy. It goes something like this.

Each of us exists in an environment of air: we breathe it, move through it, and are in contact with it continuously and inexorably. We don't see it and generally don't feel it, yet we are always using it to provide us with one of the most basic nutrients of life. So also does a personal construct psychologist (of whatever discipline) see his world through the medium of PCP. If we want to examine the properties of air, it can be broken down in a variety of ways – into atoms and molecules, suspended particles, interactions and so forth. The effects of different combinations of these on individual human beings can be studied, and altered occasionally to improve their physical states by increasing oxygen content or reducing smog causing chemicals for example. Much of learning about PCP seems to be at this level. What is a construct? How does a system structure itself? What problems can occur? But there comes a point when it is not just a collection of molecules or collisions, or constructs and experiments, but a system in which we live, like air. When this stage is reached, the personal becomes natural, expected and much more understandable.

I feel aware as I write this that it sounds rather like a cross between a Maslow-type peak experience and a religious conversion. It is very firmly neither. It is simply the same sensation anyone has who learns a skill so thoroughly that eventually they *almost* don't need to think about it any more. Many drivers have this kind of experience when they continue to drive without being consciously aware of the individual gear-changes or use of the rear-view mirror. So also can it be with PCP.

There are perhaps two sentences of caution to introduce here. The first of these is that reflexivity, and the personal use of PCP, is not an invitation to over indulgence in introspection or lengthy examination of your own navel. The use of any approach to self-examine simply for the sake of it is probably inappropriate. To use it in the situations in which we ourselves notice anxiety, or threat, or where our inter-personal relationships fail importantly, in order to understand our own role, and the contribution we ourselves make to the situation does not seem at all inappropriate. Indeed, if you found yourself attempting to analyse all your activities, you might need to consider why you felt you needed to do that very thing itself! It is worth remembering that many patients/clients take to working with PCP precisely because they find they can use it themselves, practically and helpfully. Why not make use of the tool we try to give them for our own benefit?

The second sentence of caution applies to using the techniques and approach with other people in your daily life. This is a more difficult question altogether. I have certainly had discussions with PCP colleagues who have argued strongly that you should never use it outside the therapeutic (or equivalent, depending on the discipline) role. Their argument is that it is a powerful professional tool and should only be used in the professional context. This seems to me to be much too restrictive. There is no doubt that the skilful understanding and use of this approach allows one to begin to probe another person's understanding and view of the world. But there are many occasions when I feel I want to know something of that. In a conversation where I am not clear exactly what the person I am talking to means, it seems ridiculous not to be able to draw on PCP to help me to understand him or her. I have even found myself in the middle of a dinner party trying to ladder a fellow diner's constructs to understand the political point he was trying to make.

The important point to remember, I believe, is that using PCP allows you a powerful tool with which to intrude into another's personal space. In therapy, a client gives you permission to explore himself and similarly in a research project or management exercise. The client knows you are about to explore, gives you permission to do so, and is on his/her guard to call a halt if you seem to be going further than is acceptable. I think that there is nothing wrong with using PCP in personal situations provided you make clear what it is you are trying to do and receive some kind of permission to proceed. At my dinner, I might have said, 'look, I don't really understand what you meant by that statement. Do you mind if I ask you some questions to see if I can understand your meaning more clearly? Feel free to tell me to shut up any time.' This puts my friend on his guard, and gives him the right to tell me to stop at any time. This way, there is a fair chance he will still be my friend at the end of the dinner, and I may know and understand him better, rather than his feeling aware that somehow I have got inside him without his knowing how or when.

Thus far, I have written about using PCP in my personal life, but it is just as valuable as a reflexive tool in my professional life. Encouraging some kind of self examination is already institutionalised in some parts of the caring professions. Psychotherapists, for example, are often expected to have undergone psychotherapy themselves before being approved to practise independently. Because Personal Construct Psychology is reflexive, training in its use automatically encourages some degree of self examination without the necessity to undergo a specific period of 'therapy'. The purpose here is not to enter into the fraught argument of whether personal therapy is essential to a psychotherapist or not, but to re-emphasise that PCP contains an encouragement to self knowledge and awareness for all those who try to use and understand it.

This leads on to the point that it is one matter accepting that a psychology based on individual personal views of the world is attractive and applicable in our various specialities, while it is quite another to consider the implications of its application to oneself in the context of carrying out our work. To look at our clients construing personally may make sense to us and allow more fruitful interventions or more innovative and sensitive approaches to therapy. It may also make us as individuals feel good in terms of investing our clients/patients with the human dignity and respect they clearly deserve. *Their* needs become clearer, options for achieving them more obvious, experiments more easily devised, and lo and behold, change occurs. But what of us? What of our needs, our options, our experiments, and our change? Is any time spent discussing these? My guess is that the answer is generally no. PCP challenges you and I to apply the same approach to our lives and endeavours as it does to those whom we aim to help. In many ways this is its greatest challenge, and its most difficult hurdle.

In my career there have been many times when I have been confronted by a patient I did not seem to be able to help. There have been countless situations where I felt incompetent and uncertain. Frequent occasions have arisen when I really did not know what to do next. Around me I have often seen colleagues from different disciplines as well as my own all having similar experiences from time to time. Morale, that indefinable commodity, drops so easily, and usually with protestations of not knowing exactly why. There often seemed no room to be personal because there was no structure that allowed for it. Somehow, carers are supposed to go on caring indefinitely like a battery with an infinite charge. More and more books and articles are written about 'burn-out' and 'compassion fatigue'. The caring often seems to be a one way street. For me, one of the challenges of PCP is that not only is this an unreasonable way to proceed, it is also bad psychology. What possible reason can we have as members of the so-called caring professions when we show an appalling disregard for the care of ourselves and our colleagues? Our individual aspirations, hopes, successes and failures mould our approach to our jobs. Any good personnel officer knows that. Yet, perhaps *because* we deal with the personal in other people's lives, the myth has grown that the personal in our own should be kept shrouded, ignored or disregarded.

Of course, I am painting a very bleak picture, and it is seldom quite as stark as I am suggesting. But PCP does demand that I look at my own motivations and my own concerns with just as caring a view as I would my patients or clients. Further, although I may know something of PCP which may help me with my frustrations or whatever, reflexivity ought to alert us to the vulnerability in colleagues that would be immediately visible to us if presented by a client. This is not to argue that we should all be going around 'therapising' each other. We should, however, be trying to create working environments in which each of our personal concerns can be acknowledged, and the part they play in our work taken into account. We work in a stressful arena of people's personal distress. Is it too much to ask that when we also have personal distress, this can be seen, understood, supported by our colleagues? More, is it not important that it should be so?

As I referred to above, many psychotherapists are required to themselves undergo therapy partly to learn the technique from the receiving end, but also to learn about themselves, and the difficulties they might experience in their clinical work. This is a first stage towards acknowledging the personal in work settings. Other areas of movement in this direction include matching of therapist and client for therapy (rather than the assumption that any therapist properly trained can deal with any appropriate client), staff groups, proper supervision sessions and so forth. With the increasing development of multi-disciplinary working, there is even more need for understanding the different ethos of the disciplines, the individual pressures felt by members of them, and the interaction of professional demands and personal structures.

Reflexivity provides us with the mechanism to gain knowledge of oneself; knowledge of one's needs; knowledge of one's limitations; and knowledge of how we deal with events. All this knowledge should lead us, not only to learn to function better in our personal lives, but also to let this spill over into our professional roles. It should encourage us to act remembering the personal in us, in our colleagues and in our clients and patients. It should tailor our actions and our institutional structures accordingly. It is the fundamental challenge of *Personal Construct Psychology*.

I am not sure that I have yet responded to this challenge. To have found this chapter so hard to write, and to feel as I do that there should have been so much more to say, suggests to me that this challenge remains in front of me. But perhaps it will encourage you as you read the remainder of this book to bear in mind that you take yourself along all the time, and that *you* are human too.

3 · Towards a constructive clinical psychology

DAVID WINTER

Rarely does Personal Construct Theory receive a mention in general texts on clinical psychology, and when it does it is often consigned to a categorisation which George Kelly would doubtless have found amusing. Sundberg *et al.* (1983), for example, present it, together with behavioural and Gestalt approaches, as exemplifying the 'learning orientation' to clinical problems. Trainee clinical psychologists will also be surprised to find a question on the theory in their examination papers: over the past ten years, only one of the 426 full questions and two of the 232 'short notes' options in the papers for the British Psychological Society's Diploma in Clinical Psychology have been of this type. Therefore, in organising part of the academic programme for a clinical psychology training course, I have been faced not only with the problem of where to place the theory within the system of modules which comprises the programme (its original allocation to the module on behavioural and cognitive approaches seemed singularly inappropriate and so now it rests, not entirely comfortably, within the humanistic therapies module), but also with its inclusion being perceived as irrelevant by some trainees.

Nevertheless, despite its apparent neglect by the clinical psychology establishment, practising clinical psychologists have increasingly turned to personal construct theory in their attempts to understand the phenomena with which they are confronted and to guide their interventions. In his analysis of the development of Kelly's theory, Neimeyer (1985b) reports that 54 per cent of British, and 56 per cent of American, personal construct theorists hold clinical psychology degrees, and this is appropriate enough in view of the fact that Kelly himself was a professor of clinical psychology. While admittedly much of the early interest of clinical psychologists in the theory centred on the utility of repertory grid technique, the wide range of applications of this technique stimulated awareness that Kelly's writings indicated an even more extensive clinical applicability of the constructivist perspective. My concern in this chapter will be to illustrate this potential value of Personal Construct Theory to the clinical psychologist by describing a few of the areas in which I have found it to be of use in my work. As I am based in an 'adult psychiatric' setting, most of the examples which I present will concern this field. However, it should be noted that applications of the theory in clinical psychology are by no means confined to adult psychiatric problems but extend, for example, to work with children, with the mentally handicapped, and with the physically ill and disabled. Readers who wish to explore further the use of Personal Construct Theory by clinical psychologists are recommended to turn to recent publications by Button (1983, 1985) and Neimeyer (1985a).

A purpose in confusion

In Kelly's view, we are all scientists, attempting constantly to make sense of our world by formulating, testing out, and if necessary revising, hypotheses about our experiences. This does not necessarily mean that we are all good scientists, and indeed we sometimes fail to take adequate account of evidence which invalidates our constructions and to modify these constructions accordingly. 'Bad science' is particularly characteristic of psychological disorder, defined by Kelly (1955, p. 831) as 'any personal construction which is used repeatedly in spite of consistent invalidation'. Nevertheless, even in psychological disorder, the individual's constructions and actions are directed towards the optimal anticipation of events.

One of the earliest examples of such an analysis of psychological disorder, and of the application of Personal Construct Theory in clinical psychology, was Bannister's (1960, 1962) research with thought disordered schizophrenics, whose repertory grid responses were found to be characterised by weak and inconsistent relationships between constructs. It is somewhat unfortunate, therefore, that interest in this work focused largely on the diagnostic efficiency of the grid test developed by Bannister and Fransella (1966) to detect schizophrenic thought disorder. Of far greater significance was the formulation of thought disorder and its genesis put forward by Bannister (1963) and later elaborated by other workers (Radley, 1974; Van den Bergh *et al.*, 1985). In his 'serial invalidation hypothesis', Bannister proposed that the thought disordered schizophrenic has reacted to an inconsistent, and therefore constantly invalidating, interpersonal environment by 'loosening' his or her constructions concerning other people, albeit typically after an initial modification in the content of these constructions. Loose construing, as typified by schizophrenic thought disorder, could therefore be considered to represent a strategy by which the individual avoids further invalidation, and consequent anxiety, by making their predictions too vague to be testable.

In my view, the primary importance of this work lies in its indication that, no matter how bizarre a client's behaviour may appear to the outside observer, it may still reflect the way in which the client attempts to maximise his or her capacity for anticipation. One of its limitations, however, was the use by Bannister of a repertory grid method in which the constructs were supplied to, rather than elicited from, the client, and so which may not have tapped the client's *personal* construct system. Therefore, stimulated by Bannister's work, in my first attempt to make use of Personal Construct Theory in the clinical sphere I employed both the Bannister–Fransella Grid Test and a repertory grid with elicited constructs in order to investigate the construing of chronic, thought disordered schizophrenics. I found them to exhibit significantly weaker construct relationships than did non-thought disordered schizophrenics and normal subjects when using Bannister's supplied constructs but not when using their own personal constructs. This indicated that, even in chronic schizophrenics, a level of structuring of constructs equivalent to that of normal people can be discerned if one takes the trouble to consider their own personal constructs and to ignore the fact that many of these are highly idiosyncratic, if not neologisms, including in my study descriptions of people as 'simplex' and 'mentalistic'.

The generally loosely organised construct system of the thought disordered schizophrenic may, therefore, contain residual islands of relatively structured personal construing, which Bannister and his colleagues (1975) have suggested could form a starting point from which to reverse the process of thought disorder by repeatedly validating the linkages between these constructs. Although only moderate changes were observed in the thought disordered schizophrenics with whom they attempted a therapeutic programme of this type, possible reasons for their lack of success may be found in their questionable assumption that their clients' constructs could be operationally defined as would constructs with the same verbal labels in the general population, and in their failure to control invalidating experiences in other areas of the schizophrenic clients' lives. Amongst these invalidating experiences appeared to be the clients' interactions with their family members, and the possibility that such relatives' inconsistent, invalidating behaviour may have a basis in the structure of their own construct systems was suggested by a further study of mine in which the parents of schizophrenics exhibited looser construct relationships than did the parents of non-schizophrenic clients when completing the Bannister–Fransella Grid Test (although, again, not when they used their own personal constructs) (Winter, 1975). Furthermore, the more loosely they organised the constructs in this test, the looser were the construct relation-ships of their schizophrenic children. Procter (1981) has demonstrated that it is useful to think of families, and not just individuals, as having construct systems: the family construct systems of the schizophrenics in my study appeared to be characterised by a blurring of constructs in common social usage which is comparable to the descriptions of 'schizogenic' families by workers such as Lidz (1968).

Although alternatives to the Personal Construct Theory explanation of the grid performance of thought disordered schizophrenics have been proposed, none have been able satisfactorily to account for all the research evidence or to show the same heuristic power in providing an understanding of the etiology of thought disorder and implications for its treatment. The constructivist view of the schizophrenic as actively 'attempting to maintain a consistent understanding' of inconsistent events (Radley, 1974, p. 320) contrasts with currently fashionable ideas that such individuals are the passive victims of viral attacks, hemisphere imbalance, or cerebral atrophy (Cutting, 1985). Some of the research which it has generated (e.g. Lawlor and Cochran, 1981) has also, inci-dentally, enhanced our understanding of how the structure of a client's construct system may, as we shall see, determine their response to psychotherapy.

Understanding puzzling choices

The presenting complaint

Nearly as incomprehensible as the behaviour and utterances of the thought disordered schizophrenic may appear the choices made by those of our clients whom we construe as neurotic or depressed. Mowrer (1950) referred to this problem as the 'neurotic paradox', the puzzle of why some people behave in a way which is 'at one and the same time self-perpetuating and self-defeating'. This persistence of apparently self-destructive behaviour is a considerable problem for those approaches, such as learning theory, which adopt a hedonistic view of human motivation but, as Kelly (1969a) indicated, poses no such difficulties for a theory which views the individual's behaviour as directed towards making greater sense of his or her world.

Two features of Personal Construct Theory which are of particular importance in this regard are Kelly's view that constructs are most conveniently regarded as bipolar, and his 'Choice Corollary'. The assumption of bipolarity of constructs leads the personal construct theorist always to view a situation in terms of contrast and, in the clinical situation, to attempt to understand a client's predicament by considering what the alternatives might be for the client. For example, as described by Landfield (1980), the personal construct psychotherapist may regard a client's presenting complaint as one pole of a construct and may then attempt to define the construct's contrast pole, remembering that this contrast may be highly individual and bear little relation to lexical meanings of verbal construct labels. Such an exercise may lead to the conclusion that what the clinician initially viewed as a client's major difficulty may in fact pose relatively little problem for the client given his or her particular view of the world. For example, Nigel, a student whose examination performance consistently failed to reflect his high level of ability, and whose experimentation with hard drugs was also a cause for concern, contrasted 'self-destructiveness' with being 'egotistical' and 'treading on other people to get where you want'. For him, then, to be self-destructive was preferable to what he saw as its alternatives. His predicament was also reflected in another of his constructs, which contrasted being 'conventional' with 'being free to choose from a spectrum of possibilities', these including self-destruction.

As has been indicated by Tschudi (1977) and Rowe (1971), for example, the 'payoffs' of a client's complaint can also be explained by considering its implications in terms of other constructs within the client's system, perhaps with the aid of repertory grid technique. A particular strength of the repertory grid is that it is able to combine the advantages of projective and objective methods, being idiographic in emphasis and allowing access to constructions of which the client may only be dimly aware, but also being objective in its scoring. Its use means that the clinical psychologist who is requested to carry out an assessment of some puzzling complaint no longer has to produce a report which verges on the tautologous and which, for example, explains a client's avoidance of social situations in terms of their high Introversion and Neuroticism scores. Readers who wish to acquaint themselves more fully with repertory grid technique and its clinical applications are referred to publications by Beail (1985), Fransella and Bannister (1977), Neimeyer and Neimeyer (1981), and Ryle (1975), but here it may suffice to illustrate how it may elucidate the payoffs of a client's presenting complaint by returning to the case of Nigel. For him, positive implications of his apparently self-destructive behaviour were indicated by the correlations of the constructs 'self-destructive – egotistical', 'takes acid – does not', and 'crazy – normal' with other constructs in his grid. Several of these correlations are presented in Table 3.1, and as a central assumption of repertory grid technique is that such statistical relationships reflect the psychological relationships between the constructs concerned, it can be seen that when Nigel construed himself as a crazy, self-destructive acid-taker he was also able to see himself as free, aware, thoughtful, humorous, and rather selfless and intelligent. Although the ability to pass examinations was not included as a construct in his grid, it is doubtful that it would have carried similarly positive implications. Further surprising implications of self-destructiveness for him were its strong associations with being 'evenly balanced' and 'under control'.

Table 3.1 Selected Correlations between Nigel's Constructs (for convenience, only one pole of each construct is shown)

	Self-destructive	Takes acid	Crazy
Free	0.78	0.73	0.44
Aware	0.61	0.39	0.27
Thoughtful	0.77	0.50	0.43
Has sense of humour	0.56	0.42	0.75
Selfless	0.59	0.18	0.26
Intelligent	0.20	0.30	0.24

While in some clients, such as Nigel, the persistence of a complaint may be explained in terms of the negative implications of its loss, an equally major obstacle to change may be an idealistically positive construction of life without the symptom. Fransella (1972), reporting the idealistic constructions of fluency held by stutterers, described this problem as the 'if only' syndrome: the belief that one will attain all one's ideals if only one were not afflicted with a particular symptom can be a very good reason never to lose the symptom, so ensuring that the idealistic belief may be maintained. I have found a similar pattern in both agoraphobics and their spouses in that they imagine that the agoraphobic's symptom loss would result in both agoraphobic and spouse becoming more similar to their ideal selves than they had been even before the commencement of the phobic symptoms (Winter and Gournay, 1987). One client who displayed such a pattern was Crispin, an aging hippy who had been unable to find a suitable niche for himself after the end of the 1960s and who had become increasingly agoraphobic since this time. Repertory grid assessment demonstrated that, while he construed himself as very dissimilar to his ideal self, his perception of how he was before the commencement of his phobic symptoms was also very negative in that he saw himself as having been a 'cocky', 'I'm all right, Jack type', who was 'only interested in himself' and did not 'accept responsibilities' or 'take relationships seriously'. His very favourable construal of himself if he were to lose his symptoms therefore indicated that he imagined that symptom loss would result in his becoming a much more ideal person than he had ever been. His fantasy, in fact, was that if only he were not agoraphobic he could soon become a famous folk guitarist, despite the fact that he had never performed in front of an audience. It was scarcely surprising, therefore, that he dropped out of a behavioural treatment programme, presumably choosing not to risk testing out his idealistic fantasies.

Kelly's (1955) 'Choice Corollary' further enables the clinician to understand why a client may characterise himself or herself by one pole of a construct rather than the other in that it states that the chosen construct pole is the one which it is anticipated will be most likely to lead to the individual's construct system being better defined or extended. One of the clearest demonstrations of the clinical utility of this corollary is again provided by Fransella's (1972) work with stutterers. She was able to demonstrate that for such individuals stuttering tended to carry a great many implications in terms of their other constructs whereas the implications of fluency were relatively few. Stuttering was their 'way of life', the way in which they were best able to anticipate events, whereas fluency offered far less structure and meaning, a state of affairs which for Kelly would be equated with anxiety. That a similar analysis may be applied more generally to the problems of neurotic clients is suggested by findings that constructs relating to their symptoms are particularly highly interrelated with other constructs (Winter, 1983, 1985a; Watts and Sharrock, 1985) and therefore at least afford the client some certainty.

Resistance to therapy as a constructive choice

From the above examples, it will be apparent that a Personal Construct Theory analysis of the persistence of apparently self-defeating behaviour may help the clinician to explain why many of their clients resist therapeutic change. As Fransella (1985, p. 100) put it, the client who appears to be stubbornly resisting the therapist's efforts is 'behaving perfectly reasonably from their own perspective. It is the therapist who is doing a poor job of subsuming the client's construing if they merely see the client's behaviour as resistance – and therefore something to be overcome.'

Clients' 'resistance' to therapy was considered from their own perspective in a repertory grid study which I carried out on social skills groups (Winter, 1987). An understanding of the generally poor response of clients to these groups was provided by the finding that in 80 per cent of the clients social competence carried some negative implications, such as lack of tenderness towards others, dishonesty, and egotism. Furthermore, the more pronounced these implications, the more unfavourable were the clients' responses to a questionnaire examining their perceptions of the groups. The treatment which they were understandably resisting was therefore one which they appeared to construe as training in selfishness, contempt for others and deceit.

In attempting to understand resistance to therapy, it is often valuable to consider the implications of symptom loss not only for the client but also for people close to the client. For example, repertory grid assessment of Joan, an agoraphobic, and Jack, her husband, demonstrated that they both associated the ability to go out with the possibility of infidelity, as indicated by correlations between these constructs of 0.31 in her grid and 0.51 in his. Given such constructions, therefore, it was not altogether surprising that the reduction in Joan's agoraphobic symptoms during behaviour therapy was accompanied by Jack's growing concern with infidelity, together with a decrease in his self-esteem and increase in his intropunitiveness. Neither was it unexpected that her more positive self-construal during therapy was not sustained at follow-up, her decrease in self-esteem in this period being associated with an increase in that of her husband, whose preoccupations with infidelity also lessened. These complementary changes in Joan and Jack's test results are illustrated in Figure 3.1.

A particular client group which is generally regarded as highly resistant to change is the long-stay population of psychiatric hospitals. Nevertheless, mental health policies emphasising community care have resulted in increasing efforts to resettle such individuals, often with the involvement of clinical psychologists in rehabilitation programmes.

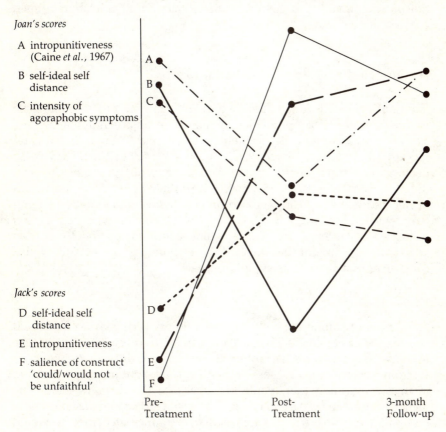

Figure 3.1 Changes in Joan and Jack on selected measures

Michael Baker and I have recently employed a Personal Construct Theory perspective in attempting to explain why a significant proportion of these clients do not feel that they can leave hospital. Dividing our sample into those who felt able to leave and those who did not, we found that their constructs concerning people outside hospital accounted for significantly greater variation in the grids of the former group than in those of the latter, whereas there was no such difference in their constructs concerning people from inside the hospital. This implied that only those clients with a subsystem of constructs capable of discriminating between people and events in the world outside hospital were able to contemplate moving into the community. Without such a subsystem, life outside the hospital gates would be likely to appear largely unconstruable and hence, in Kelly's terms, anxiety-provoking. Such results would suggest that the clinical psychologist working in a rehabilitation programme might most profitably be occupied not just in assessing dependency levels and organising training in social and self-care skills but in examining clients' constructions of the outside world and helping, where necessary, to elaborate such constructions.

A constructivist approach to therapy

If a client's constructions of their world are considered to be responsible for the persistence of a particular complaint, reconstruction will be seen as a necessary prerequisite for therapeutic change. Thus, with Joan and Jack in the example above, the clinical psychologist who adopts a personal construct theory approach to therapy might attempt to help them to reconstrue the ability to go out rather than concentrating his or her efforts on exposing Joan to previously avoided situations. Similarly, with the client who has a highly elaborated view of himself or herself as suffering from a particular symptom, personal construct psychotherapy might be directed at elaborating an equally viable construction of the self as symptom-free.

Reconstructing an erection

Psychotherapy along personal construct theory lines may be illustrated by the case of Stanley, a 25-year-old bachelor who sought help because for some five years he had found it increasingly difficult to obtain an erection. Repertory grid assessment threw some light upon this problem in that it indicated that, while his level of self-esteem was high, he imagined that if he lost his sexual problem he would become more dissimilar to his ideal self. In particular, he anticipated that he would become a more 'dishonest', 'unlovable' person, and more similar to his father. A further negative implication of sexuality for him was that he associated sexual attractiveness with a desire to dominate.

Therapy was initially directed at 'controlled elaboration' of Stanley's complaints, 'a way of bringing about reconstruction through clarification' (Kelly, 1955, p. 935). As an aid to such clarification, we discussed his repertory grid results and explored his construing of episodes which he reported in which he had felt highly sexually aroused. His initial constructions of such episodes were very negative. Thus, he said that at such times he was 'brainless', and on further questioning that this was because he could be 'undiscriminating in finding a sexual outlet' and could not 'apply myself single-mindedly to anything else'. Another undesirable implication of sexual arousal was that he associated it with 'a danger of abusing and hurting someone', such that he might not be 'safe on the streets'. By contrast, the possible payoffs of his impotence were illustrated by an incident which he recounted in which he received a sexual invitation from a woman to whom he felt indifferent but whom he imagined he would have slept with had he felt confident in his sexual abilities, despising himself the next day for taking advantage of her. To exclude such sexual possibilities from consideration allowed him to avoid not only possible guilt but also the anxiety occasioned by uncertain amorous situations.

In view of the negative implications which sexual potency carried for him, it was apparent that the recovery of his erection would necessitate reconstruction. A particular strategy which I adopted in order to facilitate such reconstruing was time-binding (Kelly, 1955, p. 1075), in which a construction is tied to a particular period of time and that period only. In his case, it seemed relevant that a major source of conflict for him as a child was that, while most of the time he had had 'immense respect' for his father's moral convictions, he also remembered often feeling very ashamed when, at dinner parties, his father would become 'flirtatious, overattentive to women, and ridiculous'. I suggested to him, therefore, that while his negative constructions of sexual responsiveness had perhaps once served a purpose in allowing him to anticipate his father's behaviour, they had now outlived their usefulness. A further construct which he employed in describing his father's rather erratic behaviour towards him and his brother was 'hard' versus 'soft and malleable', the latter condition being associated with tenderness and love. It was considered not inconceivable that such constructs had been given nonverbal expression in the state of Stanley's penis and that if they were made more explicit during therapy they could be more readily tested out and revised.

As therapy progressed, Stanley became increasingly willing to elaborate his construing of himself as a sexually active person, whereas at first the threat posed by this prospect was reflected in his concern that he might 'uncover a part of myself that I wouldn't want to uncover'.

Coupled with this, he allowed himself to sleep with women once again when the opportunity arose, and found that on most such occasions he was potent. At this stage, after some six sessions of therapy, we completed a second repertory grid, which demonstrated that, in contrast to his pre-treatment grid results, he now construed himself without sexual problems as closer to his ideal self and as honest and lovable, and sexually attractive people as not wishing to dominate. The repertory grid assessment suggested that the recovery of his sexual potency may have been due to the fact that he no longer risked experiencing the guilt with which the negative implications of potency would previously have confronted him. Also notable was the fact that he used several new constructs concerning emotional awareness (e.g. 'in touch with their emotions – more hazy about their emotions'; 'faces their frustrations – does not') and relationships (e.g. 'inquiring about the links between people – not inquiring'; 'independent of other people – dependent on being fed energy'; 'experiences ego competition – does not'). With this new repertoire, he was perhaps better equipped to anticipate the intricacies of encounters with the opposite sex.

Monitoring reconstruction

As the previous example illustrates, assessment methods derived from Personal Construct Theory, such as repertory grid technique, may provide a useful means both of focusing psychotherapy and of monitoring therapeutic change. The utility of the repertory grid as a therapy outcome measure is by no means confined to the evaluation of Personal Construct Psychotherapy, and my colleagues and I have turned to it in studies of analytically-oriented group psychotherapy and behaviour therapy when we required an instrument sufficiently flexible to be sensitive to change in these different therapeutic modalities (Winter and Trippett, 1977; Caine et al., 1981; Winter, 1982). This flexibility stems in part from the ability of the grid to tap constructions at various different levels of cognitive awareness, ranging from those which are relatively accessible and are equivalent to self-ratings on symptom measures to those, such as the construct relationships which appeared to underlie Stanley's sexual difficulties, of which the client may have little awareness.

I have enumerated elsewhere other reasons why the clinical psychologist who wishes to evaluate a therapeutic programme may find it advantageous to employ repertory grid technique (Winter, 1985b). Perhaps chief amongst these is that the grid lends itself particularly well to the derivation from it of individualised outcome measures of the type advocated by psychotherapy researchers such as Bergin and Lambert (1978) and Malan (1983). In the outcome studies mentioned above, for example, I developed a framework by which such measures, tailored to the individual client, could be derived from the client's pre-treatment grid, and which was intended to provide guidelines for the researcher or clinician who wishes to use the grid in this way. The possible value of such individualised predictions of the changes in construing which would occur in successfully treated clients was indicated by the findings that they were more likely to be confirmed than were general predictions applied to every client studied and that, while they showed some relationship with questionnaire and rating scale measures of therapeutic outcome, principal component analysis indicated that the latter were tapping a rather different level of change from the grid measures.

Therapeutic alternatives

Clinical psychology departments nowadays often include in their therapeutic armamentaria a very wide range of techniques and approaches. Their members may, for example, include Freudians and radical behaviourists, cognitive therapists and transactional analysts, and even the occasional personal construct theorist. It may seem impossible for such departments to be characterised by any unifying philosophical framework, and indeed they often describe themselves as eclectic in orientation. However, I have found it useful to employ Personal Construct Theory in an attempt to provide an underlying rationale for the therapeutic service offered by a department, such as my own, of this type (Winter, 1985c).

Personal construct psychotherapists, like psychology departments, also make use of a broad spectrum of therapeutic methods, including techniques developed from other theoretical perspectives in addition to those, such as fixed role therapy, with a basis in Kelly's theory. As has been noted by Karst (1980), however, the apparent eclecticism of the personal construct psychotherapist is only at the level of the techniques which he or she employs, whereas the goals of therapy, and the principles by which particular techniques are chosen in an attempt to attain these goals, are firmly and consistently rooted in the theory: in Stanley's case, for example, the therapeutic approaches adopted in tackling his sexual problem were selected in view of such considerations as the fact that many of his constructions appeared loose and only barely expressible in words. Conceivably, in similar fashion, the eclecticism of a psychology department might only be at the level of the therapeutic orientations of its individual members, not extending to such 'superordinate' constructions as the criteria employed in selecting a particular treatment approach for an individual client.

The series of research investigations referred to in the previous section has been primarily concerned with such selection criteria, demonstrating that contrasting features of clients' construing are differentially predictive of positive outcome in behaviour therapy and group analytic psychotherapy. For example, clients who responded to behaviour therapy were found to have relatively tightly organised construct systems, in which constructs relating to their symptoms carried many implications, and their construing appeared to show a predominant concern with their external reality. If such clients, preoccupied with their symptoms and with their external worlds, were allocated to a treatment approach, group psychotherapy, which did not focus initially on their symptoms, they tended not to respond. By contrast, responders to group psychotherapy tended to have relatively loosely organised construct systems in which constructs relating to their symptoms were less central, and were primarily concerned with their internal reality. The poor response of clients with tightly organised construct systems to psychotherapy is consistent with previous research and perhaps reflects the fact that in such clients, whose constructs are highly inter-related, any invalidation of their construing is likely to carry implications for many constructs in the system, including the 'core' constructs whose change Kelly viewed as a most threatening prospect.

Numerous other findings arose from these investigations but all led to the conclusions that individuals are only likely to respond to therapeutic approaches which are congruent with their constructions of the world, and that a therapeutic service which caters for a wide range of clients should therefore offer a correspondingly broad range of treatment approaches. A service of this type, which as we have seen is character-istic of many clinical psychology departments, would to a large extent accept the client's view of their situation, this being the central initial consideration in treatment selection. In this respect its philosophy could be considered to be entirely consistent with the 'credulous approach' of the personal construct psychotherapist, who 'starts with whatever limited conceptualization of psychotherapy the client is initially able to formulate' (Kelly, 1955, p. 567).

Constructs aren't confined to clients

One of the characteristics of Personal Construct Psychology is that it is reflexive, being as applicable to an understanding of the behaviour of psychologists, including personal construct theorists themselves, as it is to that of their clients. Such applications may be illustrated by the research studies discussed above for, as well as suggesting that if they are to be maximally effective psychology departments might usefully contain representatives of a variety of therapeutic orientations, some indication was provided of the reasons for the heated disputes which often occur between representatives of these different approaches. As was the case with clients, staff members' constructions of psychiatric treatment were found to reflect their more fundamental attitudes to life, their core constructs. Clinicians being no less resistant to changes in their core constructs than are their clients, a possible explanation was suggested for the observation that in the traditional psychiatric settings which we studied many staff members had vehemently opposed the introduction of a new treatment philosophy such as a therapeutic community or crisis intervention approach (Caine *et al.*, 1981; Winter *et al.*, 1987). These staff members were perhaps being faced not only with the prospect of learning new treatment techniques, but also more radical reconstruing involving such core constructs as those on which they had previously contrasted themselves with their clients.

Such considerations may be particularly valuable for the clinical psychologist to bear in mind when introducing trainees or members of other disciplines to new methods of intervention or when supervising their clinical or research work. Research supervision is perhaps a pertinent example in that Kelly viewed psychotherapy as analogous to the relationship between a research supervisor and their student. Just as the experimentation that occurs in psychotherapy may threaten our clients if it involves invalidation of their core constructs, so may our research students find disconfirmation of their hypotheses a very threatening prospect. These students, in their research, may be seeking validation not just for their hypotheses but for their whole view of the world. This is an issue to which I have often found it essential to attend in supervising the research of trainee clinical psychologists, not least because Kelly felt that one way in which an individual may react to threat is by hostility, which he saw as involving tampering with the evidence to make it fit with one's predictions. For other trainees the whole enterprise of carrying out research appears to provoke a certain amount of guilt, as Kelly defined this emotion, because it leads them to see themselves in the uncharacteristic and therefore uncomfortable role of relating to others in an impersonal, objective way. Whatever the problems faced by the trainee in conducting clinical research, the clinical psychologist who adopts a Personal Construct Theory perspective will proceed on the assumption that the student's research project will have a personal meaning for them which may be as important a focus for supervision as is, for example, consideration of computer packages for statistical analysis.

Constructive alternativism contrasted with current trends in clinical psychology

Although the above examples constitute a personal account of ways in which one clinical psychologist has applied Personal Construct Theory in his work, they may perhaps provide a flavour of the broader applicability of the theory in this field. While the examples cover several of the activities in which a clinical psychologist may be involved, ranging from direct clinical work to the organisation and evaluation of a therapeutic service, and from interventions with clients to the supervision of fellow professionals and trainees, they all share Kelly's basic philosophical assumption of constructive alternativism, which asserts that innumerable, viable alternative constructions may be applied to a particular situation and that none can claim to represent absolute truth. From this standpoint, it follows that effective work with a client or staff member will not involve exhorting them to adopt the psychologist's view of the world, but rather will seek to understand the other person's constructions, the purpose which they serve in the individual's anticipation of events, and the consequent emotions which may be engendered by attempts to change these constructions.

Such an approach, it seems to me, is singularly appropriate to a profession whose subject matter, and whose constructions of that subject matter, are so diverse. One of the distinguishing features of the clinical psychology profession has been its respect for alternative viewpoints and resistance to the imposition of a 'party line', this trend being exemplified in Britain by the professional autonomy of psychologists once qualified, and by experiments with democratic departmental organisation such as that at Bexley Hospital psychology department (1980), which, significantly enough, derived a major impetus from Don Bannister. There are signs now, however, that things are changing, with moves towards registration, 'professionalisation', and the barring of some clinical psychologists from speaking for the profession. In relation to the latter issue, witness the view of the chairperson of the Clinical division of the British Psychological Society that 'It does not seem, to me, to make sense simply to allow any clinical psychologist to call themselves an expert . . . It has not been unknown in the past for some psychologists to hold views which are quite bizarre and with which the Society and the Division would not want to be associated' (Cullen, 1985, p. 5). Perhaps, after all, it is not altogether surprising that a theory which espouses constructive alternativism should remain less than popular with the clinical psychology establishment.

4 · 'What can I do for you?' Personal Construct Psychology in primary care

PETER CUMMINS

The context

In the United Kingdom about one million people consult their General Practitioner (GP) every day. They do so, on average, four times every year. As each GP has a personal list of patients registered with her, doctor and patient get to know each other well. It is usual for GPs to spend their professional career working within the same practice. There is, therefore, often a long standing relationship between doctor and patient, and indeed often between the doctor and the family of the patient. It is by no means uncommon for one doctor to have treated several generations of the same family. It is equally not uncommon to find several generations of one family working within the same practice; medicine tends to be an inherited profession. There is an increasing trend in the UK for doctors to work together in groups; these are usually partnerships of three to six GPs. It is now normal practice to find a wide range of other professionals working in conjunction with primary care doctors. These will include nurses, midwives, health visitors, social workers and psychologists. In the past seven years, I have worked in a variety of group practices, on a sessional basis, as a clinical psychologist. My clinical training had included *no* experience whatsoever of working in primary health care.

Anticipation

In construct psychology terms my early experience of working in a health centre can be described as the *anticipation* phase. In this phase I was struggling to understand what actually went on within the health centre. My initial ideas of ill people being diagnosed, treated and cured did not take long to be challenged. In my early days I sat in with some of the GPs during their normal morning surgery. I was not prepared for the impact of meeting at least twenty people in the space of two hours. At the end of a morning surgery I had to struggle to remember the reasons people initially gave for coming to see the doctor. It was rare for an identifiable organic pathology to have been diagnosed in more than four out of twenty patients. These surgeries were quite typical according to the doctors I had sat in with. Just what was going on in these consultations? Since I first asked myself that question I have read much of the literature which attempts to answer my question, of, 'just what is going on in the surgery?'. The literature available is (as in many other areas) rapidly increasing. It is not my intention to even try to summarise this work. My intention, rather, is to clarify for myself, and to attempt to show you, the contribution which George Kelly's work has made to answering my question. In doing so I have written almost exclusively about the work of doctors and one psychologist (myself) in primary care. I do not intend in any way to marginalise the contribution of the other professions previously mentioned; I have worked closely with several of them. The focus of this chapter simply reflects the central role played within primary care by the family doctor.

The nature of construing

Kelly's Psychology of Personal Constructs (PCP) suggests that all people try to understand their own experience in order to improve their antici- pation of what the future holds for them. The person anticipates by using their own individually developed system of personal constructs. At this stage I think it is important to emphasize that when Kelly talks about constructs he does not only mean verbal constructs. This is one of the most common misunderstandings about PCP, a misunderstanding which has allowed people to dismiss the theory as being merely cogni- tive and unable to deal with emotion. Kelly was always quite clear about the range of convenience of construing.

> Construing is not to be confounded with verbal formulation . . . many pre- verbal or non verbal governing constructs are embraced in the realm of physiology . . . thus they (constructs) may have to do with such matters as digestion, glandular secretion and so on which do not normally fall within the ranges of convenience of psychological systems.
> If a person is asked how he proposes to digest his dinner he will be hard put to answer the question, yet digestion is an individually structured process and what one anticipates has a great deal to do with the course it takes; what we are saying is that the notion of construing has a wide range of convenience if we choose to use it that way (Kelly, 1955).

With a few exceptions (Radley (1977), Neimeyer and Neimeyer (1981)) the implications of the above quotation, implying the wide potential range of construing, have not been sufficiently explored. It is these implications which I have found central to understanding what is going on in the surgery.

The meeting

In any first consultation the central task is for patient and doctor to understand each other's construing. As we have already seen constructs are ways of anticipating events. The patient's task is to describe her present situation and to negotiate a meaning for her symptoms with the doctor. The doctor's task is to understand what the patient expects of him and to assist in 'the continuous shifting of the patient's construct system' (Kelly, 1955). The most common reason to consult the doctor is due to the patient's construing her particular symptoms as being out of her own control. In situations like this, which are difficult to construe, Kelly suggests we get anxious. Anxiety is defined in PCP as being aware that the events we are confronted with lie mostly outside the range of our construct system. The task of the doctor, seen in this light, is to help the person to bring the particular events within their own construing, i.e. to help them to understand. The family doctor will only be able to do this if he can understand the patient's construing. People usually come to see their family doctor with a relatively restricted range of constructs about their own body. It is common to find that bodily functions are construed using a set of pre-emptive, constellatory constructs e.g. pain is always bad; that it is a sure indicator of serious underlying pathology, that the doctor's job is to know always what is causing the pain; that the only appropriate treatment for physical pain is to prescribe medicine or surgery; and that treatment will remove all pain. Almost always physical is construed as one end of a construct:

PHYSICAL —— MENTAL

This implies the classical body-mind dichotomy; there is no direct connection between physical events and mental events. It is therefore not possible for physical pain to have emotional causes. Parallel to this construct is the medical construct of:

ORGANIC/SOMATIC PAIN —— PSYCHOSOMATIC PAIN

This construct allows 'physical pain' to be caused by 'mental constructs'. These two different constructs cause a lot of misunderstanding in medicine.

> The term Psychosomatic disorders is, of course, systematically meaningless. 'Psychosomatics' utilises neither a consistent psychological system of expla-

nation nor a consistently physiological system of explanation, but rather makes the gross philosophical error of presuming that certain facts are themselves inherently 'psychological' or 'physiological,' respectively (Kelly, 1955).

I am often told by people that their pain was diagnosed as due to 'nerves'. A common response to this diagnosis is to ask 'How can real pain be caused by nerves'. The alternative response is to construe the doctor as not believing that the pain is real.

The doctor-patient relationship

As previously noted, it is as important that patients understand doctors' construing as that doctors understand the patient's construct system. Kelly suggests that the degree to which they can construe each other determines the nature of the *role relationship* between them. By *role* he meant an interaction where both people are trying to understand (subsume) the other's unique construing. Such a role relationship is the essential requirement for any therapeutic relationship. It is the joint responsibility of both participants to determine the depth of the relationship.

Diagnosis in primary care

The particular significance of the doctor-patient meeting in primary care is that it is the meeting place of the biological and the social.

The GP is frequently called upon to decide upon an appropriate construing of the patient's problems from a biological perspective and to negotiate with the patient about this construing. The simplest role-relationship is one where doctor and patient construe the situation in a similar way, e.g. where both accept a purely biological perspective and a suitable remedy is prescribed. It is equally clear that when the two participants construe the problem totally differently then there is no role relationship. The different possible constructions of pain mentioned earlier imply the lack of a role relationship.

'Diagnosis is all too frequently an attempt to cram a whole live struggling client into a nosological category.' The alternative Kelly suggests is to use a set of professional constructs to subsume the construction processes of the client. 'In transitive diagnosis the clinician, instead of preoccupying himself with the question "in what category should this case be classified" immediately addresses himself to the question "what is to become of this client".'

This form of diagnosis is clearly different from the normal medical diagnosis which attempts to place a person's symptoms within an existing framework; I have spots, pain and tiredness therefore I have illness type x. In PCP terms diagnosis is a creative activity; doctor and patient are creating a new way of construing the patient's symptoms. To be creative PCP suggests we employ the CPC cycle and the creativity cycle (see Figure 4.1).

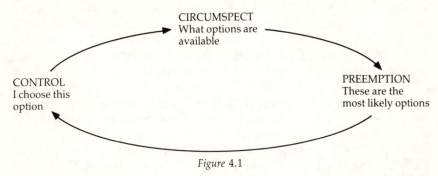

CIRCUMSPECT
What options are
available

CONTROL
I choose this
option

PREEMPTION
These are the
most likely options

Figure 4.1

CPC Cycle

The creativity cycle consists of alternate *tight* and *loose* construing. In many consultations the doctor and patient are at different points in these two cycles. The doctor has a set of professional constructs which she applies to the tale told by the patient. This can lead to the following consultation.

Mrs Smith comes to see her doctor because she has a lump in her throat.

GP
Circumspection: What does this symptom represent. What are the physical reasons for lumps in throats.
Preemption: Most likely this is not a physical problem.
Control: Prescribes tranquillisers/counsels herself/refers on to psychiatrist or psychologist.

PATIENT
Circumspection: Am I ill – lumps in throat probably mean cancer – will I choke – what if I cannot swallow – will I stop breathing.
Preemption: I know I am ill – I have a life threatening illness.
Control: I need physical treatment.

At the start of this consultation the GP had a loose construct about throat lumps.

A loose construct is one which leads to a variety of possible predictions. Thus for the doctor a throat lump may be construed as being a benign growth, a malignant growth, an infection, no physical cause obvious, etc. Very quickly the GP decides (preempts) that there is no physical cause for this 'lump', and decides that this is a psychosomatic problem. This is in sharp contrast to Mrs Smith's construing; for her there is no question about the physical existence of the lump, which she can feel. The only question for Mrs Smith is 'How ill am I?' In our culture lumps have become tightly associated with malignancy. As far as Mrs Smith is concerned the most likely diagnosis is one of cancer. It is quite possible that she already knows someone who died of a similar type of lump. When her doctor declines to refer her on to the surgeon she will probably construe this as the doctor not understanding her problem. The most likely result of such a lack of role-relationship is that Mrs Smith will either return with similar symptoms or consult another doctor. If she does return then eventually she and her doctor have to develop some understanding of how they interpret the lump Mrs Smith is worried about. Out of such negotiation often comes a referral to someone else such as a clinical psychologist. For Mrs Smith to accept such a referral involves a great deal of reconstruing of her initial constructs about her throat lump. The referral may only be accepted following the reassurance of a physical examination by a hospital specialist.

The implications of change

When I meet a person in a Health Centre my central concern in a first session is to try to understand the implications for the person of her particular symptoms. I also need very quickly to construe how she construes being asked to go and see the psychologist. This will clearly depend on the depth of the role relationship she has with her doctor. It is not uncommon to discover that the person has come to see me as part of their struggle to persuade the GP to reconstrue their diagnosis. The clearest example of this is a referral such as Mrs Smith where she construes her lump as being 'organic' and not 'psychological'.

Tschudi (1977) has developed a very useful technique to explore with people what the implications of change in their present construing would be. It is a technique I have found to be valuable as a first attempt to understand why a person has ended up coming to see me. A clinical example demonstrates this technique.

Mr Jones has had problems with high blood pressure for many years; he is now aged fifty-one. In his medical 'career' he has been seen by many different doctors and prescribed a wide range of drugs. His blood pressure has never been successfully stabilised for any significant length of time. For years he has been advised that he must learn to relax more as a means of improving his blood pressure. I was asked to see him to explore whether I could teach him how to improve his capacity to relax.

I was interested, to begin with, in exploring what the implications were for Mr Jones of being better able to relax. Tschudi's ABC technique involves asking the person firstly what would be their desired alternative to the presenting problem.

A1 Presenting problem   A2 Desired alternative

For Mr Jones, his desired alternative would be low blood pressure. The person is then asked what are the perceived disadvantages of their presenting problem and how they see the advantages of their desired alternative.

B1 Disadvantages of high blood   B2 Advantages   of   low   blood
   pressure   pressure

Finally they are asked what advantages (if any) they can see in having their present problem and what disadvantages would there be if they achieved their alternative.

C2 Advantages of high   C1 Disadvantages of relaxation/
   blood pressure   low blood pressure

This yielded the following from Mr Jones:

A1 Tense/high   A2 Relaxed/reduced
   blood pressure   blood pressure

B1 *Disadvantages*   B2 *Advantages*
   Increases irritability   Less irritability
   Long term strain on my
   body, veins, arteries etc.   A moderate approach to life
   Could promote heart   concerns especially people
   problems
                                Could be fitter and healthier

C2 *Advantages*   C1 *Disadvantages*
   While I am a driver I ensure a   Could   become   lazier   or
   job well done, plus increase   moronic which in turn would
   my finances   lead perhaps to more dissatis-
                                     faction   and   less   financial
   Does not allow one to become   reward
   slapdash in approach to life
   etc.

The rational model underpinning Mr Jones's treatment focuses on the A and B levels; there is a desired solution with desirable consequences. What is not taken into account is how the patient construes the 'desirable' change *in total*. It can be seen from the above example how important the implications of the suggested medical advice are for Mr Jones. In his job as a sales representative he works best and earns more while under pressure. If he were to relax, as advised, he foresaw a decrease in his job performance with concomitant financial problems. He was already only just managing to avoid becoming insolvent; he could not contemplate any further decrease in his income. For Mr

Jones the medical implications of not relaxing were outweighed by the implications for him of relaxing. I was not able to help him to alter this situation, but I was able to help his doctor to understand what lay behind Mr Jones's apparent 'failure to cooperate in treatment'.

A second case illustration, in brief, again illustrates the usefulness of this approach. I was asked to see Mr Brown to see if I could help him with his life long problem of enuresis. He is now in his late thirties. His problem only really occurs when he has drunk several pints of beer. The standard advice he had been given was to give up drinking beer, and indeed my initial impulse, having heard his story, was to tell him . . . to give up drinking beer! Using the ABC technique I discovered that for him drinking beer was an important part of his working-class culture. For Mr Brown to give up drinking beer had major implications for his social relationships, hence his reluctance to accept the advice about giving it up.

The ABC technique is a concise yet powerful means of exploring how change is construed by the patient. Personal Construct Psychology suggests that these *implications of change* are what determine the result of the consultation. Apart from the ABC technique there are two forms of repertory grid technique which may also be used to explore the implications of change. These are implications grids and resistance to change grids. As I rarely use these techniques in primary care I do not intend to describe them further. If you are interested in finding out about them they are clearly described by Fransella and Bannister (1977).

Levels of awareness

It is important to emphasise that it is not always possible to clarify the implications of change as rationally as in the above examples. These implications are often at a level of awareness which is not immediately accessible to verbal formulation. Many of our most important constructs are non verbal and thus are often difficult to put into words.

> We should not assume that a ready verbalisation is the hallmark of consciousness or that because a thing is not expressed we are not aware of it. Nor should we assume that what is asserted is identical to that of which we are conscious. We know from self-experience that consciousness has many levels and not all are mutually consistent. The relationship between what is asserted and what is known is a function of the relationship between speaker and listener. Indeed I have heard it said that the only two occasions when a person tells the truth are when he trusts and when he wishes to hurt (Ravenette, 1980).

Given that constructs are not necessarily verbal we are left with the task of understanding people's behaviour. Kelly suggested that behaviour is man's principal instrument of inquiry. It follows that a person's behaviour is determined by the nature of their construct system. 'If a person endlessly repeats the same behaviour then I shall suspect he is still looking for the answer to a question he knows no better way of asking' (Kelly, 1970a).

The meaning of symptoms

If physical symptoms are a form of construing then they have meaning at some level of awareness. Primary care is where negotiations take place about the meaning of symptoms. Such negotiations often take years of patient-doctor consultation to resolve. The skill of general practice is to maintain a role relationship with the patient throughout these negotiations. I often see people who have agreed to see me only because of the strength of their relationship with their doctor. Although they themselves are puzzled as to why a psychologist is relevant for their problem, if Dr X thinks it is a good idea, they are willing to give it a chance. Just as Kelly himself was very fond of asking people to try to see things *as if* so also GPs make this demand of their patients when referring them, e.g. try to look at your symptoms *as if* they have psychological implications. The particular implications of the problem will influence the person's reaction to this request. As I discussed in a previous section (*the meeting*) this may lead to anxiety, or even what PCP calls *threat* (being aware that you are going to have to make a comprehensive change in your core constructs).

Exploring meaning

Mr Black came to see me after two years negotiation with his GP. His problem is severe pain in his jaw, which is getting worse and worse. In the preceding two years he and his doctor have pursued every avenue physical medicine has to offer. He has been to dental surgeons and had a jaw plate fitted. He has had a wide variety of drugs prescribed. He has had physiotherapy to loosen his jaw muscle tension. Finally as a last resort he and his doctor agreed upon a referral to the psychologist.

By the time he comes to see me he has begun to reconstrue his symptoms in the light of this agreement. His wife has begun to comment on the phases his pain goes through. In particular she has pointed out that his pain gets worse in the week prior to his monthly visit to his son who lives with his first wife. When I ask him about this he begins to tell me how angry he is with his ex-wife. He is unable to express this anger in case he loses access to his son. I ask him whether it is important to him to be able to express anger. Mr Black replies that all *real men* are able to express their anger. I am already getting some idea of the dilemma Mr Black is in. I begin to build a hypothesis: 'I wonder if his jaw pain is providing some sort of resolution for his dilemma. It may be that the focus is now on finding a solution to his pain, which preempts the need to look at what started the pain.' At this stage I have no real understanding of Mr Black's construing system or its contents.

In forming such a hypothesis Kelly suggested that there are six basic questions to be asked.

1 Exactly what is peculiar about this client, when does he show it and where does it get him?
Answer: He has chronic jaw pain, which has developed since he was divorced by his first wife. The problem became acute about the time his ex-wife moved to another part of the country. This move meant a long journey for Mr Black if he wanted to see his son. I wonder if the pain diverts his construing into safe areas. The choice corollary suggests that people choose that option which allows the greatest possibility for extension and definition of their system. For Mr Black to define his problem as illness allows him to avoid the *threat* and/or *anxiety* implicit for him in construing his symptoms as emotionally based.

2 What does the client think about all this and what does he think he is trying to do?
Answer: His initial construing was that this was an organic (as distinct from emotional) problem. He had spent two years seeking the physical cause of his pain. The wide variety of solutions he has been offered have failed to solve his problem. He has recently begun to acknowledge that there is a pattern to his symptoms. This pattern is linked to his visits to see his son, who lives with his ex-wife and her new husband. He is currently fluctuating between organic and physical causation. Kelly described such change as 'slot movement' and observes that this change is often superficial and 'is all too likely to end up in see-saw behaviour'. For Mr Black this might imply a superficial change to a 'psychological' explanation but he might readily return to an organic hypothesis.

3 What is the psychological view of the client's personal constructs?
Answer: In primary care I often only have one hour to produce an initial psychological view. The challenge is often to produce this in such a form that the other person will accept it to the extent of returning, at a later date, to continue the process. In the course of my hour with him several important constructs emerged:

Made a success of life _____	Done nothing with life
Old fashioned type _____	A nowadays bloke
Someone who shows anger _____	Someone who hides their anger
Fatherly _____	Someone who does not accept responsibility

From these I begin to think Mr Black is in a position which he cannot resolve while he refuses to change his own self image – *guilt* in Kelly's term (see glossary). For Mr Black the proper response to his situation would be to show his anger to his wife. His main method of showing anger is to be physically violent. If he decides not to be aggressive then he becomes the sort of person he despises – in his language a 'nowadays bloke'. But if he shows anger or gets violent he knows he will lose access to his son. He therefore rationally hides his anger, but is unable to live with himself. His 'solution' was to reconstrue his dilemma in physical terms. The obvious hypothesis is that he was literally holding back his jaw from expressing anger. His continued quest, from specialist to specialist, began to become *hostile* i.e. he continued to try to get proof for seeing his problem as a physical one, despite specialist after specialist failing to find anything physically wrong.

The inability to resolve competing demands (to get angry vs to stay calm) could only be resolved by a change in his core construing which he was unable to make.

4 In addition to the client himself what is there to work with in the case?
Answer: The immediate answer to this seems to be limited to his current partner and possibly his son. At the time of our first meeting he seemed resigned to his present relationship ending due to the strain of his symptoms.

5 Where does the client go next?
Answer: At this stage I have to decide with the client what should happen next. Is Mr Black willing to make a therapeutic contract with me? Do I think he would be better dealt with by an approach other than one to one work (e.g. group therapy)? Should Mr Black be seen jointly with his current partner, or with his ex-wife (should this be feasible)? If we jointly decide to meet again, is this practically feasible for him in view of his work commitments? I work in a fairly working-class area where taking time off work usually means losing money.

6 How is the client going to get well?
The *big* question! Kelly is always very demanding of clinicians 'a therapist should check his understanding of his client by continually testing his ability to predict what the client will do'. At the end of a session I should be able to predict how the client will fare in the interval prior to the next session. For Mr Black one clear sign of his getting well would be a reduction in the degree of pain he experiences in his jaw. My provisional hypothesis is that such a pain decrease will occur as he becomes able to verbalise and to reconstrue his at present unverbalised constructs about anger, rejection and failure.

At the end of this first session I agree with Mr Black that we will meet for six sessions.

I have spelled out my first session with Mr Black to give you some idea of how I try to organise my own initial diagnostic thoughts. In such a first session I have several distinct objectives. I need to begin to try to understand Mr Black's unique construing system. I try to facilitate Mr Black in his struggle to reciprocate by understanding my construing. I have to convey to Mr Black that change is possible without catastrophe. I have to decide at every stage just how much change we should aim at. Eventually this becomes a mutual decision. Personal construct theory offers a range of strategies to continue this process of exploration. You may have noticed that I have barely mentioned its most famous technique, grids. This simply reflects how limited my own use of grid methodology is. Once or twice in a year I see someone for whom I find grids extremely useful. I hope it is obvious, however, that PCP has far more to offer than just grids. When Kelly was asked in 1966 how he would have changed his major two volume work he indicated that he would probably delete the section on the repgrid as it seemed to him that it had obscured the theory (Hinkle, 1970).

From my initial interview I have developed my own hunches. I am particularly struck by Mr Black's construct of himself as an old-fashioned type. I may ask him for a contrast and then ladder or pyramid this construct. From this I discover one of his dilemmas:

> Old-fashioned men use violence to express themselves. However women now will not tolerate violence. Therefore you cannot both have a relationship with a woman and remain an old-fashioned man.

Mr Black's first wife left him the day he first hit her. He did so because he suspected she was being unfaithful. This suspicion had never been discussed by him with his wife; apparently old-fashioned men did not discuss suspicions.

I have often found that the second meeting is the crucial encounter. One reason for this is that it is not uncommon for a person to fail to turn up for such a second meeting. In primary care there is an almost automatic follow up by the GP: sooner or later the person returns to see the doctor. When the person does turn up the first thing I am interested in is what impact our first meeting has had on their construing. When Mr Black came to see me for the second time he had clearly thought deeply about our first session. He spontaneously told me that his jaw had not been quite so painful since we last met. What he did not tell me was that he had been back to see his doctor, four days after our first session, complaining of his jaw pain, thus emphasising the importance of my link with his GP. He had thought about the pain and realised its onset was precisely at the time he first made the long journey to see his son. As he made this journey he could feel tears well up from inside him. The actual length of the trip intensified his sadness about the potential loss of his close relationship with his son. He had previously seen his son every weekend. The journey now meant he would see him, at best, monthly. This decrease in contact increased the risk that he would fail in his role as father. It also increased the risk that he would be usurped, by his ex-wife's new husband, in his role as father. This fear of being usurped clarified another aspect of his present situation. Almost all women Mr Black met already had children. Any relationship with such a woman was not feasible for Mr Black in case he would end up usurping the children's natural father. To do this would obviously do to another man what he was afraid of having done to him by his ex-wife's husband.

In these first two sessions we have begun to construe verbally what was previously non-verbal. Mr Black is beginning to acknowledge that 'real pain' can have non-physical causes. His ideas about the nature of pain are beginning to become less rigid and able to encompass new ideas. I have also had to amend my initial hypothesis which turned out to be rather limited. Mr Black was not only holding back his anger, he was also holding back his tears. To further clarify my hypothesis, at this stage, I often ask the person to write a self-characterisation. I find this a useful way of getting to know the person's self-constructs. Asking them to do this also conveys to the person that I expect them to work on their own in between our meetings.

My encounter with Mr Black has only been possible due to my role relationship with his GP. It is often not acknowledged how important the family doctor can be in the process of counselling on psychotherapy. Patients often visit their GP in the course of being seen by a therapist. This gives the family doctor an important role in facilitating or undermining the process of therapy. It is therefore essential to reach a mutual understanding with the GP of how to construe the patient.

Choice

Fundamental to PCP is the recognition of the dignity of another's construing system. Fundamental to primary care is the frustration of watching people failing to alter potential (or actual) destructive patterns. Again and again all three of us, doctor, patient and myself, have to go through the CPC cycle as we struggle to resolve a particular problem. One of the nicest (unsolicited) compliments I have had from a GP colleague was the statement 'I can now understand more why people do not change and so I do not get so frustrated'. The frequency of consultation is one of the particular features of primary care. Again and again the doctor meets a person for the first time and experiences the anxiety of not understanding the implications of the patient's problem.

Gradually as doctor and patient develop a role relationship their mutual anxiety decreases. Frustration often develops gradually as a person returns repeatedly, with symptoms which never form a clear diagnosis for either doctor or patient. GPs often begin a consultation by asking 'what can I do for you'. With people who attend frequently the doctor's frustration often changes the greeting to 'what is it *this* time'. As previously mentioned PCP suggests people choose those constructs which most extend and define their construing system. This often means that people choose not to alter their circumstances for their own good reasons. A visit to see the family doctor is often an important part of maintaining the status quo.

People who work within the primary care setting are often worried about the implications of really coming to know the patients they work with. Their fear often seems to be that they will unwittingly damage their patients by stirring their emotions. They are also often concerned that they themselves will be unable to cope with deep emotions. What is not sufficiently understood is that it is not always necessary to challenge fundamental core constructs. It is however important to understand such constructs, if only to avoid the person being *threatened* (defined by Kelly as the awareness of imminent change in one's core structures). The challenge of primary care is to find ways of dealing with subordinate problems of construing, while understanding how such problems fit into the person's construing system. The example of Mr Brown previously quoted demonstrates what I mean. To stop drinking beer may have implications for core construing despite appearing a relatively subordinate activity. What is often required in primary care is the ability to assist the patient to find their own way of reconstruing at a subordinate level. Given a structure to work within people do find their own ways to reconstrue.

Conclusion

I have tried in this chapter to convey some of what I have learnt from working in a primary care setting using a PCP approach. Writing this has made me feel quite vulnerable, inevitably it is not the perfect chapter I intended to write. A similiar vulnerability is at the centre of primary care. In referring a patient the primary care worker has to reveal their own assessment of the patient's problem. This assessment will be scrutinised by specialists in the particular diagnostic category. In a similar manner, you, my reader, will make your own assessment of my way of working.

In making your evaluation of my work you must obviously do this from within your own professional/personal framework. My professional framework is that of clinical psychology which gives me a particular role to play within primary care; George Kelly was himself a clinical psychologist. There is however nothing about Personal Construct Psychology which is unique to clinical psychology. In describing my own work I hope I have helped you to begin to assess the potential contribution of Personal Construct Psychology to your own work.

In my own workplace I am often asked 'what do you anticipate achieving with this person?' I am expected to answer this in the space of a few minutes. In one sense the only honest answer I can give is to say I do not know. I cannot anticipate how our meetings will eventually work out. In another sense I know exactly what I anticipate happening. We will struggle jointly to describe and understand our mutual construing. We will seek to discover what it is that is causing the person's problems and work out ways in which the problem can be reconstrued. Like everyone else I, my colleagues and our clients succeed in this task to varying degrees. PCP is no magician's bag of tricks, but it does provide a coherent framework within which every person is challenged to develop their own creativity. The common GP question 'what can *I do* for you?' should be replaced by 'how can I help you?'

> For me, Kelly's work is not an end in itself nor a place to stop but part of a longer tradition. In this tradition Kelly is offering a meeting place, for the moment, where he is suggesting the getting together of issues in science, the arts, religion and a number of other disciplines. It is his claim of being concerned with man's continuing quest to know that strikes me with such particular force (Mair 1985).

I hope I have helped you in your own individual quest to know.

5 · Personal Construct Psychology and speech therapy in Britain: a time of transition

PEGGY DALTON

Coming out of speech therapy training in the mid-1960s, one was supposedly equipped to deal with everything from a deviant /r/ to a massive loss of language skills resulting from a stroke. We had studied disorders of articulation in fine phonetic detail, become experts in the counting of stuttered-syllables-per-minute and could tell an afferent from an efferent aphasia a mile off. Speech, language and voice assessment procedures were becoming more and more complex with the introduction of electronic devices for measurement. While the dominance of anatomy and physiology as major areas of study receded, the intricacies of linguistic analysis advanced. It was taken for granted that the *disorders* we were to *treat* belonged to people but very little was made of the links between the two.

Psychology was, of course, on the syllabus. My most vivid memories are of rats in mazes and cats in boxes. There was a term devoted to personality theory, where we skimmed across Freud, Jung and Adler, with a nodding reference to Skinner and Eysenck. We fared a little better perhaps in child development lectures, where Gesell, M. M. Lewis, Bowlby and Piaget at least gave us the opportunity of considering alternative ways of viewing the processes of a young person's growing up. 'Abnormal Psychology', however, was presented quite separately and a psychiatrist outlined the symptoms of various psychoses and neuroses, glancing at clinical depression and anxiety states as he went along.

It was always acknowledged that speech problems might have their psychological aspects, but the message to the newly-qualified therapist was mixed: on the one hand we were to 'counsel the patient' on these psychological matters, on the other, we were not to dabble and a swift referral to a psychiatrist was advised where problems emerged which were beyond our scope. There was little guidance as to the counselling and no attempt to define our scope. Such knowledge, presumably, came intuitively to anyone with a leaning towards helping those with speech and language difficulties.

That was the mid-1960s and, of course, it was not all bad. There was a real need for speech therapy to develop from the rather hazy mixture of the remedial and the empathetic. The growth of a more scientific approach to assessment and more carefully structured therapy programmes was, in many ways, progress. What was missing, however, was any psychological framework, placing our treatment of disorders firmly in the context of a theory about the people who experienced them.

In my own view at that time such a need was by no means elaborated. I only knew that what I had learned was not enough. I recognised that occasionally a deeper understanding of the person I was working with seemed to enhance communication between us and lead us to be more creative, going beyond the immediate task. There was a sense of development from the experience on both sides. These occasions were too rare, however, and I had no idea what made them special. I wanted to know more what the processes were. I couldn't wait for some kind of magical chemistry to 'happen'. It was only when I came upon Personal Construct Psychology that I began to see that it had something to do with being able to subsume the other person's approach to life to such an extent that this knowledge, rather than my training, became the governing factor in the choice of what we did together.

Many qualified therapists have sought postgraduate training in counselling of various kinds. And in the last few years at least more attention has been paid to counselling skills in undergraduate training. My proposition here, though, is that the personal construct approach to speech therapy does more than enhance a therapist's capacity to deal with the psychological problems associated with speech and language difficulties. It provides him or her with the means for self-reflexion in dealing with life as a whole and the role of therapist in particular; it facilitates a deeper understanding of the people with whom we work; and it forms a basis for hypotheses which must be made and tested out if our therapy is to be creative and effective.

The role of the speech therapist

In the public mind a speech therapist is construed variously as an elocutionist (still), a teacher of speech-sounds to the inarticulate young and a restorer of lost language in the elderly; there is also some vague notion that s/he can sometimes do something to stop people stuttering. I was informed by an amiable ophthalmic surgeon recently that, of course, my job was largely done by machines these days. The profession itself, although rightly depressed by such evaluation, seems to be no better at clarifying the speech therapist's role, if the continuing saga of what we should be called is anything to go by.

It is not an easy task, of course, especially if we simply look at what a speech therapist working in a hospital or health centre might *do* in a single day. This may quite properly include articulation work with a young child, vocal rehabilitation procedures with someone after laryngeal surgery, activities to help restore verbal comprehension for a person who has suffered a CVA. These details in themselves, however, say little about the larger purpose of speech therapy, which is to facilitate communication between people. This implies concern for the development of children unhampered by linguistic disabilities. It places great value on all forms of communication for the enhancement of life and the growth of relationships. Above all, there is recognition of the devastating effects of loss of speech, voice and language on a person's sense of self.

It is probably not possible to capture all this in any name. And while *speech therapist* may be limited in its implications, it may continue to serve as a verbal label representing a construct which is far more permeable and capable of change. Each person who practises will need to define and redefine his or her role as experience throws new light on the work s/he is doing.

The therapeutic relationship

When the personal construct approach was first introduced into speech therapy by Fransella in 1972 perhaps the greatest challenge came with the change of emphasis in the therapeutic relationship. Up until then, however concerned the clinician might be with the life issues and feelings of 'patients', s/he had become essentially a teacher. *Programmed learning* of everything from speech sounds to fluency techniques predominated. The idea of a partnership between therapist and client, with Kelly's analogy of the research student and supervisor setting up experiments together, was new.

For therapists to take full responsibility for their own part in the enterprise and at the same time recognise the value of the clients' own expertise was clearly threatening for some. It had always been rewarding to work with those who brought their own imagination and energy to bear on what the therapist offered. To start with what the client had to offer and focus on *their* construing of their situation was another matter. To acknowledge that a person's theories about himself, his problem and his world in general was the basis from which to create change needed considerable reconstruction to the therapeutic stance and many still find it difficult to construe the importance of the largely unexpressed theories of children or those who, for some reason, cannot verbalise how they view events.

From assessment to exploration

For those to whom such a change in therapeutic relationship made sense, the current assessments of communication abilities, for all their refinement and thoroughness, were not enough. One of the many significant ideas which Fransella brought to our work was that the study of speech should be carried out within the same framework as the study of the person who is using that speech. Only through understanding the client as a whole can we expect to plan with him or her appropriate measures for alleviating the problem as s/he experiences it.

The use of repertory grid technique, self-characterisations and other means for exploring a person's world were first introduced into work with people who stuttered, following the publication of Fransella's findings from her research project. It had long been recognised that attitude to stuttering and themselves as stutterers played a large part in disfluent people's difficulties. Attempts had been made over the years to assess these attitudes and self-concepts but still in 1980 American, Canadian and Australian clinicians were dissatisfied with their usefulness (see Boberg, 1981). By this time in Britain personal construct procedures had to some extent taken the place of these measures, giving as they do a far broader and deeper picture of the context in which these people are trying to deal with their problem. It took some time, however, for therapists to move out into other areas with any confidence.

There seem to be two main reasons for this reluctance. First, there was the assumption that 'psychological' exploration was only appropriate where problems seemed to be largely 'emotional' in origin. There was a failure to make the connection between behavioural change and psychological change, whatever the circumstances bringing a need for that change. Second, there was the common over-valuation of grid technique as if it were the only means for subsuming a person's construct system. Since speech and language problems can represent special difficulties in setting up grids in their usual verbal form, there was a tendency for clinicians to feel that construct therapy could not therefore be undertaken unless the client were fully articulate. Only as therapists began both to be more inventive in the modification of grid technique and to use other means of eliciting and observing their clients' construing of things did this kind of exploration begin to form a basis for understanding the person whatever his or her communication problem.

Modifications of grid technique

There are many examples in the literature of the use of various forms of repertory grid technique with those who have no specific speech or language problem. And there is now more discussion of the usefulness of the procedures in relation to people who stutter. Here, therefore, the focus will be on situations where speech and/or language difficulty has called for some special adaptation, always bearing in mind that the aim is one of subsuming, not of setting up a grid against all odds.

In work with adults, modification is necessary where there is severe reduction of expressive speech in a person with dysarthria or dysphasia, together with comprehension problems in the latter. Where comprehension is relatively intact but expressive speech and writing severely impaired, the skill lies in presenting appropriate material within the clients' range of interest and convenience and supplying verbal labels to their construing in such a way that they are truly meaningful, rather than imposed.

Sets of pictures of people, for example, can be offered for the client with no speech at all to sort into piles of those s/he would like to know, those s/he would not like to know and those to whom s/he is indifferent. By studying the pictures the therapist can make suggestions as to why the person liked one and not another: 'He looks quite cheerful, relaxed, bright . . . etc. Is that why you chose him?' 'She seems a bit humourless, silly, hard . . . is that why you wouldn't care to know her?' If suggestions are made in a propositional way, the client feels free to accept or reject. When a number of poles and their opposites are agreed upon, the constructs can then be applied to elements/people in the client's life and rated in the usual way.

One method for eliciting constructs where comprehension is severely limited is currently being developed. A set of photographs showing someone looking 'depressed', 'anxious', 'happy', 'gentle', 'interested', 'welcoming', 'rejecting', etc. is presented to the client for pairing in opposites. Starting with a clear contrast such as 'depressed . . . happy' it has been found relatively easy to convey what is required without words. Although people naturally differ in how they construe the opposite of someone looking anxious, for example (and the construct for them may not even *be* anxious), there does not seem to be much difficulty in finding a sample of pairs which the client is satisfied with. They are then asked (by gesture) to place photographs of their family, friends and themselves between the two pictured poles to indicate roughly where they see them in relation to the visual construct. Here, of course, the therapist can only guess at the client's meaning from his or her choice of opposite and, often, the facial and gestural behaviour which accompanies choice. Whether or not it is useful to quantify these discriminations into grid form by attaching ratings to positions between the poles has yet to be explored. As a means of sharing something of the client's view of those around him or her, however, this method does seem promising.

Clinicians attempting to understand the meaning of events for people as severely handicapped as this report a change of emphasis in their therapy. Although direct work is quite properly still done on the restoration of speech and language, there seems, for these therapists, to be a move away from drilling specific sounds and teaching correct vocabulary and grammar into something broader and more personal to the client. One result does appear to be that, with the emphasis *off* accuracy of expression and onto personal meaning, more spontaneous speech is forthcoming and comprehension on a broad level is facilitated. We need, of course, to find some way of testing out this apparent trend as more personal construct work is undertaken with people who are dysphasic. And the part such an approach can play in helping these clients to come to terms with massive psychological change will be considered later.

Exploring the child's world

For some time now clinicians working with children have found the many procedures developed for exploring the construing of young people of great value in setting their therapy for speech, language, voice and fluency problems in the context of the personality as a whole. The imaginative work of Ravenette, Salmon, and Bannister and his colleagues, in particular, has brought a new dimension to our understanding of the child's view and a very clear sense of the value of children's own theories about themselves and their worlds. Not only have these authors presented ideas for the modification of grid technique and self-characterisations with young people, but in procedures such as Ravenette's Portrait Gallery and Troubles in School we have the means to help children express some of their construing hitherto not available to them. On the basis of such exploration it becomes possible to facilitate the psychological reconstruction which for them too will be a necessary part of changes in communication.

One small boy saw himself largely in quite positive terms, isolated from his friends only in being 'teased about my speech'. Addressing this common issue of being teased within the context of this child's way of looking at things we first made the construct more permeable by considering children who were teased for other things – one for being fat, another for having red hair and a third because he always came top in religious knowledge. The construct became 'has something to be teased about' as opposed to 'never teased'. This led us to look at and role-play all the ways in which one could deal with teasing: verbally, behaviourally, internally; and reflect on what made some people tease you when others did not.

The boy showed himself to be a great experimenter, especially in managing one particular bully. He came up some weeks later, with some fairly shrewd ideas as to why he behaved as he did. Then it ceased to be a topic of interest. When he came to re-rate his grid a year later the construct had very little meaning (had moved to last in order of contribution to variance). He did not see himself as having something to be teased about, the fat boy had gone on a diet and was much admired for his self-discipline. He could not apply the construct to any adults or to the members of his own family.

In this instance, as so often in working with young people, the boy's mother was involved in his process of reconstruction, together with her own. With a problem of cluttering, he came to regard clear speech as an important factor in relating easily to his friends and put as much into practising an alternative way of speaking as he did into his beloved model aeroplanes. His mother, for her part, shifted her emphasis from a wish for her child to do her social credit to encouragement for him to have an enjoyable share in family communication. She understood him well to begin with but learned more of his priorities from working closely with him.

Sometimes, however, parents find it hard to put themselves in their children's shoes and may unwittingly be compounding the problem by imposing their own constructs on the child. The mother who is 'a worrier', sees her child as taking after herself and therefore assumes that she is equally anxious, can transmit that anxiety to her. A military father whose main concern was for his five-year-old son to be 'strong' and not 'soft' was putting undue pressure on him and adding to his growing sense of inadequacy. One mother, reacting against her own punitive parent by going out of her way to be lenient with her two girls, learned from comparing her eight-year-old's self-characterisation with her character-sketch of the child that they had very different views about what being 'strict' or 'not strict' meant. It was clear that structure, rules to follow, were quite positive for her daughter. (The use of such sketches and exchange grids by parents is discussed in more detail by Dalton, 1986.)

Apart from helping parents to construe their children's views of things there is often much work to do with the adults themselves. The anxiety and guilt present in so many parents of children with problems of all kinds is very much the business of the therapist, though s/he may have to tread warily if the child's difficulty has become the focus of all that is wrong in the family. It may take some time, as in the instance of a six-year-old with Down's syndrome, for the mother to begin to talk about her own desperation. At first she wanted me only to produce more and more 'stimulation' for her son – to teach him to read, to *make* him use full sentences and so on. This was in line with everything she had done all his life until the boy had no space left for his own creativity. Only when she was willing to talk about her fears for his future, her shame about bringing him into the world and to some extent ease her own guilt, was she able to adopt a new approach to his development, combining the structure that he needed and facilitation of his own spontaneous construing of things.

Content and structure in the development of therapy

It should be clear that exploration, be it with child or adult, is an on-going part of therapy and that reconstruction may occur simply through involvement in these procedures. Clarifying the contrast between the 'Self Now' and the 'Self Without a Problem' in a grid, for example, or elaborating one's current situation in a self-characterisation may be the first step forward a client takes. We may discover from eliciting and laddering constructs just how central the communication problem is to the client. Our approach will be very different where, for instance, a person is completely dominated by the role of stutterer, as opposed to one whose voice problem is shown to be fairly peripheral, with a well-elaborated sense of self in other roles than that of speaker.

The early stages of therapy for the former may need to focus on the development of sociality, a greater understanding of the themes and preoccupations of others, if all constructs are related to their reactions to the client's disfluency. A dilation of view in their approach to speech situations which they may be anticipating solely in terms of fluency/non-fluency, will help to diffuse the intensity of feared events. Elaboration of the self in a wide range of roles will also be needed, so that they approach life offering to others their capacity for friendship, work skills, enjoyment of art or sport – not just awareness of speech behaviour.

For a young man whose voice has failed to develop, therapy will not only consist of exercises to deepen the register but, perhaps, attention to any fears he may have about growing up and help in dealing with the reactions of others to that 'girl' on the other end of the telephone. People with 'functional' voice disorders having little or no organic cause have always been seen as needing counselling. A personal construct approach to the problems which trigger off the particular individual's recurrent voice loss, for example, should lead to alternative ways of dealing with stress. There is nothing in the literature to suggest that 'minor' articulatory deviations, such as an interdental /s/ or a labio-dental /r/, might have any effect on a person's construing of self. But if we trouble to understand the meaning of them to the people themselves we may find considerable distress, certainly far more significance than is usually attributed to them. And this should be taken into account when we plan measures for change.

Apart from a growing knowledge of the *content* of a person's construing, my own more recent work with construct theory in speech therapy has highlighted the importance of subsuming aspects of the *structural* nature of a particular individual's system for dealing with the world (see Dalton 1986). The *processes* employed as a person develops networks of meaning around certain events are clearly crucial to our understanding of them. Our plans for therapy will be as much influenced by such knowledge as they are by our grasp of the meaning itself – is indeed part of it.

We become aware quite soon, for example, of a general *tightness* or *looseness* of construing or of sudden tightening in the face of threat. The kind of experiments we help the client to set up will need to take account of this. If a client approaches life and his or her problem in a chaotic way, clarification of the issues and careful structure for action will be needed. Someone who is trapped in the certainties of too tight construing will benefit from some help with loosening their current anticipations of events before creative experiment is possible.

Awareness of the *level* at which the client construes most meaningfully is also important. For some, events may be most clearly discriminated in quite concrete, physical or behavioural terms, while for others, more abstract, philosophical constructs come most readily to mind. We must both tune in to the level at which the client is comfortable and, where necessary, work with them on the development of a fuller hierarchy of construing. Laddering and pyramiding are useful here as clinical techniques but need to be followed through by the client in the context of life. A person may have difficulty in coping with others, for example, if they are limited to making sense of them largely by what they look like. Another may find it hard to relate to those around them if they are construed exclusively in superordinate abstractions. In either case, extending to other levels of the system may be an important part of our work in helping those whose communication problem has restricted their experience of relationship.

There is considerable reference in construct theory literature to the process of *fragmentation*, expressed in Kelly's corollary as a person successively employing 'a variety of construction subsystems which are inferentially incompatible with each other'. A certain amount of inconsistency in the construing of all of us is merely human, the capacity to keep separate one set of beliefs from another. It can prove quite useful where, for instance, a 'socialist' parent believing in equal opportunities for all, nevertheless sends his child to a public school because he also believes in doing the best for his son or daughter. Where it can cause trouble, however, is in a situation where two networks of meaning are in open confrontation. A client had strong feelings about her duty to become actively involved in a political movement. She also feared more than anything revealing that she stuttered. The incompatibility of these two subsystems caused her to experience enormous guilt and resolving this proved one of our most important priorities.

There seems also to be another, perhaps opposite, process which has not received much attention to my knowledge. This is where a person, far from separating aspects of his system from one another, tends, when threatened, to draw massive implications into an apparently quite minor event. It is as if suddenly connections are made which load the moment with unbearable significance. This process can often be seen in situations which are anticipated with fear. The person who stutters approaches a reception-desk as if his whole life were at stake and experiences that brief and mundane exchange as though his credibility as a person has been lost for ever. One young woman with a slight labio-dental /r/ related the failure of her marriage to the moment when she had to say the word 'ring' at the ceremony. She felt that from then on her husband's family had put her down as 'childish' and 'stupid' and she could never come to terms with any adverse comment they made about her. We have not really understood another person unless we are aware of what form this 'overloading' process may take for them.

If, in the course of learning to use Personal Construct Psychology in therapy, we are, as suggested, truly reflexive then knowledge of our own processes will enhance our understanding of others. Realisation of my own not too effective decision-making for instance, in the light of Kelly's CPC cycle, has hopefully made me more sensitive to the difficulties experienced by some clients in the face of choice to do with any number of life issues, including how they approach therapy. Impulsivity can be anticipated, perhaps, or help given to someone immobilised in the circumspection phase and unable to commit themselves to control and action.

Therapy for the person

It should have emerged from what has been said so far that how we may help a person to reconstrue will depend more on aspects of the individual's view and approach to life than on the 'disorder' for which s/he has been referred. Nothing in this is incompatible with the many excellent treatment programmes for articulation, fluency, voice or language work. The major difference is that these programmes will be presented within the context of a much broader concern for the client's well-being. Very often, where clients have been held back in relation-ships through a communication difficulty, there will be a need for work on construing others, by learning themselves the 'credulous approach'. If they have focused mainly on their own performance in their struggle with language or articulation they may gain much from listening more perceptively for the meanings of others and observing non-verbal signals more sensitively.

Many situations which they have anticipated with dread or avoided altogether may have to be reviewed as a whole before the person can approach them with a change of behaviour. Even with the capacity to use a voice level appropriate to his age a fifteen-year-old boy found himself embarrassed at the thought of the family gathering at Christ-mas, just *because* he knew that the change would bring as much comment as his former 'peculiar' voice. A girl who had avoided public speaking due to her lateral /s/, although knowing herself to have much to say in a particular cause, needed to experience all the other aspects of exposure in role-play in a group before she was able to transfer her modified speech pattern to such an event.

When any person, child or adult, changes the way in which s/he communicates, however trivial that change may seem from the outside, there will be some reconstruction of the self. In the examples discussed so far the changes on the whole will be in a positive direction, although clients (and those close to them) may experience considerable threat in the process. It will be clear that someone who becomes fluent after a lifetime of stuttering will have much to do to come to terms with his or her 'new self'. A person who has felt ineffective due to an apparently minor articulation problem may also need help in coping with what for him or her is a significant change in self-image as that problem is overcome. One aspect of reconstruction in most cases does seem to entail some diffusion of intensity around the whole issue of speaking. This does not occur when speech only is the focus of attention in therapy. It can take place, however, if work on speech change comes within the context of the personality as a whole.

Reconstruction of the self after brain damage

The speech therapy clients for whom help with reconstruction of the self is most needed are those who through CVA, head injury, brain disease or cancer of the larynx have suffered loss of speech, language or voice. These are the people who have experienced often sudden and violent change, which has a devastating impact on themselves and their families. So far, relatively little personal construct work has been undertaken in these situations and development in these areas must be our next priority if we are to offer a comprehensive psychological as well as behaviour modification service.

Brumfitt (1984) in her investigation into loss of communicative ability in the aphasic person, considers the experience in relation to loss, grief and mourning. She looks at the effects on core role construing of grief in such a situation, where guilt, threat, fear and anxiety, Kelly's constructs of transition, are all involved in the process. She elicited constructs for a grid with the help of photographs of scenes depicting some sort of human condition (handicapped v. non-handicapped, lonely v. involved with people, happy v. sad, old v. young, etc.). Finding that for most people the 'Past Self' and the 'Ideal Self' were construed very similarly, she suggests that there is a real yearning for the 'lost' self following a stroke. It is important, she believes, for the therapist to 'work towards some personal understanding of the aphasic's construction of his past self so that therapy can focus on what is lost and indeed, more positively, on what has stayed the same'. It may also be possible later to help the client to construe some new aspects of the self.

Tightness of construing in most of her clients suggested a predictable constriction in the face of anxiety. 'This anxiety needs to be acknowledged. By acknowledging it, the patient may feel more substantial and be able to construe himself differently rather than just sinking into an immovable anxious state.' She draws our attention to the need for many aphasic people to reconstrue their own bodies, which may now be hemiplegic. Most sadly, she reminds us of the person's loss of what John Shotter describes as the ability to talk to oneself as a means of maintaining a sense of self.

Brumfitt and Clarke (1983) discuss ways of helping the aphasic person come to terms with all this loss. Despite difficulties in verbal communication, receiving full attention from the therapist may in itself be the most crucial factor in establishing a caring and personal relationship. Trying to share 'what it is like in there', they suggest, can be done by using tentative statements like 'I wonder if it feels you are completely alone now?'. Where there is severe communication loss, even the tone or touch of the therapist can convey something of this wish to understand. One quite significant way of making contact I have found can be to share a client's likes and dislikes. By looking together at objects, pictures of clothes, houses, food, people's faces, handling textures and, above all, listening to music, the therapist can form a profile of the person's taste in things and, at the same time, reciprocate by conveying his or her own. Thus a 'conversation' at a gestural and feeling level really does take place.

As has been said, work in this area is still very new. We can learn much to help us develop our skills in subsuming from work such as Luria's *The Man with a Shattered World* and some of Oliver Sack's papers in *The Man who Mistook his Wife for a Hat* (for all its sometimes sensational style). David Green (1986) takes us through his experience with three young men who had suffered head injury and reveals a sensitive understanding of their plight through approaching them credulously. All such accounts can help us to put ourselves in the shoes of someone who has suffered not only loss of communicative ability but changes in perception and memory which can grossly affect their construing of their world.

Just as in our work with children it is important for us to subsume the construing of parents, teachers and others involved, so our therapy for people who have suffered a CVA will inevitably demand an understanding of their relatives. Often the spouse of someone who has become dysphasic is as shattered as the person him or herself. S/he too will experience sudden loss of role at having to readjust to many aspects of their joint lives. Guilt, threat, anxiety are great. Mourning for them too often lasts a long time. Groups for relatives have been run for many years and it is hoped that here also the personal construct approach is being introduced. Sharing meanings, exchanging ideas for experiments to cope, learning together how their dysphasic family members might be experiencing life, all have a place in rehabilitation.

So far, I believe, no such work has been done at all with people after laryngectomy. It has always been acknowledged that loss of voice means loss of a very important part of the self. The contribution Personal Construct Psychology might make here is potentially enormous. The impact of the loss, the psychological upheaval involved in learning oesophageal voice or using some other means for communicating calls for complex reconstruction personally and socially. How one comes to terms with remaining fears of cancer may be the difference between a satisfying though altered life and constriction into depression.

Training the personal construct speech therapist

We end where we began, with the issue of training. It was recognised that more attention is now being paid to counselling skills in undergraduate training and that more experienced therapists are seeking to enhance their therapy by undertaking counselling courses. However, this does not seem enough. If we are to get away from the emphasis on the assessment and treatment of disorders and reach a position where the person truly comes first, we need more than the attachment of counselling skills to the rest of our training. Speech therapy has been described as currently being in a time of transition and, as we have seen, transition can mean threat, anxiety, even guilt. A major change in our approach such as has been suggested here, with Personal Construct Psychology as the superordinate framework within which we work, will threaten, make anxious and certainly cause guilt in those set in their ways.

As one who rated herself quite high on the construct 'open to new ideas' in her very first grid, I have by no means been immune to the alarming experience of challenging many dearly held notions about my work as a therapist and myself as a person. Nor do I expect this challenge to cease. I have found, however, that it is possible to retain a good deal of what I had already learned and will continue to learn from other sources and, indeed, for that learning to be enriched by being set in a new context. Not the least, perhaps, the reflexive nature of Personal Construct Psychology should help a profession such as ours to understand more clearly how we interact with one another and how those from other disciplines view themselves and the clients we are all trying to help.

Fransella and her colleagues at the Centre for Personal Construct Psychology have contributed much to the development of construct theory within speech therapy by training many clinicians to various levels. These therapists have shown themselves to be aggressive and creative in their application of the ideas. It remains, perhaps, for those who teach to acknowledge the need for a more comprehensive understanding of Kelly's approach.

6 · *Speculative adventures: the social work setting*

HILDA BROWNING

Behaviour is an experiment – an attempt to anticipate the future, not merely a response to the past. Although much of what happens to a person in life may be outside his control, his construction of those events will determine what he makes of life. States of mind such as anxiety, threat, hostility and guilt serve as indicators of the need for change. Each person views the world from a unique standpoint, developing networks of meaning which are based on discriminations in his mind between the similarities and differences of those things within his experience.

These are some of the assumptions on which Personal Construct Psychology is based, and which I have found provide a useful framework for examining what takes place between people who meet as client and professional worker in a psychiatric setting. I am not a personal construct psychologist, nor any longer a practising social worker; that lends me, in one sense, a clearer perspective from which to view both, and in another way perhaps restricts my vision. It depends upon which way you look at the matter and upon the opinions of those you are addressing – the balancing between subjective and objective. This, it seems to me, is what Personal Construct Psychology is about – looking at things from different angles, tasting, trying out; evaluating and learning from experience; absorbing the creative and positive outcomes into daily living. The flavour is one of optimism. Man is not the victim of his circumstances but has an active role in determining the quality of his existence.

Certainly there are events and circumstances which are beyond our sphere of influence, but there are many areas in life over which we have more control than may sometimes be acknowledged. All of us, in our separate ways, have to manage experiences of loss – failed relationships, death, redundancy, financial hardship, mental or physical illness, the aging process – those phenomena which bring people to the attention of social workers. We need to acknowledge the inevitability of these life events and to be sufficiently aware of how we ourselves deal with them if we are to be of use in helping other people. The reflexive nature of this process is explicit in Personal Construct Theory; there is no hierarchical difference between the helper and the person seeking help. There are, however, differences in task and role.

Before giving illustrations of practical ways in which I have applied some of the methods relating to this theory, I want to say something about the ideas which are evoked in me when considering its application to the field of social work. The quality of relationship to be established between client and worker has been emphasised throughout the literature of social work, usually under the heading of casework (Hollis, 1966). A basic tenet of Personal Construct Theory is that the relationship is mutually examinable; a joint venture. Here the distinction between those involved is in the roles adopted, described by George Kelly as that of supervisor with researcher; in this instance a social worker with a client. This indicates that what takes place is in the nature of an experimental undertaking.

Social science?

The proposition of 'man the scientist' is a base-line of Personal Construct Psychology – man who attempts to predict his future and to control it by engaging in constant experimentation – making hypotheses, testing them and evaluating the outcome. What has social work to do with science, and how can we equate with scientific method the piecemeal processes in which we engage? Peter Medawar (1984) speaks of misconceptions of scientific thought, describing what he sees as the false polarization that exists between creative and inductive approaches, the art and the sciences; the distinction between having an idea and trying it out. He outlines on the one hand the romantic conception – the search for truth – as seen through the mind of the searcher: ' . . . every advance in science being the outcome of a speculative adventure, an excursion into the unknown . . .'. On the other hand he poses the alternative view of a scientist's task as being ' . . . an act of discernment, which can be carried out according to a Method which, though imagination can help it, does not depend upon the imagination. The Scientific Method will see him through . . .'. He proposes that what appear to be paradoxical are, in fact, accounts of two successive and complementary episodes of thought that occur in every advance of scientific understanding. Whereas a scientist must be freely imaginative, he must also be sceptical; creative and yet also critical: ' . . . there is poetry in science, but also a lot of bookkeeping . . .'.

This seems to me to bear a very close resemblance to what, in construct theory, is termed the CPC cycle (Kelly, 1955), the sequence of construing which involves a system of open attentiveness, followed by the adoption of a possible position, and culminating either in control of the phenomenon by that means, or in moving forward into a new cycle if the first proves unprofitable. This cycle of circumspection, preemption and control, then leads to further choices precipitating a person in a particular direction. Again, Kelly speaks of the cyclical nature of creativity, of the successive tightening and loosening involved in productive thinking. In order to be of use in prediction, creativity needs to be directed purposefully. An idea or hypothesis which leads to an experiment (a contrived experience) may need to be repeated a number of times before it can be discerned how useful this may be for future predictions.

If we extend this to the practice of social work, this implies an awareness of the sequential nature of thought processes. In order to be creative, we require open minds, the ability to float ideas and to think tangentially. Yet, to be able to harness these ideas, we must also be able to tighten and draw boundaries, imposing a structure which in turn may be modified when no longer adequate to that situation. Today, in the mid-1980s, social work spans a broad field of operations and expectations, where there is a good deal that is undefined and indeterminate in the assumptions made of the social work task. At the same time, there is greater prescription relating to the 'controlling and policing' part of that role – fresh legislation sought, and new directives issued constantly. Can social workers cover the range which spans intensive, credulous championing of individual causes at the same time as acting as agents of social control?

Why Personal Construct Psychology?

It was in the 1970s that a psychologist first mentioned to me the theory developed by George Kelly and later elaborated and applied in this country by Don Bannister, Fay Fransella and others working in the clinical field (Kelly, 1963). I was airing the difficulties that I found as a social worker in accepting one or another psychological base while working with a multitude of people who differed radically from each other, each having his own context and unique situation – some of which might be within my own range of experience, although much was quite outside my own environment or manner of daily living. Each person, it seemed, demonstrated different capabilities and required an understanding and a relationship which bore little resemblance to the way in which I had engaged with the previous person, or to the possible needs and demands of the one who might succeed him. None could be fitted, in a procrustean way, to a particular framework; rather, as I listened, did I detect something of the framework by which he ordered his life, whether or not to his or others' satisfaction.

Whereas there might be a common theme – a person with a problem meeting a person trained in certain skills directed towards alleviation of social distress – it was evident to me that only by coming to know someone's dilemma *as he saw it*, from within, and in his own terms, could one offer a quality of help which might be acceptable and of lasting value to that person. To base assumptions on half-digested analytical or behavioural theories that had formed part of the psychology input of social work training appeared to be denying the diverse needs of the people who arrived at the door labelled Social Worker, as well as the range and inclinations of the practitioners of that agency. Whilst psychoanalytical models might be useful in interpreting current actions in the light of early patterns of upbringing, the practicality and immediate applicability of behavioural methods seemed equally relevant on other occasions. I felt that in the time-pressed context of social work the first approach delved too deeply into areas of unconscious motivation, requiring a disproportionate time commitment and a distance between helper and supplicant that I found alien. It also demanded the acceptance of premises based on a mythology which I found questionable. The second – though it offered more immediacy in terms of results – seemed to be preoccupied with surface behaviour, the inner feelings of the subject appearing to be subsidiary to the establishment of acceptable social behaviour. Procrustes again. It was difficult to move far in any direction without entering the esoteric and rather restrictive world of professional psychology, where language and methods of schools of thought differed radically from one another, and where it appeared to be heretical to acknowledge the positive aspects of any one in the camp of the other.

It is an exaggeration to polarise these theories or to speak of them as being barricaded in well-defined camps – each with its hierarchical battalions of practitioners – but that is the way it felt to me at the time, with myself in a sort of no man's land between. Moreover, I saw the roles of 'helper' and 'helped' as being inherently linked, each with his own skills, dependencies and vulnerabilities. The boundaries between the roles, and the balance of giving and receiving was a good deal more reciprocal than the textbooks or training courses acknowledged.

To revert to my discussion with the psychologist – he murmured something about 'constructive alternativism' and arrived later with a book which outlined personal construct theory. In becoming more familiar with this over the past few years, I have found it a useful guide in a variety of social work settings. While not denying the validity of other ways of working, it provides a comprehensive structure within which to operate, allowing the flexibility that is essential if one is to remain open to new ideas and revision of old ones. Human communication is complex and diverse; we are social animals and our relationship with other people begins with our views of self and whatever 'world' constitutes reality for that self. That reality is adaptive and changeable.

Looking for themes

What issues are likely to preoccupy a person who has come with an undefined emotional problem? There are varied ways in which we may discover themes which recur, some of which may be developed in discussion, and others tackled as a task between sessions, such as the self-characterization that I shall describe. This method is explained more fully in another part of the book (p. 11), but two features need emphasis. Firstly, it is suggested that a person write a character-sketch about himself in the third person, as if the description were written by a friend who knows the client well, perhaps even better than he knows himself; secondly, the imagined friend is required to emphasise the positive qualities and strengths of the subject.

Many people, faced with writing about themselves, exclaim how impossible it would be to find anything to say which might be favourable; however, it is surprising how many return saying that the act of writing some of their thoughts, however painful or laborious the process, has helped them to see things more clearly. Somebody who has the commitment to self-exploration, and the trust to engage in this, already demonstrates his capacity to experiment. The 'distancing' dimension of writing in the third person is helpful in indicating new viewpoints, and in considering perspectives which might otherwise not have been considered. Our sense of individual identity depends not only on how we view ourselves, but is associated with how we see ourselves to be viewed by the people around us.

In the self-characterisation, the worker is initially looking for clues to construction processes, trying to find bridges between a client's present and his possible future, in order to help him to select and act on those connections which might lead to desired change.

Ann's self-characterisation

Ann was in her late thirties, and she had a drinking problem which, so far, she had managed to hide from the family. At the stage at which she feared she was on the verge of 'being found out', she went in desperation to her GP. Communication between her husband and herself had broken down; he was staying away from the home longer and later, and when he returned she berated him or punished him silently. Her children, too, spent their time at neighbouring houses – for one thing, the atmosphere at home was oppressive and tense, for another, they were usually invited to have whatever food was being prepared at other homes, whereas there seemed to be an inexplicable lack of provisions in their own kitchen. Much of the housekeeping money went on the vodka that Ann kept hidden at the back of a cupboard. She was accumulating debts. It was this last fact which was likely to emerge soon and was the triggering point at which she capitulated and decided to seek the help of her doctor.

The GP recognised the extent of Ann's difficulties but was unable to persuade her to use the local alcohol-abuse organisations, or to share her problem with her husband. Ann was referred to a psychiatrist for further assessment, but refused the offer of admission to day hospital or the suggestion that she attend a self-help group which had been initiated specifically for people with drinking problems. She did, however, agree to see the social worker, believing that she might be able to get advice and possibly some help towards payment of the overdue bills.

A number of professionals, then, might have been able to help, but this was the route that Ann chose. I listened to what Ann had to say. Although the imminent cutting off of the gas and electricity could be avoided through discreet negotiations with the services involved, there was, of course, little that could be done about the accruing debts without looking at broader issues, including ultimately the involvement of Ann's husband. I made plain my own view of this, outlined the practical steps that she and I might take in the interim, and offered to spend some time with her, trying to work out with her some ways in which she might help herself out of the predicament.

As she talked, gradually the underlying theme emerged, centring around her sense of isolation and lack of self-worth. Whether that perception caused the drinking or the drinking caused the tarnished self-image seemed less important than the need for us, together, to discover how to break the cycle. From the message Ann gave me, I knew that the drinking provided an escape from her low opinion of herself; the anxiety generated by her fear of 'being found out' led her to dull her senses with habitual drinking, and she was caught in a hostile and repetitive mode. She was 'guilty' in that her present way of living was alien to that which she would feel was her 'true self'. Guilt in Kelly's terms, is 'dislodgement of the self from one's core role structure' (Kelly, 1955, p. 111). Ann's guilt was evident in how far she was falling short of her own ideal, of the way in which she felt she should be looking after her family – in not fulfilling what she saw as her role in life. She appeared to have little perception of her own separate existence outside the sphere of wifely and mothering duties.

During our meeting, in spite of the fact that no easy solutions could be offered, some rapport was established between us. Ann was relieved to have voiced some of her anxieties and the imminent catastrophe was seen to be avertable, although it had not disappeared. She agreed to return the following week, at the same time emphasising that she was a victim of her circumstances, and seeing no way of changing her situation. She was adamant that her husband must not become involved. I wanted her to take some responsibility for what was happening in her life, and to know something of the person behind the roles that she felt she was fulfilling unsatisfactorily; with this in mind I suggested that she write a little about herself, preferably day by day and in the third person. 'I haven't written anything except shopping lists for years, and in any case, nobody else could possibly write anything good about me if they knew the truth', she said. However, the idea intrigued her, and she warmed to the attention that she, as an individual, was being given.

The next week Ann returned, bringing the following. The first paragraph had been written on the morning after our talk together:

> Every time I try to put things into words, I find I'm so confused and bottled up that I can't even begin. Although I now haven't had a drink for three days, I'm on the edge of a precipice all the time. My nerves are shattered. I'm jittery and edgy with people, and their clatter and hurrying is almost unbearable. I can't stand being with them and I can't bear to be alone. All the same, it's easier when the family is around because there is always something that has to be done immediately, and this makes me feel I am useful. It is during the day when I am on my own that I feel desolate. As soon as the children go out of the door, I get the craving and go to the cupboard where I keep the bottle. Drinking is like love. It is all or nothing. I can escape for a short time with a drink. I hate myself for doing it but it helps me to get through the day. Sometimes I blot things out and curl up on the couch and go to sleep. But with a drink or two I can escape the awful loneliness that engulfs me. I can't bear the thought of what my family or friends would think of me if only they knew. How my husband would despise me. I'm trapped and feel there is no way out, because I can't manage and fall to pieces without it, but if I have been drinking I don't do all the things I ought to be doing for Bob and the children, and the house gets into a terrible mess. Then, when it is nearly time for them to come home from school, I panic and get so strung up that I'm awful to be with when they do get home, so off they go to their friends and I'm alone again, feeling desolate, a failure, and useless to anybody.

On the morning of our next appointment, she wrote some more. This time in the third person:

> She drinks because she is anxious and apart from the money she is spending

on drink there is no reason why she should be in such a state. She has not much confidence in herself and feels she is too shy to be of interest to other people. She has a good husband and two lovely children but she is driving them away because they can't understand what is wrong. She used to have a number of friends who thought her worthwhile and they are still pleased to see her if she makes the effort to go out. She makes a point of being the life and soul of the party, listens to their troubles and hides her own in case she loses their friendship by showing just what a sad person she really is. She is rather like those clown's faces that have a broad grin one way up and if you turn them upside-down they're in the depths of misery. The happy and the sad. But people never see the sad side. Except the family, in the past year or so, then they keep away. She feels misunderstood because friends think she is flighty, and feels desperately alone because they don't know the real Ann.

Ann was diffident about her writing, but at the same time eager for me to read it. It seemed to me to be a vivid and articulate portrayal of her state, highlighting her need to be seen as a cheerful, buoyant person, the darker side of her nature being for home consumption only.

Although she had reverted to her drinking pattern during the rest of the week, on the day after our meeting she had used my suggestion in the terms that she could manage at that particular time. On the morning of our second meeting, perhaps in anticipation of being told she had 'not done it right', she wrote the paragraph which described herself objectively.

In my opinion there is not a wrong or a right way for a person to use these exercises; rather, it is the quality of commitment to exploration and experiment that is significant. The fact that she followed up my guidelines for viewing herself in that way did, however, give her sufficient distance from her usual view of herself to allow some strengths to be acknowledged, and provided an opportunity for self-assessment.

When on the third week I presented Ann with the typescript of her writing, she was pleased and surprised that what she had written was regarded by me as sufficiently important for that treatment. Seeing her work in print helped in further distancing. She remarked on the different feelings she experienced as she read the subjective and then the objective paragraphs. 'I despair when I'm reading that first part. I feel as if I'm drowning; but when I think of myself through the eyes of a friend, I realise I'm not such a bad person after all.'

The writing provided some keys for exploration, in her own language, of the 'all or nothing' of love and drink; of her dependence on her family; of the need to find ways of expressing the 'happy/sad' dimension both inside her home and when with friends. Over the next few weeks we continued to work with her writing from time to time, listing some of the constructs that appeared, and adding others that arose in our discussions. She began to use the 'desolate' mornings at home for writing. One of her home tasks was to supply the opposite poles of the constructs:

confused	v. to have life, feelings, neatly understandable
bottled up	v. unmuddled. At peace with myself and my surroundings
unbearably alone	v. to feel wanted, loved and love back all the time
escaping with drink	v. no need to escape

We smiled together over the phrase 'bottled up'. She remarked that it seemed that with or without drink she was bottled up, therefore it did not appear to be a very useful means of escape. These were her words we were using, and her own 'interpretations'. We looked at possible bridges that might link the contrasting poles – at what 'feeling wanted, loved and to love back all the time' might mean in her day to day existence. She saw what demands that might be placing upon those around her, and began to look at the areas in between – recognising that the attainment of the cherished ideal could be somewhat cloying, and that its non-fulfilment on a twenty-four hour basis did not necessitate the radical swing to being 'unbearably alone'.

In our sessions, we 'laddered upwards' (Hinkle, 1965) some of her less articulated thoughts. I asked why she chose a particular pole of a construct in preference to the opposite, and continued to pose the question 'why?' until we had built a picture together of what she felt she stood for – her highest aspirations. Among these was 'openness and honesty', and this, in which she felt she fell short, appeared to her to be at the heart of her sense of being unbearably alone. How could she be true to what she stood for if she was hiding her predicament from her husband, the one from whom she most required the love?

In answering the question 'why?', Ann was faced with defining what was most important in life for herself. In attempting to discover practical ways of doing something about the conflicts in her ideal view of herself, I used the 'laddering down' procedure described by Landfield (1971), in which the question eliciting the more tangible possibilities is 'how?'. How might you be more open? How would you go about that? How could you try to put that into practice in the coming week? Gradually she defined small practical steps of a manageable proportion which she felt able to act upon. When these achieved the required effect, this resulted in a growing sense of achievement and control, which in its turn lessened her self-condemnation.

Ann confided in a friend and was surprised to find her friend both sympathetic and aware of what Ann had thought an undetectable secret. After some weeks she divulged to her husband what had been troubling her. At first he found her story inexplicable. His own constructs of his wife had not accommodated her as 'an alcoholic who has been throwing all the housekeeping down her throat'. However, he was relieved to have some explanation for events which had been disquieting and mysterious.

At this stage, Ann felt safe enough to agree to my making a home visit. I met the children briefly as they swooped in and out of their home, with other friends in tow. I felt as she, her husband Bob and I talked together, that the work would be continued by the couple, and that the children would respond in their turn to the relief in tension that I hoped would result from greater understanding between the parents. Bob recognised that he himself might have to alter not only his views of life but his own way of escaping, which was in switching off and leaving the family to their own devices.

There was a good deal of plain speaking between them as they thrashed out their views of what had been happening in their relationship, but I judged that there was sufficient commitment, too, for them to be able to tackle difficulties together, including the problem that had brought Ann to my door. I continued to visit Ann for a number of months. Progress was not always smooth, and there was one area in which she had to make permanent change. She could not trust herself to drink again, even socially, and both she and her husband had to come to terms with having no alcohol in the house. As she reconstrued her 'ideal Ann', she was able to risk more self-disclosure. She joined the local community group which had initially been suggested, and began to feel of use to others outside the family, not only in the group but through the part-time work she found in a home for the elderly. This was a source of income from which she steadily repaid the financial debt.

Although the ultimate aim of this type of social work is similar, whichever framework one uses, the methods and route may vary. By use of the self-characterisation early in our relationship, it seemed to me that Ann was able to address her own needs and to find some sense of power over what happened in her own life. The acknowledgment of herself as being individual and important helped her both to encompass a broader view of life and to reconstrue herself as parent and partner.

Defining the opposite pole

If we are to subsume the construction processes of another person, this requires us to have some idea of what lies at the other end of a verbal label. Ann's 'unbearably alone' might have led along a dimension to 'contentedly alone' or 'having good friends'; her 'escaping with drink' might have encompassed a contrast of 'finding a less harmful escape' or 'expressing my anger'. It was necessary to know the contrast in order to help her to move nearer to a central and obtainable position.

The bipolar nature of constructs was made particularly apparent to me by Richard. He was an attractive and intelligent nineteen-year-old who, as he progressed through adolescence, appeared to have a bright and uncomplicated future before him. I first met him when asked to visit him at home to prepare a routine social report prior to an out-patient referral. He had shut himself into his bedroom for the previous nine months, withdrawing almost entirely from family and outside life and emerging only for meals. His parents had the sensitivity and toler-ance not to hound him and eventually he agreed not only to see a psychiatrist but to attend the day hospital on a trial basis. He refused any suggestions of medication, but gradually, with the combined help of the team, began to take part in the sheltered life of the Unit. My own contact took the form of individual weekly sessions in which, at first, he was rambling and tangential – loosely construing – and the structure and regularity of these sessions afforded him safety in which to voice some of his fears and anxieties.

Richard was keen to work on his difficulties. He wrote a biographical sketch which was guarded and, I felt, offered little opportunity for exploration at that stage; there was need for caution in approaching his private world, where any intrusion might seem an invasion. There was, however, a theme which dwelt upon the significance of place and territory, and I suggested that we look at what 'being in my room' might mean for him, as compared with 'being with the family/friends/day hospital'. It was only when he began to define the opposite poles of these constructs that he started to articulate for himself and for me a picture of the terrors that the outside world held for him. My own contrasts when trying to put myself into his shoes might have been:

'being in my room'   v.
outside, not depending on my parents
taking responsibility
having a satisfactory job
enjoying social activities

As his own alternative, Richard came out starkly with one word, 'suicide'.

I myself had construed the room as something of a prison. For him it was not merely a haven but a place of survival. I realised the percep-tion his parents had had in allowing him to take his own time. Together he and they sensed the stage at which he was ready to emerge from the security of his room, which for many months had been the only place in which he felt he could exist.

Grids

For some people, Personal Construct Psychology is synonymous with grids. In my definition, we are employing a form of mental gridding all the time we are discriminating, selecting and making decisions about life. The attempt to capture and identify those processes can be made in many ways, of which one is the creation on paper of a network of lines, a diagram which has the purpose of illuminating an area of thought which may be inaccessible by other means. The relevance of grids depends on the practitioner's experience in devising and administering a format appropriate to the occasion, and in understanding the use to which it is to be put. This may appear to be an unnecessary statement, but there is a sense in which such a technique can become an end in itself, and a practitioner may be carried away into the land of numbers, lured by the seductive prospect of measuring and quantifying human behaviour. This is not to deny their value as instruments of research and diagnosis. If a worker is computer-literate and sufficiently at ease for the technology not to cloud the process, then a print-out may be a valuable diagnostic tool. There are, however, many uses of grid forms which are not dependent upon computer skills.

Ann, the woman with the drinking problem, was able to see her situation more clearly through defining her roles as elements – wife, mother, daughter, housekeeper, drinker, ideal self and so on. This is similar to the approach described by Miller Mair as 'The community of self' (1977). From her roles, Ann elaborated constructs which created a picture of her world. By rating these constructs in relation to their significance for herself as represented by her different roles, she was able to focus on what changes she wanted to make in her life. She also evolved a structure in terms of a hierarchy of prerequisites to the recovery of her self-respect.

For Richard, the withdrawn young man, his territories were the elements. Through these we were able to build a map of his world from which he could look at possible routes out of his constriction.

The importance of grids is in the process involved – in the dialogue which goes along with elicitation, and the thinking which is evoked in both workers. A grid framework may be used as a tightening mechanism, as in Richard's case. Equally, where for instance a person is finding difficulty in seeing a problem from any perspective other than his own, then his vision may be extended by elaborating the likely responses of other people: 'How might your best friend/parent/neighbour/employer see the situation?' Grids and their design can be as involved or as simple as the practitioner chooses. The vital consideration is to recognise that what is noted on the paper in the form of words or numbers is representative of a 'slice' of construing which appertained at the time at which it was elicited; repetition may lead to the emergence of quite a different set of characteristics. This repetition may in itself be helpful in diagnosing the movement of a person's thought processes. One danger to be avoided is the tendency to interpret grids as holding constant validity; numbers in themselves do not constitute a sort of fixed truth. The range of devices and stimuli to self-expression is limited by our own inventiveness, and creativity is essential if they are to provide suitable tools for a diverse spectrum of people and situations.

One young man who stammered painfully when trying to talk about his family situation, forgot his self-consciousness when offered a box of small wooden counters which I suggested he move about on the table to represent the allegiances he felt with the people who were closest to him. He clustered the counters, moved and realigned them, sometimes silently, sometimes describing what was going through his mind in the process. For a number of sessions during the next weeks he continued to ask for these, using them as a means of objectifying where he was, within a family context which was fragmented and fraught with conflicting emotions. During this time his parents separated and he illustrated his position graphically, coming to see them as separate persons, both from one another and from himself, distancing himself from them and drawing some supports from a wider network.

Iris, a woman aged sixty, was overwhelmed by anger towards the senile father who lived with her and made her life a misery through his aggressive and irrational behaviour. After his death she was guilt-ridden and self-accusing, seeing herself only as being despicable and selfish. When I felt that the anger had gone on long enough, I asked if she was willing to bring photographs of herself and her family, at various stages of their life together. Over the next six to eight sessions these provided a focus for her expression of anger against her mother also, who had died when Iris was in her teens, leaving her to cope with a father who expected of Iris the whole-hearted attention that he had received from his wife. Gradually Iris began to reconstrue herself as daughter, and as a person in her own right, allowing herself some compassion for the difficult last years during which she had managed, as best she could, the extreme situation of her father's senility.

For Iris it was important to develop a network. During her fraught life with her father she had also been very dependent on his dominating and controlling presence, and in the vacuum caused by his death she found herself bereft and lonely. In working through a dependency grid, she was given a structure in which to explore her social field. She reconsidered approaching friends who had withdrawn through the years, whom she had cut off in shame over her father's behaviour. She took up again with a church group to which she had belonged. Although other ways of working might have evoked these changes, by mapping her world in this way she made visible to herself her own needs, and felt responsible for the implementation of the paths indicated by the map. A dependency grid is useful in exploring such questions as: Who does this person rely on, and who relies on him? How broadly based are these supports, and how reciprocal? Where does the social worker or other 'carer' fit into this? How can the elements in his natural environment supply what he is wanting, or is a different social setting likely to be preferable? Frequently, of course, strong dependency may be related less to people than to such objective elements as alcohol, violence, a tenet of belief or an institution.

Social work and change

The examples I have given are from the field of psychiatric social work, and I want now to look briefly at the more general picture. Broadly, the task of social work can be described as an attempt to assist people who have problems or who are seen by society to be 'causing problems' of a social nature. Some internal or external change is expected to be the outcome of the interaction. This can involve the provision of practical services or information, such as assistance with welfare rights, benefits or accommodation, or advocacy on behalf of a person or section of the community defined as under-privileged – the linking of available resources with the people who need them. Even at that practical level, however, there may be discrepancies between the expectations of the requester, the services available and the capacity of the particular worker to provide what might be useful. Immediately we are dealing with different perceptions of need and priority. Value-laden judgments are made, dependent upon the combined constructions of those involved.

Social work is a hybrid, based on practice which has evolved through a number of routes – political morality, charity, economic necessity, religious scruples. The Barclay Report (1982), in reviewing the role and task of social workers, identifies two major strands: counselling and social care planning. The counselling process involves 'direct communication and interactions between clients and social workers, through which clients are helped to change, or to tolerate, some aspects of their environment'. Social care planning is aimed primarily at 'solving or ameliorating existing social problems' and secondly at 'prevention and community work'.

Diversity and ambiguity

In looking to a theoretical base within social work itself, we refer to sources 'owned' by other disciplines – to psychology, to philosophy or to sociology – subject areas which are themselves loosely defined and overlapping. We borrow medical terminology and talk about diagnosis and treatment plans. We call ourselves caseworkers, welfare workers or therapists. We propound in our code of ethics the duty to uphold individual rights; we are increasingly expected to act as controllers or watchdogs on behalf of the public who have elected the councillors who form the committees who employ us. Like the Lord High Everything Else in *The Mikado* (except that our status is considerably more humble) our roles are multiple and frequently conflicting. Our jobs are at risk if we fail to meet individual needs, and equally if we challenge the system in which we are required to operate.

The nature of social work incorporates holding differing and perhaps opposing ideas simultaneously. This applies equally to those people who have come to us in the role of client. A person who is attempting to reconcile conflicting views, both within himself and between himself and his social milieu, is likely to experience similar tensions. Each person has an approach which may in part conform or conflict with others, in part remain distinct and unique. The extent to which there is a shared area of understanding of that world determines how much of a role it is possible for one person to adopt in relation to another. The helping role depends not merely upon empathy but upon the capacity of the worker to anticipate the possible needs and behaviour of a client, and to be able to work with him in managing those needs. Whilst a social worker might have detailed knowledge of resources and how to gain access to them, and might also have a broad understanding of human behaviour, it is the client himself who is 'expert' in what he wants of life, and in the way he goes about everyday living.

Working in a team

Let us now look at a situation where client and social worker meet in a multi-disciplinary setting – the first contact, perhaps taking place in the ward round of a psychiatric unit. Already there may be a number of people involved, representing different roles and with distinctive tasks – nurse, doctor, occupational therapist, physiotherapist, psychologist – not forgetting those who may already know the patient outside the hospital in some professional capacity – health visitor, general practitioner, teacher, community nurse or divisional social worker. Ideally there will be a team approach and a common purpose in helping a patient to feel at ease, in assessing what has brought him here at this stage – what his present state is, what strengths and capabilities he appears to have, what is the likelihood of change, and how the combined skills of these people can assist with this process.

In the role-bound institution of the hospital or the social service department a person is deemed 'patient' or 'client', and these are terms that I, too, continue to use, while remaining uneasy over the depersonalisation bestowed by these labels.

Every team member brings his professional perspective – his reading glasses as well as the everyday spectacles with which he views the world at large. Leaving aside the question of personal bias, the staff in their various roles may be asking themselves such questions as: How is this patient similar to/different from others we meet here? What sort of management will he need in my understaffed ward? What medication might best suit him? What activities have we to offer here that might be suited to his needs? What signs does he give of being out of touch with reality? Is he a suicide risk? What family/community network appears to surround him? How does his apparent mental state relate to what can be deduced about his external circumstances?

In an acute unit the social work role involves representing the client's social dimension, as accurately as possible, to the multidisciplinary team. Here the emphasis is on what can be done by the client *outside* the clinical situation, in the context in which the changes need to take place. Although much of the groundwork can be done during the inpatient period, the social worker's real scene of activity is outside the hospital. Through the tradition of home visiting, social workers have a privileged perspective compared with most other hospital practitioners; they have the opportunity to make some assessment of how a person appears to be managing within his own particular context. By far the greater proportion of patients seen by social workers in the psychiatric unit where I last worked – something like 80 per cent – were outpatients, and apart from the initial consultation with the psychiatrist a number of those had no further contact with the unit.

In that situation, the worker is trying to help a person to function in his own environment, with referral back to team and supervisor where appropriate; attempts and exploration leading to the investigation of further possibilities. Not only, however, is the hospital social worker trying to forge links with a person with particular needs, she is also representing, and is seen to represent, both hospital and social service agency. There is, therefore, the necessity for a worker to subsume a number of collective ideas of task and role.

Entering the patient's world

While accepting that advocacy and the provision of resources are integral to the practice of social work, I have concentrated on themes which relate to less tangible areas – the emotions – where changes are sought within the individual person himself, by attempting to help him to alter his own environment or his attitudes towards that environment. How much we can be of positive influence depends upon our ability to enter the world of another person sufficiently to offer him currency that he can use in his own country.

Within a particular and necessarily restricted field, any practitioner gathers information to enable him to make an initial prediction as to what possibilities might be helpful to this person, assuming it is agreed that he has been referred to the right establishment in the first place. The mixture of considerations is complex, subjective and fluid, just as the person under scrutiny comprises a multitude of interacting processes, physical and emotional, being not simply 'a patient etherised upon a table'.

The process is a questioning one; the mood is 'propositional' (Kelly, 1955, p. 564). The question is not: How does this person fit into my/ our framework?, but, what framework does he himself use which might be creatively extended? While the worker is required to have some very clear notions of her own professional boundaries and their implications, she needs also to be in an 'open' state, ready to look at a situation with an outlook uncluttered by preconceptions or at least an awareness of her prejudices. This is particularly important, for instance, where norms of culture, race and religion might differ widely from one's own.

Interviews are a form of mutual exploration, in which decisions are made on both sides as to how far work appears mutually possible. Each is scanning the other for clues: how is this person like myself/others that I know/what I expected? Can I offer what he is wanting/can she provide what I need? However propositional we like to be, as a short cut to making sense of what would otherwise be a chaotic world, we classify. Given that some labelling is inevitable, it is well for us to remind ourselves that others will hold varying views of us, of the function we are there to fulfil, and of the agency we represent.

Classifications, then, are made on both sides, based on the clusters of constructs that go to make our own personal assumptions. Such constructs as hospitalisation, disease, mental illness, carry powerful collective messages which may have very different meanings for each person involved. If labels are imposed, then let them be continually open to question and modification.

Patient as expert

The patient himself is the one who carries inside him the greatest amount of information about what has happened to him in life so far – his feelings about those events and how earlier problems have been overcome; whom he trusts; which areas he is willing to reveal to others and which may be as yet unarticulated even to himself. Although he is the subject of this investigation by a number of (one hopes) well-intentioned and qualified professionals, he is sometimes the person who is given the least explanation, the least opportunity to speak, with whom there is the least information-sharing or invitation to express an opinion, in a setting within which he is the least familiar of the party.

A social worker can offer options, listen, form her own opinion, fit the client into a number of classifications, liaise with colleagues, follow procedures, act politically, try to alter the environment – but where the needs are emotional rather than strictly practical, it is the client's understanding of his situation, and his own wish to alter, that is the basis of anything other than a temporary palliative. It is the aspect of *partnership* which seems to me to be distinctive about the personal construct approach – a collaboration rather than a hierarchical meeting of supplicant and holder of power. This demands an openness and ability to risk on both sides, and an acknowledgment that without the active participation of both there may be little headway made towards understanding and remedying the problem.

Managing the future

At best, all we can do with the past is to attempt to reconstrue events and to learn from them. Personal Construct Psychology places emphasis on the present and future rather than on the past. Energy is directed towards trying out different options which might enable us to handle future events. Perhaps this is one of the fundamental differences between construct approach and those based on psychodynamic theories in which current difficulties are seen largely in the light of past events, unconscious material is brought to the surface through the acquisition of insight, and linkages are made between past and present by the intervention of an interpreter. Certainly our chronology is useful in helping us to reflect on patterns we have developed in responding to the world, and in indicating directions and pathways which might lead to more favourable outcomes. Some of these patterns have resulted in the achievement of what we find fulfilling; others have triggered frustration and a sense of *'déjà vu'*; but the cost of changing our ways seems greater than we can face, and we become stuck in repetitive modes which make us feel powerless, push the responsibility outside ourselves, and perpetuate an existence which, although it might be uncomfortable, feels safer than the turbulence which could result if we were to risk changing. We may never discover *why* we are as we are, and the question may in itself become a diversion into history which blocks the ability to live freshly day by day. We as practitioners may be able to enter – albeit only in part – the world of someone else; this limited entry may be sufficient for us to join in helping a client to predict for himself more accurately, and within his own context, courses of action that give him the strength to manage the dilemma that he is facing.

George Kelly's initial proposition and its corollaries provide a descriptive framework for identifying and attempting to modify individual construct systems where change is necessary. His underlying philosophy reflects a respect for individual variety and personal autonomy. He suggests a wide spectrum of methods devised for the purpose of discovering these personal meanings that people give to their lives. His view of the counselling process is of an active partnership, where the practitioner is openly engaging in an experimental and creative way, and acknowledging the uncertain outcome of the quest while bearing professional responsibility for the ways in which she goes about attempting to help. The admission of that uncertainty might be painful; the routes that people take and the solutions they generate may differ greatly from those that she herself might choose. However, in my view there is room for change in the paternal and prescriptive attitudes which pervade the services set up for people who require care and intervention because of physical, social or emotional deprivation.

7 . Enlarging horizons: Personal Construct Psychology and psychiatry

GAVIN DUNNETT

I want to try, in this chapter, to show some of the influences Personal Construct Psychology has had on my practice of psychiatry. The first major implication of this opening statement is that to some degree this chapter is also autobiographical. I make no apology for this: PCP is by definition reflexive, and since the point of perspective is my own, it seems right and proper for you to know something of how it came about. The second major implication is that reading about the influences PCP has had on me and my work may be of some use to you in your own work. This is a prediction, partly born out of the fact that this book is being published at all, and partly from my own experience of teaching, lecturing and supervising PCP to a wide range of disciplines in psychiatry and finding enthusiasm and a desire to use it themselves in return. My hope is that a similar enthusiasm and desire to use PCP may be engendered in the readers of this chapter, and indeed, the whole book.

History

I entered the field of psychiatry in the early 1970s following the normal six years of medical training. I had always had an interest in matters psychological, and had predicted my choice of career in psychiatry for myself as early as my second year of training. Many of my subsequent desires and attitudes were already present then: a feeling that much of my study was divorced from the people I had entered medicine to help; that medicine was the application of facts and techniques to a collection of organs in an unsuspecting human being; and that whatever else my training was designed to achieve, the ability to think creatively was not

part of it. Many of my views were naive and idealistic but the effect
they had on me was to encourage me to seek out pastures outside
medicine to complement the sterility within. One of the more powerful
areas of involvement was that of politics through which I became a local
government councillor before finishing my training. This experience of
practical grassroots politics overlapping as it did with my entry into
psychiatry (indeed for a time I had the dubious distinction of representing the district in which my local psychiatric hospital stood!) made
me aware of just how similar the people were who presented at either
'psychiatric' or 'political' surgeries. On detailed examination, the case
of depression presenting at the former had almost exactly the same
symptoms and problems as a constituent pouring out their housing
problems at the latter. It seemed not so much that they had different
problems as that the route chosen to present or deal with them was
different, and so the eventual response was too. This phenomenon did
not seem to accord well with my new psychiatric training with its
emphasis on discrete psychopathology, specific mental illnesses, hospitalisation, and a medical approach to management and treatment.

It is strange, looking back, that although I began my psychiatric
career in a service with a strong psychological and psychotherapeutic
orientation, I still felt alienated from my everyday practice. The process
of eliciting symptoms assiduously, and then assigning them (and the
patient) to what felt like arbitrary diagnostic pigeon holes followed the
medical model carefully but without the anticipated benefits. Because
psychiatric diagnosis was phenomenologically based (that is to say,
the 'illnesses' were diagnosed by the presence or absence of specific
symptoms assessed by the examiner) rather than physiologically based
(where the symptoms are directly related to underlying physiological/
organic change) it suffered from the subjectivity of the examiner on the
one hand and a myriad of alternative remedies for the same symptom-
cluster on the other. The overall impression I gained was of confusion
together with a sincere but rather desperate effort to make the medical
model work better by refining the diagnoses; eliminating the subjective
(in both examiner and patient); and encouraging research into the
underlying physiology and pathology.

It is perhaps not surprising that although I had entered the field in
part *because* it was not all cut and dried, this feeling of confusion encouraged examination of alternative ways of making sense of what was
going on. Initially there were two paths for doing this. The first was
the 'psychotherapeutic' approach. Then, as now but to a lesser degree,
the psychoanalytic/psychodynamic approaches held sway within the
medical psychotherapeutic fraternity. It certainly offered a radically
different angle and I can remember initially espousing it strongly. But
increasingly it seemed difficult and ultimately impossible to incorporate
it into my day-to-day work.

It felt like an 'either/or' choice; one was either for a biological or a psychological argument. It was one *or* the other – there seemed no middle line. Although I wanted to be psychological, I could not keep it up in the face of the flood of problems that kept on arriving remorselessly. With this kind of psychological approach I simply did not have enough time. Further, it did not help me when I felt I had to be 'biological'. I simply felt guilty, that I was letting my principles down, and that I was not helping my patient as I ought.

Around about this time, anti-psychiatry was beginning to appear. This was the second possible path. Authors such as Thomas Szasz, Irving Goffman and Ronnie Laing burst into print and were promptly seized upon. Here was the answer. Let us ditch the whole idea of mental illness altogether – it obviously does not work, has deleterious effects on the people it is supposed to serve by labelling them and institutionalising them. It is time to jettison the entire approach and start again!

But what with? This seemed to be a different and rather more difficult question. Certainly there was a need to put the *person* back into psychiatry. Certainly the social and cultural dimensions needed to be incorporated. But how to put all these together to make some corporate sense? The answer did not appear to be forthcoming. The then current practice of psychiatry was terrible, dreadful even, came the trumpet, but an awful silence seemed to reign thereafter.

At this point two important events occurred for me. I read a book by Jan Foudraine called *Not Made of Wood* in which an American psychologist related how he had taken over a unit of institutionalised chronic schizophrenic patients and had attempted to rehabilitate them by treating them as *people* rather than as *patients*. It is powerfully written and seemed such an obvious way of going about the task. The other event was that a psychologist with whom I was working decided to administer a grid with one of my patients.

It will already be apparent that at this stage in my career I saw myself rather as a rebel without a cause. In a much more minor way, it felt similar to the experiences of Dr William Sargant which he described in his survey of the psychiatric scene in his youth in *The Unquiet Mind* a generation before. Like him, I felt there had to be more. Matters were better; much, much better than in the old institutions he described, but it was not enough.

It is ironic, upon reflection, to realise that my contact with PCP came through the repertory grid which is now the part I invest with least importance. Ironic, but not surprising. Even then, repertory grids were an accepted tool in the armoury of the clinical psychologist even if their knowledge of Kelly and his theory was thin or non-existent. I do remember well being lucky that this particular psychologist spent time with me not only explaining how to administer a repertory grid, but also why it was useful and what it might show . . . and that it derived from Personal Construct Psychology. This was a psychological theory that put the person on the centre of the stage; that encouraged, even demanded, that we look at the world through *his* eyes (rather like the anti-psychiatrists and Foudraine) but also told you how you could go about such an endeavour constructively (unlike everyone else!). It seemed too good to be true.

Over the ensuing years, I have had the good fortune to learn more about PCP and its uses from a variety of teachers and practitioners, as well as being given freedom to develop its use in both theoretical and practical clinical work. This chapter can only touch on many of the areas in which I have found it valuable. As a starting point, it is worth remembering that 'psychiatry' is itself one pole of a construct, and I have chosen to structure the rest of this chapter around a pyramid of constructs derived from this point (see Figure 7.1). Clearly Figure 7.1

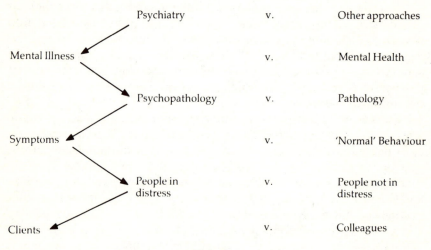

Figure 7.1

is my own pyramid, and the limitations of space have denied it a proper pyramid shape or the pyramiding of each of the contrast poles. Nonetheless it demonstrates effectively that PCP has something to offer at each of these different levels of activity, as well as providing an insight into the fact that there *are* different levels. Many of the apparent divisions and arguments within psychiatry seem to me to derive from the problem that individuals argue from different levels. One person may be discussing the differences between a mental illness or a mental health service, while another sees this as an attack on the whole idea of psychiatry. However, to stay with the structure, let us look at each level in turn.

1 *Psychiatry v. other approaches*

When I began my training, psychiatry seemed always to be under attack. Either the methods used were inhumane, or the facilities were degrading to human dignity, or psychiatrists were supposed to be as mad as their patients. Much time seemed to be spent defending psychiatry against these arguments which became most powerful when deployed by what came to be known as the school of anti-psychiatry. It felt as though those of us in the profession needed to defend it as hard as possible, while those outside attacked it equally mercilessly. Although this attitude has changed considerably, and many of the criticisms made during that period are now enshrined within the new directions psychiatry is taking today, there is still a view around that psychiatry is somehow right, or the true and correct way of sorting out problems.

I find this a curious approach. Historically, society has dealt with people whose behaviour it did not understand or did not approve of in a variety of ways. Possession by the devil or evil spirits, having holy visions, simple-mindedness and so forth, are ideas not so far from us in time, as were the 'remedies'! Many of the people so described clearly would nowadays be referred to the psychiatric services and would be treated as for an illness. The modern discipline of psychiatry is therefore one model for coping with a set of problems – one way of construing the problems in fact. There have been other models in the past which we feel we have improved upon. Logically, therefore, it is reasonable to assume that there may be other models in the future that could be considered an improvement on what we are doing now.

With this approach there ceases to be the need to see matters in terms of attack and defence, but more of a variety of different ways of construing similar problems. All of us, both from within and outside the profession of psychiatry, will benefit for the airing of different constructions, as indeed the current move away from institutions and into the community has proved. It is not a question of being right or wrong, but of attempting to sift through the available approaches and use the methods and skills most appropriate to the problem being addressed.

This leads on to the further point, which I believe psychiatry has utilised more than many other professions. This is that psychiatry does not exist in a vacuum, separated from other disciplines by an unbridgeable divide. I have always taken the view that effective psychiatry involves a knowledge and understanding of medicine, psychology, philosophy, sociology, anthropology, politics and many others besides. Increasingly, as the community dimension grows, psychiatric staff have to work alongside colleagues in old related specialities such as social work and probation as well as new ones such as housing, planning, information technology and so forth. Practical use of PCP allows the practitioner the means of looking at 'their' problems through the eyes of practitioners with different priorities, different sets of values and sometimes totally different sets of philosophies. It does not always produce easy relationships, but it does encourage an open-minded outlook and give some structure for what otherwise often becomes heated disagreement. As psychiatry moves further away from the comfortable confines of traditional mental hospitals, so these 'other approaches' will have more influence and need greater attention. PCP gives us a system for putting it all into the same perspective.

2 Mental illness v. mental health

Many words have been written elsewhere about the value or otherwise of the notion of 'mental illness': whether it exists at all; whether it is an artefact of the society in which we live; what its boundaries are; whether the medical-type model is right to treat it; and so forth. I have argued elsewhere (Dunnett, 1981) that mental illness is but one way of construing many of the problems our patients present to us with, and that developing a service as a 'mental illness' service is only one kind of service which could be provided. Personal Construct Psychology does not come up with alternatives of itself. The possible alternatives lie within our own ability to create and invent them. What PCP does do is to encourage us, rather like the concept of lateral thinking, to loosen our constructs of what constitutes 'illness' and consider what other phenomena may be occurring. It may be that even when this has been done, the 'illness' model may provide the best explanation open to us now. But there have been many occasions when I have been presented with a patient by a colleague with a description of 'chronic schizophrenic' when the subsequent questions – why? and what else could this behaviour represent? have unearthed useful answers once the respondent had overcome the shock of the question. There are frequently assumptions that a particular form of behaviour indicates relapse, or unwillingness to participate in treatment or similar, when encouraging an alternate viewpoint provides a quite different line of management. This is not an encouragement to abandon the mental illness model; merely an admonition that alternatives to it do exist, and examination of some of them may help the person who is requesting it.

Constructs being dichotomous, mental illness has to have a contrast pole, and in my case I have chosen mental health. I am not really sure I am very happy with this as a contrast, but it is worth remembering that to some extent mental illness may be defined as what mental health is not, and vice versa. This dichotomy is not precise; few people are *totally* mentally ill or *totally* mentally well. How one goes about placing the line in some circumstances is very difficult. The construct of *mad* v. *bad* crops up often in my practice where it seems difficult to ascribe some behaviour to being due to a mental illness or to being the responsibility of the individual to control. No one denies that prisons are full of people who should not be there because they need 'treatment' and I suspect that most of us in the field consider there are people in hospital who should not be there because they are not truly ill but manipulate the circumstances to engineer admission to hospital rather than an appearance in court. Examination of my construct system around *mad* v. *bad* would probably have some similarity to others in my profession (at least I hope so) but also some differences. These differences are not exact, no lines can be drawn and no battles should be fought. I do not believe that there *are* objective data available to define one group from another. Mental illness in part is subject to the whims and fancies of the society in which it is based along with all our other personal constructs. Alcoholism has traversed the spectrum almost within my lifetime of Badness to Illness to Social Problem. The phenomenon may be the same, but what we call the problem, and how we ascribe it for action may change. This system of ascription is based fundamentally on each of our personal construct systems, acting in commonality to provide a societal view. One day, we may ascribe everything to Social Problem, and nothing to Illness. Or, better still, we may have new categories altogether to ascribe to.

The purpose of this argument is not to confuse you, but to illustrate that the differences of opinion which rage around in psychiatry at all levels down to team meeting, and care plans for individual patients, are not part of an *either/or* system. Psychiatry must be aware of this and remember that it too is continually changing and moving just as the overlapping disciplines along its boundaries do too.

A Mental Health service, of course, may provide quite different priorities to a Mental Illness service. In my construct system, it suggests prevention rather than response. And that begs the question of how to go about prevention. Again it is not the purpose of this chapter to continue that debate – merely to suggest that such debates are the legitimate concern of the personal construct theorist within psychiatry and should be encouraged, and that for those already concerned with such issues but not having a structure within which to address them, to say that PCP provides such a structure.

3 *Psychopathology v. pathology*

Psychopathology is defined (*Dorland's Medical Dictionary*, 1965) as: 'The pathology of mental disorders; the branch of medicine which deals with the causes and nature of mental illness.' This is clearly subordinate to a construct of mental illness itself, while being superordinate to examining the symptoms with which individual people present. This is the level that asks what schizophrenia is rather than how it is diagnosed (below) or whether it exists (above). Much of the work done in the field of mental illness in the Personal Construct Psychology framework is excellently outlined in Button (1985). Examination of schizophrenic thought disorder in terms of looseness of construing (Bannister, 1962) is but one of many examples that can be given (and is chosen by virtue of being one of the first). But most of the work is actually at the next level down, at the level of the symptoms and behaviour individual patients present.

I believe Personal Construct Psychology invites us to consider specific illnesses within its framework. Here I am encouraging a specifically psychological view of these illnesses (for the moment accepting the existence of the superordinates of psychiatry and mental illness) and am suggesting that exploring them from a PCP angle could be valuable. To some extent I believe that Bannister has done this with schizophrenia in that there is a broad suggestion that much of the illness is explicable in terms of loosened construing and the effects this has on the functioning of the individual. I say to some extent only because schizophrenia is such a vast and apparently complex disorder that no relatively simple explanation in this chapter would remotely cover all the possibilities. But if, for the sake of argument, a prediction that what people presenting with the disorder called schizophrenia actually have wrong is a disorder of their construing processes such as extreme loosening, then this has implications for a treatment plan. This new treatment plan could be radically different from many we currently operate for schizophrenia, or it may run in parallel. Personal Construct Psychology provides an excellent environment for examining old psychopathological entities from a new angle.

This is especially exemplified by Dorothy Rowe's wide-ranging examination of depression (1978; 1983). Dunnett (1987) has also carried out such an exercise looking at phobias beginning from a theoretical standpoint and producing a hypothesis that is clinically testable, and exciting in its possible application.

I consider that the whole of existing psychopathology could be re-examined in this way, providing different and new insights which could themselves lead to new and exciting methods of treatment.

4 Symptoms v. 'normal' behaviour

Within the field of psychopathology, disease entities are distinguished by the presence or absence of various symptoms. These are generally easily distinguishable from that considered normal in the relevant society. Delusions, hallucinations, passivity phenomena, thought blocking and ideas of reference are some relating to mental functions, while elation, over-excitability, flatness of affect, retardation and so forth are more objective physical observations. It is easy enough to see these purely as indicators of illness; a certain combination suggesting a diagnosis of schizophrenia and a different combination, severe depression for example. But each of these symptoms can be examined in its own right. After all, what exactly is a delusion?

It is defined as 'a false belief which cannot be corrected by reason. It is logically founded and cannot be corrected by argument or persuasion or even by the evidence of the patient's own senses.' If you begin to examine this statement from the PCP perspective, there are several immediately important observations. First, the fact that the patient believes in his/her delusion is discounted. It is simply wrong, because everybody else agrees it is wrong, or because it is so patently ridiculous as to *have* to be wrong. This objective criteria of thought content is of paramount importance in classical psychiatry but fails to look at the position from the patient's angle. Perhaps this 'delusion' has some real meaning for the patient which if *we* were clever enough, or credulous enough, or loose enough in our own thinking, we might begin to be able to understand. How many of our own beliefs might, in fact, be considered delusional if they were not shared by many other people? One individual's delusion may be another group's belief.

Delusions are not entities, available to be picked up and examined at will. To the person suffering from them, they are not delusions at all. They only become delusions when a second, or other person, deems them to be so. This is an important point, because PCP by encouraging us to examine things from the patient's position, rather than from prepared vantage points based on our own professions, may make us have to consider different kinds of 'symptoms' in trying to help people. This may in turn produce different kinds of diseases, with possibly different treatments, and so forth.

Before anyone thinks that I am advocating a total free-for-all, let me remind you that the classical approach in psychiatry to diagnosis and management by examination and elicitation of symptoms, remains a perfectly valid and well tried method of dealing with the variety of problems under the heading of mental illness. There is no suggestion that it should be abandoned as such. But in the same way that Kelly suggested that his theory might be useful just until somebody came along with a better one, so also the use and definition of symptoms such as delusion continue to be useful just until somebody comes along with something better. Consideration of the alternative ways in which the psychological phenomena presenting as delusion could be viewed, in this case using PCP, is one way of looking for it. Perhaps we will find something, perhaps not, but not to look at all, or to be self-critiquing in the methods we use daily, is to be complacent. It also encourages us to slide unwillingly and unwittingly into the dangerous trap of becoming a means for society dealing with members it does not like, approve of, or understand.

The value of PCP at this level is to make us look outwards from the system we employ; to measure it against the patient's own perspectives rather than that of an abstract discipline; and to remember that our objective criteria are somebody else's subjective psychological processes. These can be sobering thoughts.

5 People in distress v. people not in distress

It seems amazing that it has taken so long to actually reach people in this system, but I believe that this is indicative of the reality of psychiatry. Indeed, with the increasing technology and developing sciences with medicine, the distance between the carer and the patient in distress seems to becoming greater. There are often many members of a team involved each with differing skills employed on behalf of the client. It is increasingly easy for none to see the person as a whole individual rather than a collection of parts, needs or symptoms.

People in distress are the *raison d'être* of psychiatry. It is a deliberate mistake to call them 'people' rather than patients because psychiatry has enlarged its horizons beyond those of traditional mental illness to try to help a myriad of different types of problems. These include, along with classic illness such as schizophrenia and manic-depressive psychosis, marital and family dynamic problems, difficulties with interpersonal relationships, aggression, socially induced problems such as the effects of unemployment, psychosexual problems, and so forth. The range is almost endless. It is indeed one of the fascinations of working in this field that no two people present with the same difficulty.

Much traditional psychiatry works on a reductionist basis. That is to say that despite the individuality of presenting patients, we are encouraged to reduce their problem to something identifiable in one or other classificatory system. In Britain this is usually based on the *International Diagnostic System*, ninth editions, while the USA bases its system on the *DSM* III (*Diagnostic and Statistical Manual*, third edition). This approach tends to lead to the old criticism of labelling whereby the individual patient is consigned to a catch all descriptive diagnosis which then hangs around their neck like an ill fitting collar that cannot be removed. Most psychiatrists and their colleagues in related disciplines agree that this system needs to change and attempts have been made to introduce multidimensional models of diagnosis, taking into account not only symptoms, but also social and interpersonal relationship factors amongst others. Although this is a way forward, it tends to be a patch-work method, rather like extending an old house with additions as necessary in the prevailing mode of architecture. The result, to continue the analogy, is a draughty, inconvenient building, not really suited to any special function, but which tends to feel familiar and comfortable to those who have spent their lives in it!! To abandon this for a new purpose built edifice is never pleasant, and when the alternative build-ings are generally equally old structures with questionable improve-ments, the incentive is miniscule.

This is where I believe PCP has a large role to play. As I have described in various sections above, it can be used to explore and extend the very fabric of psychiatry in all its various levels. This might be considered in the recent analogy to exploring different plans for a new building. However, even while this process is going on, it offers us a methodology for understanding or, perhaps better said, trying to understand, the problems of the people who do come to us in distress. To illustrate this, I have mentioned below a few areas where I have seen it used directly and beneficially.

(a) Rehabilitation

Much work in rehabilitating old patients back into communities has been achieved over the past ten years. Many of those who were veget-ating in large mental hospitals but wanted to move on have done so. Two problems remain. The patient still in the hospital who seems totally unmotivated to leave, and people currently living in the community who survive only because of enormous support from parents or rela-tives, and who may well be unable to cope if this support is reduced. Most rehabilitation programmes are based on good behaviour theory principles, and have worked well. But there have been many patients who simply have not benefited as staff or relatives expected them to. The reaction in these cases tends to be either to examine the programme which is deemed faulty, or to claim the patient 'unrehabilitatable'. What seems to happen rarely, is to look at the person and ask why s/he is not making the most of this opportunity.

PCP offers practical methods of doing this. Eliciting constructs related to the hospital environment, the community, the kinds of activities expected of them, the programme they are on, and the kind of accom-modation they aspire to often reveals vast differences between their view of what is happening, and the well intentioned staff's view. Without some commonality of end point desire, all the best efforts of a rehabilitation team are likely to come to naught; and even if the patient does end up outside the hospital, they are often the ones who return quickly. PCP offers a valuable input to the rehabilitation process, encouraging the development of more accurate and more individual programmes, and providing an alternative method of analysis of apparent failure from the clients' own point of view.

(b) Psychogeriatrics

There are at least two areas in which PCP may be of use in helping the elderly who present to the psychiatrist. The first of these relates to the view the individual has of being elderly and its implications for them. Indeed, they may have strong views about being labelled 'geriatric' simply because of their age! Many people have problems connected with retirement and the massive change in their lifestyles, expectations, financial circumstances and so forth. Some 'expect to be looked after' either by family or by institutions. Although this may only be a part of the presenting problem, knowledge of this kind is almost invariably useful in providing appropriate support, identifying future difficulties before they occur, and in planning for possible accommodation needs before a crisis occurs. Although all these points are as valid in other branches of psychiatry, especially perhaps adolescent work, the increasing numbers of elderly people presenting to the psychiatric services demand particular attention.

The second special area of usefulness is in dealing with relatives. Whether the patient is functionally ill, or dementing, relatives have often a variety of concerns and feelings. Guilt, anger, concern that they may have to look after the person, despair at the problems already encountered in looking after them are just some which vie with affection, natural concern and the wish to support and help. Increasingly, with a community oriented service, relatives and close friends are vitally important as part of the network of support and help. Knowing their concerns, and making a positive attempt to understand them, is an increasingly important aspect of caring for the elderly in general, and the elderly mentally ill in particular. Again, PCP offers us both a framework for beginning this kind of work, and justifying it, as well as methods of actually discovering the views, attitudes, concerns of the relatives.

(c) Psychotherapy and counselling

There are chapters elsewhere in this book covering individual psychotherapy, group therapy and counselling. There used to be a view that this kind of work was extremely specialised and beyond the scope of many working within the field of psychiatry. Many psychiatric nurses in particular have extended their range of work to include counselling, and involvement in group therapy, but in my experience, are often looking for a model which they can use and learn for themselves which fits in with their role.

PCP has always seemed to me potentially valuable for nurses in this context as much of its ethos fits in with many of the concerns expressed by psychiatric nurses. This is a field still to be explored (as the lack of a nursing chapter in this book exemplifies) but which shows some signs of developing activity.

These are just some areas PCP can be useful with people in distress. If nothing else, it reminds us incessantly that *people* in distress is what they are.

6 Clients v. colleagues

I have added this level into my ladder for two reasons. First because it is important to remember that some colleagues may also be 'people in distress'. The description does not only apply to clients. Second, PCP has much to offer us in our working relationships with colleagues.

In the second chapter, dealing with reflexivity, I pointed out that we should always be observant and concerned about our own distress, and that in those we work with. I would not wish to labour the point for fear of sounding neurotic, but I am acutely aware at times of the insensitivity of our profession to the traumas existing in the 'carers' lives which we would be much more understanding of if they were occurring with a client. I remember myself, at a time of immense trauma of an interpersonal relationship, being expected to continue to work with a large number of seriously disturbed marital problems as though nothing were happening to me personally. Of course, our professional and personal lives are separate, but they also overlap. Do we really remember to ask of ourselves or our colleagues the same questions we might ask of our clients or patients? The reflexivity inherent in PCP encourages us to do that to the advantage of ourselves as individuals able to help others, and to the advantage of our working environments and relationships. Indirectly, these all benefit the people we are trying to help professionally by maximising the potential available to them.

Psychiatry today is a wide ranging, multidisciplinary affair, crossing not only boundaries in medical and associated disciplines with the health service, but also local authority services such as social work and housing, and a wide variety of voluntary agencies. The concept of the multi-disciplinary team (MDT) has been around for many years, but still remains in many areas ephemeral. One of the reasons for this is the lack of understanding of the roles each member sees themselves having, and the lack of any method for negotiating changes while minimising threats. PCP has much to offer in the field of team-building, providing a structure for looking at the perspectives of different disciplines while reducing the anxiety of those participating. As psychiatry proceeds to devolve further into the communities it attempts to serve, so the range of different constructions of the same set of circumstances increases greatly. A problem perceived in one way by the NHS resources may be considered quite differently by social services; differently again by the probation service, the housing authority, the police, and the local branch of MIND. As members of the community, we can no longer exist within our own institutional walls, and we have to develop methods of understanding various equally valid methods of making sense of a problem, and find means of reaching an agreed consensus between them. I believe that the philosophy and psychology of personal constructs provides a framework for community psychiatry unparalleled by any other.

This chapter has ranged widely over the various uses of PCP in psychiatry at various levels. It has only skimmed the surface of the actual and potential value of this approach, but I hope it has provided much food for thought and discussion, and perhaps the stimulus to explore further.

8 · *Personal Construct Psychology in the practice of an educational psychologist*

TOM RAVENETTE

Introduction

The practice of an educational psychologist takes place in a context in which the role is shaped by the twin expectations of those who employ him and those to whom he offers a service. Each of these is also a function of their perspectives. Training provides a formal institution whereby role and expectations are transmitted. It was my good fortune not to be tied by either of these constraints. My training took place in a hospital context and seemed primarily to be a preparation for answering the questions of other professionals rather than taking a direct responsibility for dealing with clients' problems. Furthermore, the area in which I received an appointment had for many years had no psychologist working in the schools, and the director of education gave me effectively a free hand to work out my own salvation. Thus, at one and the same time, I was both at an advantage and at a disadvantage. On the one hand, I was not really prepared for the role of carrying sole responsibility, on the other hand the possibility was there to develop the practice which seemed to me to be relevant to the task. I had, indeed, recollections of what educational psychologists previously had done and I was determined not to repeat a style of work which appeared limited in conception and doubtfully illuminating to clients. By great good fortune, I was able to become conversant with Kelly's two volumes whilst studying for my professional qualifications and recognised that the Psychology of Personal Constructs offered a stance which was positive to people as human beings (children, teachers and parents) and a theoretical basis from which it might be possible to respond meaningfully to the dilemmas which my future clients might present. Needless to say it has taken most of a professional lifetime to work out its implications, and doubtless the work is not yet finished. To anticipate what follows in the succeeding pages, the adoption of a personal construct approach effectively meant the creation of both a role and task which proved to be considerably at variance with the existing pattern in the practice of educational psychology.

In this work what are presented as problems are children who fail to learn, who fail to behave appropriately, who show anomalies of development or disturbing features of personality. People making referrals will usually be teachers, sometimes parents, sometimes other agencies, and the work will usually be carried out in schools. On occasion a referral may be passed on to some other agency if the facts of the case make this seem more appropriate. The Child Guidance Clinic in particular may be used if the problem seems essentially to be related to acknowledged tensions within the family. As will be seen later, Personal Construct Psychology invites the psychologist to take more than a casual look at any referral.

The appeal of Personal Construct Psychology

It is a proper question to ask what is so special about Personal Construct Psychology that I should see in it a basis for work as an educational psychologist. A number of themes which Kelly put forward made an immediate impact and provided the inspiration to adopt a Kellian approach:

'Behaviour is an experiment' provides a way of giving a positive aspect to that which others see as a problem.

'Constructive alternativism' the insistence that there is always a different way of construing events, provides a challenge to the imagination and loosens the bonds which the notion of 'cause and effect' so often creates.

'No man need be a slave to his own autobiography' points away from the determinism of history whilst still acknowledging its importance.

The fundamental postulate and its corollaries provide a basis for making sense of an individual's behaviour within a framework of relative simplicity.

The implication running through the theory, that importance lies in meanings rather than events, leads to evaluating a person's history in experiential terms, thereby undercutting the view that personal history is a set of facts, each of which puts its mark on the individual.

Kelly's simple suggestion that if you want to know, then ask, his observation that 'A pat answer is the enemy to a fresh question' together with the corollary 'A pat question is the enemy to a fresh answer' all provide ideas for an overall style of enquiry. His stress on sameness and difference as the basis for all discrimination then suggests specific tactics for eliciting an individual's constructs and constructions.

Over-riding all of these, his insistence on the provisional nature of psychological findings gives a freedom from the expectation placed upon us as 'experts' that there is always a correct explanation to be found and the consequent feelings of guilt when we fail to match up to those expectations.

In what follows I present the thinking and resulting practice which stem from my own interpretation of a Kellian approach to being an educational psychologist. Although it is put forward in a number of sections each section is reflected in each of the others. The whole represents one psychologist's attempt to develop a practice out of a theory.

A restructuring of practice

Problems

By way of a preamble to this section something needs to be said about what, in the context of a referral to a school psychological service, constitutes a problem. This is a difficult topic to resolve since in construct theory terms, problems can only arise from a person's construction of events. Let us say, quite simply, that there are events, and that individuals, out of their construction systems, impose meanings, or constructions, on those events. When a person cannot make sense out of an event, *and feels that he should*, then he has a problem. The problem comes from the feeling that he ought to make sense, not from the event itself. Without that feeling there may be irritation, but not a problem. For example, a child fails to make the progress in school that a teacher expects. The teacher cannot understand why, but feels that he should. That teacher then has a problem. Alternatively, and not untypically, a teacher may construe a child as, for example, wanting to learn whereas the child has no such view of himself. His behaviour then becomes incomprehensible to the teacher, who in consequence may label him as 'lazy' or 'unmotivated'. If the teacher is satisfied with such a formulation, perhaps she does not have a problem. If she wants a cure for laziness then she has.

The personal construct psychologist therefore seeks to disentangle events from the constructions which people put on them in order to tease out precisely what the problem is. If we choose to see a person's actions as purposeful we may in fact go one step further and pose the question 'for what problem is this behaviour a solution?' But this is already a move towards problem resolution.

Clients

It follows from this argument that when a teacher makes a referral of a child, for whatever reason, the person with the problem is the teacher, and it is the teacher who is asking for help. The logic needs to be pressed even further. If things are proceeding relatively smoothly between teacher and child, no matter how little the child meets teacher's expectations, there will be no referral. It is at the point where a child's behaviour defeats the teacher's expectations that a problem arises and a referral might be made. When this is put the other way round, i.e. that a teacher's construct system cannot comprehend the child or his behaviour, it is clear that the teacher is the client.

This notion runs contrary to the popular view that the child is the psychologist's client, a view which at one time led to moves whereby educational psychologists should be subsumed under the label 'child psychologist'. Such thoughts take no account of the fact that a psychologist needs to be equally skilled in dealing with the teacher's problems which a referral reflects. To argue that the teacher is, at least in the first instance, the psychologist's client is not to deny that the referred child has problems, but I shall elaborate that later.

Teachers' problem

Returning to teachers and their problems, we have been able to recognise and categorise four types of teacher referral, and these hold whatever complaint is put forward as the basis for the referral. Sometimes the category can be inferred from the ways in which the referral is couched, at other times it needs to be elicited through subsequent questioning.

The first category reflects a failure in understanding a child and this failure represents a threat to the teacher's sense of knowingness about children. The request with this referral is for understanding.

The second category reflects a teacher's inability to make any difference to what a child does; the child continues not to learn, or continues with behaviour which is disturbing to the teacher. This relative inability is a challenge to the teacher's sense of competence and his request to the psychologist is to know how to act effectively.

With the third category, a teacher will speak 'with authority' that a child has 'special educational needs'. It is not this teacher's job to try to meet those needs because he has not been trained to. The child challenges the teacher's sense of who he is by making demands which the teacher considers inappropriate. The request here is for the child to be placed in some special provision.

Children referred in the fourth category are recognised by the teacher to have problems but that these can be handled by the present teacher in the here and now. The teacher is concerned about what will happen with the next teacher or the next school. Typically these referrals are made towards the end of a child's stay in a school and the teacher is asking for some guarantee that the child will have special considerations in the next school. By making a referral the teacher himself will not hold to be guilty of not taking action to have the problem dealt with. The referral represents an insurance policy.

Although I have identified four categories it is often more useful to look at any referral as carrying characteristics of more than one category. What follows is an instructive example. A teacher referred a child towards the end of the summer term of her last year in the junior school. The reason he gave was that some years earlier, in a different local authority, a psychologist had said that the girl was 'borderline' and should be followed up at six monthly intervals. This had not been done but should be done now. When questioned further he said that although the girl could now read reasonably well she was impaired in her conceptual development and pointed to her inability to 'conserve length' and that she was not very good at 'numbers'. He claimed that he was not qualified to help the girl with handicaps such as these and that there should be some recognition in a formal statement that she had 'special educational needs'. My response to the referral was that at this point in her career there would be no action but that should there be problems in the secondary school action could be initiated from there. This decision, correct in its appraisal of the situation as it affected the child, was unsatisfactory since it did not recognise the teacher's problems which underlay the referral. In fact he became quite angry arguing that we were ignoring the referral (and of course the girl's 'needs'). Only when I recognised for myself that the referral was a combination of categories three and four ('it is not my job' and 'insurance policy') was I able to respond to the teacher in a way to deal with his annoyance. In effect this was to give him an assurance that the girl would not be 'lost' in a comprehensive school.

So far this discussion has been pitched at an interactive level. There is, however, a more profound way in which referrals are related to teachers' constructions, especially constructions of themselves.

It is a simple fact that any one teacher is unlikely to make more than a few referrals during his professional lifetime, he is quite likely however to grumble about many more in the staffroom. Nor when they do make a referral is it usually the child who is worst behaved, the least mature, or the most chronic non-learner in the class. We are entitled to ask, therefore, what is so special that leads a teacher to refer an individual child.

Central to my argument is that the view the teacher has of herself will be based on peripheral and core constructs and these constructs are always open to invalidation. The invalidation of peripheral self constructs will certainly lead to grumbles but the invalidation of core constructs is a much more serious affair. It seems to me, that a referral of a child does in fact mean that a teacher's core constructs are being repeatedly invalidated by just that one child.

Two examples will illustrate the argument. A teacher referred an eight-year-old boy because of his continued failure to make progress in learning to read. She also described him as a boy who withdrew from contact with her, did not initiate communication and was generally distant. When I asked what, in her deepest sense of self, made her a teacher she had to struggle for words and then said quite simply that she saw herself as a caring person. Having said that, she immediately recognised that it was the boy's distancing behaviour which upset her rather than the failure to learn to read. This was invalidating a core construction of herself. Significantly, a month later she said that she saw him now just as a remedial problem and that was something she could deal with.

The second case involves a teacher of a nine-year-old boy. His complaint was of the boy's impassivity and unpredictability both in terms of work and behaviour. My own interview with the boy confirmed the description of impassivity. The teacher said that even when he put on exaggerated behaviour in order to provoke a response, the boy remained unmoved. I asked the teacher what it was about the boy that got under his skin and his reply was that he saw himself as essentially good at making relationships with his pupils. This boy's lack of responsiveness and implicit denial of relationship, therefore, invalidated an essential construction which this teacher had of himself.

It follows from this analysis that Personal Construct Psychology leads to an insistence of taking the teacher aspect of a referral very seriously. The psychologist needs not only to look where the teacher's finger points, but to the teacher behind the finger and the constructions which lie behind the teacher. In effect we ask of the teacher 'What is the problem for which this referral is a solution?' recognising that behind the obvious answer, i.e. the complaint, there is an unverbalised, because unrecognised, answer which is personal to the teacher.

Children's problems

When a child is in school he is in a situation from which there is no escape. It is not of his choosing and it is a place where he is expected to meet the requirement of teachers that he should acquire skills and knowledge, become a social individual and progressively have control over the expression of negative feelings. The situation is essentially interactive and for this to run smoothly the child needs to have a reasonably comfortable sense of who he is. To some extent he is prepared for this by his parents who give him instructions as to how to behave such as 'do as teacher says, be a good boy, work hard'.

Out of all that he has heard about school (and the sometimes pious exhortations of parents) and his own perceptions the child makes some sense of school as a context in which he will spend much of the day. He will also develop simultaneously a construction which has predominantly been shaped by the validations and invalidations of his family.

Just as a teacher's problems arise out of his constructions of himself and his situations, so too does a child's problems arise out of his constructions. Initially his sense of self-will probably takes some hard knocks from his social experiments with others and from his failure or success with the demands made by the teacher. In particular, there will be massive difficulties if the parents have created different and sometimes opposing identities for the child, leaving him in grave doubts as to which identity is appropriate in school. This, therefore, will be a ground for behaviour which is confusing both to his teacher and other children. Alternatively, a child may be striving to refute the construction which his parents wish him to be, and if parents and school are congruent in their views the child will then strive to refute the view of him which teachers not unnaturally hold. Yet again, where family values are in opposition to those of a school, the child will be forced to go along with the parents in seeing the school as a hostile environment, or, if he sees the school as good, develop attitudes which are disloyal to his family. In either case divided loyalties will lead to behaviour which is not easily understandable.

The ground for a child's problems is his constructions of himself and his circumstances, and the expression of those problems will be various, ranging from non-learning to disturbing behaviour, from self-isolation to excessive dependence on the esteem of his peer group. It is the exploration of these issues which provides a personal construct intervention with the child parallel to the enquiry with the teacher.

The aim of intervention

Stemming from the central proposition of Personal Construct Psychology that an individual's construct system and constructions are at the heart of behaviour, the aim of intervention is simply to promote changes in that individual's construing. A referral from a teacher, therefore, calls for an exploration of that teacher's construction of the child, and of herself, in order to promote change. Interviewing a child in order to find out something of his construction of himself and his circumstances, and the communication of this to the teacher, provides a means whereby the teacher may change his constructions. At the simplest level a teacher who initially views the child with some hostility may, by being given a different construction, become sympathetic. The exploration of the child's constructions will, in fact, reveal something of the problems which underlie his actions. And the problem will not be the one which the teacher has put forward. This dual exploration, of teacher and child, is already full of potential for change since it brings into the open undisclosed problems both in the teacher and in the child. At least when they are in the open, it may be possible to do something about them. Moreover, the exploration carried out in a non-judgmental way is frequently felt by the client as an experience of being understood, often for the first time.

I have described the need to interview both teacher and child. There is a further component. As I said earlier the child is an extension of his family and carries their values and attitudes into school. The older he gets, the more he also carries his own feelings about them. Thus, to make an optimum sense out of the child's constructions, it is often necessary to interview the parents as well. In this way, we may learn something of their expectations of the child and of the school and the family construction systems which the child is living out. When this is carried out in the presence of the head teacher, the possibility arises of further modification of the head teacher's constructions, and consequently an improved understanding, of both child and family. In many ways, the joint interview, family, head teacher and psychologist, provides the most beneficial form of intervention.

Not the least important aspect of the construct psychologist's intervention is to remind the client (teacher, child or parent) that the responsibility for change is theirs not the psychologist's. It is the teacher who must find a way of maximising her influence in promoting a child's educational growth. It is the child who has to master his learning in school. It is the parents' task to ease the child's load in school by finding better ways of understanding him and his dilemmas. It is the psychologist's responsibility to help each to achieve that end.

Questions and answers

The major, and perhaps the only, interviewing tool is the question. It is important, therefore, to elaborate principles whereby we may acquire a skill in questioning. Personal Construct Theory suggests a number of principles to promote this end, and in the process invites the psychologist to take very seriously the use of language, his own and that of his client.

The first principle is quite simply to go along with what the client says.

The second principle is to be prepared to challenge what he says in the pursuit of meaning. These two principles imply an attitude of sceptical credulity in the interviewer.

The third principle poses four questions, the answers to which lead to a clarification of what the client has to say. We need to ask:

1 What does the client's answer deny?
2 What does it further imply?
3 What does the answer presuppose?
4 What is the context within which the answer is valid?

The fourth principle takes care of the possibility of the client giving a pat answer by asking for a second and third.

The following dialogue illustrates some of these principles. All questions follow the first two principles. Q.1 uses the fourth. Qs 5, 6 and 7 all reflect the third. The dialogue is part of an interview with a thirteen-year-old boy.

Q.1 Tell me three things about a boy who you respect or admire.
A.1 He trusts his family and his mates.
Q.2 And the second?
A.2 He shares things.
Q.3 And the third?
A.3 I don't know another.
Q.4 You say 'He trusts his family and his mates'. How would you describe someone not like that?
A.4 He doesn't trust anybody.
Q.5 Is it important to trust family and mates?
A.5 Yes.
Q.6 Why is that?
A.6 Then they will trust you.
Q.7 Why is that important?
A.7 It just is.
Q.8 Is it important not to trust anybody?
A.8 No!

In this dialogue what the final answer presupposes and the context within which it is valid were not taken up. They might have been by asking what experiences led him to that belief and were there any situations in which he would give a different answer to that particular question.

A fifth principle requires that a client should respond to a precise question with an appropriate answer. Not uncommonly a client will answer a question which was not put, giving a construction for an event or a diagnosis for a description. Not to take this up with a client leads to sloppy interviewing in which the interviewer and client do not come to grips with issues and this in turn reduces the chance of promoting change. The following is an example:

A teacher complained that a boy continued not to learn and whatever special help she offered made no difference. I asked her what specifically the boy did when she offered him help. Her reply was that he found it difficult to settle down. Unwittingly the teacher here gives a construct of events, not the events themselves. This I pointed out to her and asked again what the boy did. Her reply this time was very different. She said that he sharpened his pencil unnecessarily, he moved paper around, he went to sharpen other boys' pencils and generally declined to sit down and get on with the task in hand. I suggested to the teacher that an alternative way of understanding the boy's behaviour was to see him as deliberately avoiding the task. This construction, in the light of the teacher's overall knowledge of the boy, made rather more sense to her than the one she had previously tendered and moreover led her to feel less guilty about her own relative failure with him.

The structured interview

With children the structured interview provides an efficient way of exploring their constructions. Since a child lives in a variety of different contexts and, since problems arise out of his constructions, it is necessary to explore with him the sense he makes of himself and those contexts: himself and his family, himself and school, himself and other children, himself and his experiences, both in the outer world and within. The interviewer will need to sample some or all of these content areas, introduced, however, by an essential inquiry, namely, does he know why teachers are worried about him? Does he agree with their observations? Is he also worried? He needs to be told who it is who is interviewing him and why. Without this preliminary enquiry the child will be at a loss to know how best to respond to questions and the psychologist will not know how to interpret his answers.

The process of interviewing is questioning and every question refers to some issue or event about which the psychologist is seeking the child's constructions. These referrals can be real people, such as his family, or pictorial representations of situations, such as school, or they can be himself and his experiences. Just as the referrants to questions can be various so can the mode of response. A child can be asked to give verbal answers, to demonstrate an action or to produce a drawing. The choice of referrant, content area and mode of answering is part of the skill of the interviewer in weighing up what he judges will be both productive and within the child's communicational skills. Out of a number of interviewing techniques based on these parameters, I have chosen three to describe in detail, each of which I will illustrate with interview material.

'Who are you?' (WAY): This technique represents a very direct request to a child to say who he is. The invitation is made along the following lines:

> I would like to know who you are. If I were to ask you to say three things to describe you, what would you say? Who *are* you?

When these answers have been given the child is asked to elaborate each by saying what is special or important about them. A further elaboration can then be achieved by asking for the opposite of each of these responses.

The technique was used at the beginning of an interview with Timothy, a twelve-year-old boy who had twice been found unconscious after sniffing an aerosol. Only the first of his descriptions is given because of the dramatic revelation which it produced. This self-description was, quite simply, 'Myself'. His threefold elaboration of this was:

1 'I'm human,' the opposite to which was 'Dead'.
2 'I can move my body about,' the opposite to which was 'Can't move'.
3 'I can move my arms and legs about,' the opposite to which was 'Still'.

I then asked Timothy to describe the sequence of events involved in aerosol sniffing. He said 'you sniff, your head goes buzzy, you get lifted off your feet, you fall down unconscious'. He was rather shaken when I then pointed out to him that the end product of sniffing was, in his own words, tantamount to a denial of himself. (Later in the interview he said, in fact, that at that time he wished he was dead!)

The family interaction matrix: This technique focuses on family interactions using as a construct the two polarities 'easy and difficult to get on with'. It draws on the fact that the child has lived many years with his family and by now knows fairly well the ease and difficulty with which members get on with each other. He is reminded of this and then asked to say for each member who they find it easy and difficult to get on well with. The child's answers are entered into a matrix which is drawn up and explained to him as part of the interviewing process. When the family has five members the child is asked for two choices for 'easy to get on well with' and one choice for 'difficult to get on well with'. With larger families two choices for each polarity is invited. His spontaneous answers were also recorded. The technique is not useful for small families. The grid can be analysed immediately by studying the reciprocal connections between pairs of members and drawing them graphically. The technique is illustrated here by a matrix produced in an interview with a girl of whom the mother complained that she had made progress with reading up to two years ago but had made no progress since then. Assessment of her reading attainment supported this complaint. In a family drawing she had omitted to include herself but had created her two-year-old brother as a miniature version of her father.

The interaction matrix (Table 8.1) and its graphical representation (Figure 8.1) suggests that she has a neutral relationship with her parents

Table 8.1 Family interaction matrix for Jo

		M	F	S	B	Jo
MOTHER	M		+	+	−	
FATHER	F	+		+	−	
SISTER	S	+			+	−
BROTHER	B	−	+			+
	Jo		+	+	−	

+ 'Finds it easy to get on well with'

− 'Finds it difficult to get on well with'

Figure 8.1 Geographical representation of Jo's matrix

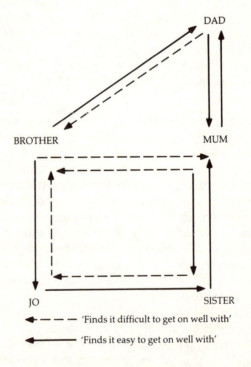

+ --- 'Finds it difficult to get on well with'

+——— 'Finds it easy to get on well with'

and is in a state of misunderstanding with her brother and older sister. Moreover, the girl's judgments place her brother in a position of some influence in his family if she sees him as difficult to get on well with by both his parents. If her judgment is less on objective grounds but more a reflection of her feelings about him, then it is not an unreasonable inference to see her cessation of learning as coincidental with his arrival and growth.

Personal troubles: The content area for this technique is times when a child feels troubled or upset. The mode of response is drawings. A sheet of paper is folded into six compartments. The child is reminded that everyone has times when he feels troubled or upset, and asked to draw five pictures to show times when he felt that way. When he has completed that, or drawn as many situations as he can, he is asked to draw in the sixth space a situation when by contrast he felt good.

After the drawings have been completed he is asked what is happening in each situation and what his feeling would be. The next question is to ask him to say three things about a boy who would not be upset in those situations, followed by 'what would upset such a boy?' The final question brings the child back into the situation by my asking when in fact he has been this boy who would not be upset. In this way, the child produces both the view of himself which he feels relatively comfortable with but also the alternative view which is its polar opposite.

As an example, I include Brian's response to the technique. Brian is twelve years old and is in temporary care because of persistent school refusal. At the beginning of the interview he strongly asserted that there was nothing wrong with him. He gave a free description of his family where everyone got on well with everyone else except father who lived elsewhere. On the other hand he produced a free drawing which was of Frankenstein, which he agreed was a person with no feeling, and a contrasting picture of a girl who he said would have feeling.

With the personal troubles technique he chose to interpret the word 'would' in the instructions as pure imagination by denying any possibility that he might commit any of them.

His drawings were:

1 Taking money from his mum's bag. He would feel bad after it.
2 Nicking someone's bike.
3 Ripping a chair in a house with an axe.
4 Mugging an old lady.
5 Picking on a little boy – spitting.

The contrast picture was:

6 Playing for Arsenal and scoring a goal.

Even though these situations are imaginary they could actually be committed by an individual. He was asked, therefore, to say three things about a boy who would not be upset in those situations. The responses he gave were:

1 He has no feelings (c.f. his drawing of Frankenstein).

2 His mum doesn't care about him (c.f. his cosy description of his family).

3 He doesn't worry about anything he does (c.f. his assertion at the beginning of the interview that there was nothing wrong with him).

The boy thus described would himself be upset if someone took something from him but he was unable to say when he had himself been this boy.

The technique, therefore, despite Brian's distancing himself from his own answers, seems to have produced responses that are of a piece with the rest of the interview and which suggest aspects of himself which he would like to ignore.

Two illustrative cases

I shall now illustrate some of these matters with edited material from two cases. In the first case, change is promoted through discussions with the teachers and an interview with the girl's mother. The method of interviewing is conversational but at the back of the interview is the question 'what construct of the mother will the material exemplify?' In the second case, a boy is invited to take stock of himself as a means of generating change. A formal structured interview which includes the 'Who are you?' technique and a 'self description grid' is used.

Case 1

Sasha is a twelve-year-old girl attending a school for children with physical handicaps. She has considerable problems of speech, hearing and mobility. She had attended the school from the age of five years, but for a variety of reasons the family had moved away. Sasha returned to the school some months before the referral. The staff were very worried about her and had been given advice from a number of professional workers who served the school. Their reports only added to the confusion so that the teachers were at a loss as to how to help this pupil. I was asked to carry out with them a review.

Interview with the teachers: I met the head teacher, the deputy head and the class teacher and asked them what it was about Sasha that troubled them. Each time I put the question they described the girl's history, which involved not only moves to many schools but also to a different country. Alternatively they talked about the girl's mother. They described how, when the girl first attended the school, the mother always brought her dressed more like a doll than a child, she had extravagant claims about what the child would do, and presented herself as a '*grande dame*'! Although this information was interesting it did not answer my question. At this point, I asked the class teacher to say the three things which best described Sasha. After a long pause, all she could say was that the girl was isolated. I then turned to the deputy head who was equally at a loss but then said that she was a very different girl from the one who had previously attended the school. When I asked the three ways in which she was now different, I was given the answers 'Then she was eager to initiate communication', 'then she enjoyed coming to school', and 'then she enjoyed school activities'. By implication, therefore, the girl's attitude represents a deterioration. A deterioration of performance based on known physical conditions was something they were accustomed to and, therefore, could understand. A deterioration of attitude without such an explanation was something with which they were not so familiar. The problem, which they were unable to articulate, arose out of failure to put a meaningful construction on the girl's change of attitude. The change was the enigma, not the behaviour.

It seemed to me that the 'non-description' given by the deputy head, together with the teacher's feeling that Sasha was isolated, was consistent with the girl behaving as though she no longer felt able to make any meaningful impact on her life situation. In order to communicate this construction the teachers were invited to imagine how Sasha might experience the constant moves to which she had been subjected. These were listed in sequences and set in the context of her handicap. The teachers were then able to recognise the validity of such a construction and realised that their first task was to recognise and validate any initiatives which Sasha might make. Out of such validation she might become aware that she was not necessarily ineffective in promoting her own interests.

It became obvious that for me to interview Sasha could serve no useful purpose and might, to the contrary, merely add further conflicting information. It would be more to the point for me to attempt a further understanding of the situation in the context of what Sasha's mother might say. My next step was, therefore, to interview Mrs P. (Sasha's mother).

Interview with Mrs P.: Mrs P. was interviewed in the presence of the deputy head teacher who had known her since Sasha was five years old. Although we were agreed that we were meeting because of a concern for Sasha's education my own purpose was to listen carefully to Mrs P.'s construction of her life experiences in order to sense the polarities which gave them meaning. Right at the outset she said that *she would be frank*, a statement that did not take on full significance until after the interview had been concluded. In response to my questions she gave a full account of her background and her experiences. She was a Kenyan Asian married to a Punjabi Muslim, a matter of some importance since there were considerable religious and cultural differences which would not readily be recognised by the outsider. Her first employment had been as a cosmetic skin specialist. Her husband had trained as a lawyer but only did two or three days work at a time. This was a cause of friction since it meant that she was effectively the financial mainstay of the family. Eventually, after a number of moves and financial ventures, they went to the Punjab with the husband but this only made matters worse. She then returned with her two children to England leaving her husband behind. Despite these marital problems she still argued that he was a good father and that she would willingly be the breadwinner even if it meant that he did the housework at home. The handicapped daughter's birth was medically traumatic and mother did not see her for ten days whilst she was in intensive care. The father had then described the daughter as like a doll.

At the end of the interview the construction was put that the girl and the mother had much in common in relation to the various uprootings but whereas Mrs P. had an adult range of resources, and could act in her own interests, Sasha had very few resources. Almost the mother might say to herself 'There but for the grace of God go I'. Mrs P. was grateful for the interview especially that she had been able to talk about her daughter. When I suggested that a tape recording of the interview might indicate that she had talked about herself she smiled and concurred.

The sequel: Reflecting on the interview, it became apparent that a construction which would integrate much of the interview would recognise that it was crucially important for mother to *put a good face on things.* This made sense of her early work as a cosmetician, the way she had presented her daughter in school, her own expectations of her daughter, her defence of her husband and perhaps her membership of a minority race in Kenya. If that represented one pole of an important construct she had already given its opposite when she had said that *she would be frank.* Since to be frank means revealing the worst face, it was then significant that Mrs P. turned up at the interview without make-up, something that had never happened before. A communication of this understanding to the school gave immediate relief for the anxiety generated by their inability to understand. Moreover, with considerable insight, they saw that a further way to promote positive change was by using the mother's knowledge of cosmetics for the benefit of the older children. Subsequent reports show that this has in fact happened. Sasha is now much more relaxed and is learning Makaton sign language quickly and creatively and the teachers feel more than competent in meeting her special educational needs.

Case 2

Whereas the interviews in Case 1 were basically conversational, the interview for Case 2 used two highly structured techniques, namely 'who are you?' and a 'self description grid'. As will be seen the interview ran into a hiatus early on but it was possible to turn this to good use.

Peter, a fourteen-year-old, presented problems to the school. These were a failure to present adequate work, but more importantly that he seemed to set up the world of his peer group against him. This led to behaviour in school which was disturbing to other teachers as well as the other boys. There had been a preliminary meeting between parents, Peter and the teacher who was the head of year. Whilst not giving the details of the interview it can be said that Peter was an only child since the others had all died very young or as miscarriages. He was, therefore, somewhat special in his parents' eyes. The interview with Peter was intended to be the next, and hopefully the last, step in dealing with the case. The detail of the interview would be shared with the head of year in order to help her reconstrue Peter and the problems.

The interview with Peter: The aim of the interview was, quite specifically, to help Peter construct the different versions of himself as he thought he appeared in other people's eyes. In the process, he is of necessity, involved in developing a construction of himself.

Peter conceded that the teachers were worried about him because his 'work was suffering' and his behaviour was 'not good sometimes'. At home he felt that he was being 'pushed aside'. His elaboration of this was that other boys 'took the mickey' out of him when he could not discuss late night films on the TV with them because he had to go to bed at eight o'clock. They said he was a mother's boy. I then explained that the purpose of the interview was to help him work out who he was because this might help him disentangle his problems. I then moved into the WAY technique. 'If I were to ask you who you are what three things would you say?' Peter gave his name and then said 'I don't know what else I would say'. I recorded this as his second description adding that perhaps when we got to the end of the interview he would be in a better position to say who he was. This was the hiatus but it gave point to the decision to use a self description grid. Its constructive use was to relocate the WAY inquiry to the end of the interview in order to see what difference the intervening part might make.

The self description grid requires three stages, construct elicitation, completing the grid and joint analysis.

In order to elicit constructs out of which he would describe himself, he was invited to give three descriptions each for two boys who were his friends, one boy he disliked and one boy he admired but did not know very well. In the event he would say nothing about a disliked boy. After he had completed this task he was taken in turn through each description in order to find its opposite. This is a procedure for eliciting constructs. His responses are those listed below. He produced nine constructs altogether but one was considered of less importance than the others and was omitted. The final eight were:

1 Good friend to his friends	– Can be quite nasty.
2 Asks 'What's wrong, are you all right?'	– Doesn't pay any interest in who you are.
3 Has lots of ideas	– Boring.
4 Doesn't hang around all the time	– Bit of a nuisance, he's always there.
5 Not too caring	– Doesn't care at all.
6 Never ignores his friends	– Never says hello when they talk to him.
7 Always talks to you even though he doesn't know you well	– Would say 'Go away, I don't know you'.
8 Would sponsor you even though he didn't know you very well	– Will deny the smallest request for help.

The aim of the self description grid is to obtain from an individual the ways in which he thinks different people will judge him on a number of constructs. The judgment is given on a linear eleven point scale.

When this technique was used with Peter, he was asked how the following people would see him: his mother and father, teachers he liked and disliked, boys he liked and disliked, girls and last of all how would he see himself. These are represented in Table 8.2 respectively by M, F, T(L), T(D), B(L), B(D), G and S.

The analysis of the grid was carried out by simply drawing Peter's attention to his responses. He recognised that the values 5, 6 and 7 represented a neutral zone of non-entity between polarities. He was asked to draw the boundaries of this zone and observe for himself where most of his entries lay. A count shows that 52 lie in the neutral zone and 12 outside, 11 of which were given by people he did not like. Thus his assessment of himself was essentially that of a non-person.

In order to turn this material to advantage he was asked to locate in the grid the profile of himself when he was being a 'pain in the neck' and by contrast the profile of what he thought would be his parents' ideal. These two profiles are shown by the letters P and X respectively. Both now fall outside the neutral zone and are almost diametrically opposite to each other. Peter could see this for himself and conceded that he did indeed have a problem as to who he was. In fact, by becoming a 'pain in the neck' he ceases to be a non-person, but the

Table 8.2 Peter's self description grid

1 Good friend to his friends — Can get quite nasty

1	2	3	4	5	6	7	8	9	10	11
		X		B(L)	S / M / D	T(L) / G	B(D) / T(D)		P	

2 Asks 'What's wrong, are you all right' — Doesn't pay any interest in how you are

1	2	3	4	5	6	7	8	9	10	11
			P	D / M	S / B(L) / T(L)	T(D) / G	B(D)	X		

3 Has lots of ideas — Boring

1	2	3	4	5	6	7	8	9	10	11
			X	B(L)	S / M	T(L) / G / T(D)	B(D)		P	

4 Doesn't hang around friends all the time — Bit of a nuisance, always there

1	2	3	4	5	6	7	8	9	10	11
		X		G	B(L) / M / T(L)	S / D	B(D) / T(D)	P		

5 Not too caring — Doesn't care at all

1	2	3	4	5	6	7	8	9	10	11
			X	B(L) / M / D	T(L) / S	G	B(D)	T(D)	P	

6 Never ignores his friends — Never says 'hello' even when they talk to him

1	2	3	4	5	6	7	8	9	10	11
			P / X	B(L) / M	S / D	T(L) / G	B(D) / T(D)			

7 Always talks to you even though he doesn't know you well — Would say 'Go away, I don't know you'

1	2	3	4	5	6	7	8	9	10	11
			X	M / D	B(L) / T(L) / S	G / T(D)	B(D)		P	

8 Would sponsor you even though he didn't know you — Will turn down the smallest request for help

1	2	3	4	5	6	7	8	9	10	11
			X	T(L) / B(L)	M / D / G	S / B(D)	T(D)	P		

alternative, to be the parents' ideal, could hardly be seen as acceptable as he was already judged by his peer group as 'mother's boy'.

It was now possible to return to the abandoned 'who are you' inquiry in order to see how his responses might change. This time he is able to give three descriptions and these appear below:

1 My name is Peter . . . with the elaboration:
   (a) You've got a name.
   (b) If people want you they call you by name, not 'Here you'.
   (c) If someone sends you a letter named Mr Blank, you wouldn't know who the letter was for.
2 Even though I don't know a person I can talk to him . . . with the elaboration:
   (a) You can make new friends.
   (b) You can find out more about a person.
   (c) You can build up friendships all the time, not just give a greeting.
3 I would try to help people if they needed help . . . with the elaboration:
   (a) Say a friend says 'will you help me with my homework or else I'll be in detention and my mum says I must get home early' then I would help him.
   (b) Someone cuts his knee, I would help by taking him home.
   (c) Someone lost his keys, I'd help him find them to get in.

These answers confirm that positive relationships with other boys are important. It is clear, however, that instead of giving a description of himself he has written a prescription for what he might be, and moreover, outlined concrete situations where this might be exemplified. To end the interview, I pointed this out to him and said that perhaps it would not be long before he would become this boy. He left the interview cheerfully and with a smile.

The sequel: I discussed the contents of the interview with the head of year who quickly grasped the essence of what Peter had said. She was a teacher of considerable acumen and when a boy was newly admitted to the school (described by his previous school as 'wet'), she recognised that this presented a ready made experimental situation for Peter to work out in real life the implications of what happened in the interview with me. She asked him, therefore, to be responsible for helping the new boy become established in school. So far things seem to have gone well.

By way of a conclusion, six hard won lessons

1 Any intervention to assess is at the same time an opportunity to promote change. The first interview, and it may be the only one,

should therefore always be seen as an occasion for potential reconstruction.

2 Language is the medium through which constructions are communicated. It is, therefore, a bridge. But language also comes between the experiencing of events and its communication. It may, therefore, be a barrier to the communication of that experience. It is the fact that a person has a problem which provides an authorisation for a psychologist to challenge and explore his client's language and its referrents.

3 Just as problems in chemistry and physics may be resolved without necessarily isolating molecules and atoms, so many human problems may be resolved without necessarily isolating a client's constructs, which are the units behind his constructions. Thus it is frequently more appropriate to look for the client's constructions and let his constructs look after themselves.

4 In a free association test it is highly probable that the name Kelly would be linked as much with grids as with Personal Construct Theory. Nonetheless, the grid is but one way in which a client's realities may be explored. For many problems, especially with children, there are other productive ways of exploring their constructions.

5 Personal Construct Psychology does not bar the use of any technique from an interview, even psychometric tests, since it regards techniques as providing events to which a child is asked to respond. The immediacy of a child's behaviour then becomes an event for the psychologist to construe. He will seek an understanding out of the raw material which the child produces before his eyes.

6 Finally, Personal Construct Psychology is for the benefit of the psychologist as a means of helping him make sense of his task. It does not necessarily benefit the client. That a client fits neatly into the theory must be considered a bonus rather than a requirement.

Acknowledgments

I would like to thank my colleagues, R.B., A.H. and R.v.M., who at various points provided constructive observations and criticism in the preparation of the finished manuscript.

9 · Occupational therapy: from soft toys to Personal Construct Theory

GINA SELBY

Whilst working as an occupational therapist it became more and more obvious to me that what I needed was some sort of theory in order to understand people, especially patients, so that I could know, rather than hope, that the treatment I was offering was definitely beneficial to them, and inspiring to me.

Having thought more about this, I realised that if I obtained a psychological framework from which to operate, I could then offer my patients realistic, individual therapy programmes, designed to assist them define and find their own solutions to their particular problems, as they saw them and in their own way. This eliminates guesswork however well informed, and does not offer *my* solutions to *their* problems: it does establish what these people require and uses their way of seeing the world.

After examining various theories in psychology, I eventually came across George Kelly's Personal Construct Theory, and was impressed by it, particularly as it offered the concept of *hope* – change is possible, if not always easy. As you have made yourself the way you are, you also have the ability to change.

This was a thrilling discovery. I had found a theory that I could use, and enjoy. Yet how was I going to be able to incorporate the theory of Personal Construct Psychology with the practice of occupational therapy? This was where the hard work came into it; but let me hastily add it was well worth it. I set about learning Personal Construct Theory, and how to apply it to occupational therapy. This was a challenging and creative process.

Gradually I mastered the theory, and recognised how this framework would help. I realised how important it was to understand the difference between *process* and *content*. Process is the continual motion of why people behave (their experiment), while content is the specific thing they do. After all what would offer more scope? Knowing the fundamentals of cooking (process) or baking a sponge cake (content). I had found a theory with which I felt comfortable. I could endeavour to incorporate this with the rationale of occupational therapy.

Occupational therapy is not an instant life-death issue as is perhaps surgery. It is a life-saving issue, saving the person from the living death of inability; the inability of not being able to live a normal life, of being independent, of being completely crippled by the frustration of not being able to do well 'What I want to do when I want to do it'.

Occupational therapy can offer many alternative solutions to a problem. After all does it really matter that the method is not in the text book? Maybe the book was not written for that person. The important thing is that the person finds a way of coping with day-to-day situations the best way he can.

Personal Construct Psychology is a theory about how a person gets on with the business of living. Occupational therapy considers the whole person not just the disabled part of the body or mind. So the personal construct occupational therapist will endeavour to work with the individual to accomplish the changes which that particular person needs and desires. She also is aware of the implications of such changes for that person.

What does Personal Construct Theory offer occupational therapy?

Personal Construct Theory offers:

1 A universally workable theory of personality.
2 A theoretical framework from which to work.
3 A process of understanding self and others.
4 Various useful techniques – e.g. the repertory grid.
5 Clarity and flexibility in understanding people.
6 An invitation for the person to change.
7 Hope: no one has to be the victim to his own history.
8 Understanding of the implications of change – what if this or that happens?

Personal Construct Theory offers a tool bag of techniques and methods for understanding the person; for getting into his shoes and seeing through his eyes. The personal construct occupational therapist has the ability to translate the information of the medical diagnosis on one hand and the theory of personality on the other into the everyday language of behaviour – the patient's experiments. This allows understanding of how the patient construes his world, how he is managing to cope with his now changed life, and helping him to reconstrue his situation. The occupational therapist must construe the patient's constructions (know what makes him tick). She can offer him assistance discovering the best possible way for him to manage his life, and reclaim his right to be responsible for himself.

After the intensity of any trauma life continues, often drastically different than before. The hospital's flying squad moves on to the next emergency, leaving the patched-up patient to struggle with the residue of his life. At this point the occupational therapist comes on to the scene. She works with the patient, and together they struggle to change and develop the patient's life.

The occupational therapist's special quality is seeing and relating to the person as a whole person, who is able to cope with everyday life, not as a damaged or incomplete patient, who is unable to do anything for himself.

The occupational therapy definition of caring is: 'to help the person in his struggle to gain a more useful way of life for himself.' (It may not necessarily seem better from the occupational therapist's point of view.) He should not be stuck in the role of a dependent patient, but is liberated within his own boundaries. It may not be the situation that can change but his interpretation of it. This is in marked contrast to the custodial care, often practised in hospitals and institutions, which means doing everything for the patient so that he becomes *more* dependent not less.

The occupational therapist has both theoretical and practical ability, and so can enable the patient to form his own hypotheses and test them out, by finding different ways of seeing the world, and thus behaving differently.

The occupational therapist and the patient work together

The occupational therapist brings to the partnership his skills and expertise:

1 His ability to analyse the activities used in treatment.
2 His understanding of task orientated assessment procedures – why the person is asked to do a particular activity.
3 His understanding of the theory of personality – Personal Construct Theory.
4 His professional role – putting aside her personal view of the world.
5 His understanding of self as a person (this is the same as the patient's expertise).

The patient brings to the partnership his expertise in:

– Himself:

1 His experience of life.
2 His understanding of himself.
3 His wish for the future.

Together the occupational therapist and the patient need to become aware of, and understand, the patient's construct system. Then they can choose alternatives with greater understanding, and have better predictive ability and control.

Personal Construct Theory explicitly states that a person can change and grow as his life continues. Living and changing are in *continual motion*. This can be shown in Figure 9.1, a circle in continuous motion.

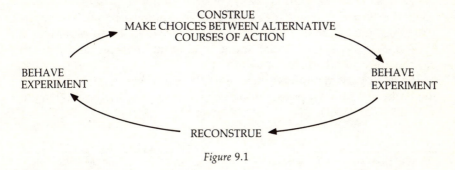

Figure 9.1

Unfortunately a person can become hostile, and have the problem of being stuck repeating the same experiments over and over, unable to discover an alternative way of behaving. This can be shown in Figure 9.2, where the same experiment is done repeatedly.

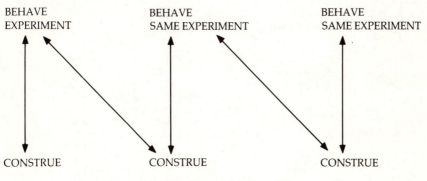

Figure 9.2

The occupational therapist's job is to get the patient to reconstrue by both theoretical, and practical means; so that he can escape from his vicious circle (Hostility – see glossary).

The differences between occupational therapists and other therapists is that occupational therapists have the practical/behavioural/exper-imental knowledge which enables them to work literally together with the patients designing and testing out their behavioural experiments. The occupational therapist must remember the patient's constructs so that he can choose an activity which is useful to the patient, not just something to keep him occupied.

The occupational therapist will *assess* the advantages of using a particular activity; and with his knowledge of Personal Construct Psychology will find it easier to *explore* or *discover* the patient's world and so design the most suitable treatment programme for him. (The term assessment implies that the therapist knows more about the person, and has the right answers, but this is not so. Therefore I have used the terms discover or explore when finding out about people/patients, and assess when discussing activities or programmes.) Explore/discover suggests that both the partners (therapist and patient) are seeking to find solutions together.

I have already mentioned the skills of the occupational therapist and the patient, so I have put them in a chart to show how the sections fit together (Table 9.1).

Table 9.1

Skills of a personal construct occupational therapist				The skills of the patient
ASSESSMENT OF THE ACTIVITY	TASK ORIENTATED ASSESSMENT OF PATIENT	PERSONAL CONSTRUCT PSYCHOLOGY	OCCUPATIONAL THERAPY	PATIENT
How the OT breaks down the activity for treatment purposes	The task categories which the OT uses to decide what the patient is capable of	The OT's understanding of the theory of personality	The person using the role of a professional	His understanding of self
1 COMPLEXITY OF JOB e.g.: Can this job be graded from simple to difficult?	1 DEMOGRAPHIC INFORMATION Name, age etc.	1 AN ABSTRACT THEORY A theoretical framework from which to work	1 USE PROFESSIONAL Suspend personal way of seeing the world. Adopt credulous approach	1 HIS OWN SCIENTIST He makes a hypothesis from which to work. He designs and tests out his experiments
2 DURATION OF JOB e.g.: Time spent at work	2 PHYSICAL DETAILS e.g.: Can he walk, see, hear?	2 PROCESS How people 'tick', make a transient hypothesis	2 REFLEXIVITY We are all struggling to make sense of the world	2 HISTORY His experience is unique to him. He doesn't have to be a victim to his history

Table 9.1—continued

Skills of a personal construct occupational therapist				The skills of the patient
3 PUNCTUALITY	3 PERSONAL CARE	3 CONTENT	3 ASSESSMENT	3 THE POSSIBILITY OF CHANGE
e.g.: Is it important for the person to be on time – not matter if he is late?	e.g.: The patient is asked to carry out tasks which assess how he can look after himself	What people do, how they behave	Understand assessment procedure of activities. Assessment of patient's needs in community	He made himself so he can change himself
4 SKILL	4 HOME MANAGEMENT	4 REFLEXIVE THEORY	4 AS PERSON	4 LIVING LIFE NOW
e.g.: Does the job need practical skills or thinking skills?	How could the patient manage at home?	This means that it fits everyone, including you and me. It helps you understand self and others	We all are experts of our self	He is alive and kicking trying to find better solutions for his problems
5 ROUTINE	5 WORK	5 TECHNIQUES TOOLS	5 INTEGRATION	5 HOPE
e.g.: Is the job boring, repetitive?	Does he work and if so at what and how?	Offer methods of finding out about the person as the person sees life eg. self-characterisation, eliciting, laddering, grids. ABC Fixed role enactment	Fits all aspects of the role together into a whole	Growth and change is always possible
6 CONSISTENCY e.g.: Work has to be at constantly high level of achievement. Does there always have to be a high standard of work?	6 SOCIAL SKILLS How does he relate to others?	6 METATHEORY It offers a theory which may be able to encompass all other theories of personality		6 RESPONSIBILITY He is responsible for himself
7 WORKING WITH OTHERS e.g.: Does the job entail working closely with other people?	7 INDEPENDENT LIVING SKILLS e.g.: Can he cope with day to day problems?	7 HOPE Man is the scientist you make yourself so can change		

Table 9.1—continued

Skills of a personal construct occupational therapist			The skills of the patient
8 RESPONSIBILITY Does the person have to be responsible for – tasks people/ workers?	8 LEISURE How does he spend his spare time?	8 FLEXIBILITY There are as many ways of seeing an event as can be imagined	
9 TOLERANCE OF OTHERS Does the person need to cope with others?	9 SYMPTOMATIC BEHAVIOUR Has he any problematic behaviour – violence etc?		
10 EXPECTATION OF PERSON What does the person expect of the job?	10 DISCHARGE AND FOLLOW UP In which type of accommodation would he be able to live most happily?	10 GROWTH PCP is a useful theory at present, but can be superseded by a different theory	
Analysis of job will give a breakdown of the required ability from the person wanting the job. NOT a certain person in the job.			

To recap, the occupational therapist's main categories of expertise are:

1 Assessment of an activity – to analyse the integral parts of the activity so that the therapist can use this activity beneficially for the patient.
2 The task orientated assessment of the patient, i.e., how the person is observed to behave given a specific task or the professional's view of the patient's behaviour.
3 Having the knowledge of the theory and techniques of Personal Construct Psychology, which enables the occupational therapist to stand in the shoes of the patients and understand the patient's view of life.
4 The occupational therapist as expert of himself:–

(a) – as a professional person,
(b) – as himself.
5 The patient as expert of himself.

The therapist should try and understand how and why the patient interprets the events in his life. The adage that 'you can take a horse to the water but you can not make it drink' must be remembered. One can plan the most impressive, elaborate treatment programme imaginable, but without the co-operation of one's partner (patient) it is just an academic exercise. Thus one *must* discover how the patient views his world.

WORKING PARTNERSHIP

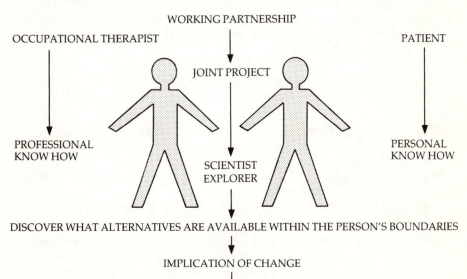

OCCUPATIONAL THERAPIST · JOINT PROJECT · PATIENT

PROFESSIONAL KNOW HOW · SCIENTIST EXPLORER · PERSONAL KNOW HOW

DISCOVER WHAT ALTERNATIVES ARE AVAILABLE WITHIN THE PERSON'S BOUNDARIES

IMPLICATION OF CHANGE

STEPS TO ACHIEVE DESIRED CHANGE, AS BEHAVIOURAL EXPERIMENTS

Figure 9.3

The therapist has to assimilate all the information gained which is:

1 Understanding the analysis of the activities chosen
2 Understanding the medical diagnosis and the implications
3 Understanding the needs of the person in society
4 Understanding the task orientated assessment of the patient
5 Understanding one's self as a person/professional
6 Understanding the patient as a person

A medical diagnosis will have been made about the patient. A personal construct theory diagnosis/hypothesis should also be made about the patient as a person (why is he as he is?) *but* remember a diagnosis is *not* like a forename that is given to the person for his life. It is *only* a transient diagnosis. People *change*, so *do not* label the person by the diagnosis.

If you are working successfully with a patient you will have made a good relationship with him as a person *not* as a diagnosis. All the information about the patient is to help him cope with his life more successfully, not as a specimen to be pinned to the notice-board.

When working with patients remember to collect information *from* the patient, not just the opinion of the medical staff, relations or neighbours. The way to obtain this information is by the techniques already described in the book. The patient is his own expert. If you want to know what his problem is ask him. He may well tell you, but in his own language not yours, so look behind the words. Collect enough information before making a workable hypothesis.

These two brief case histories illustrate how the occupational therapist explored the patient's world in order to help the patient's reconstrue.

Case 1

Joan is a woman of 65 years old who has had her second right hip replacement. At first her progress was good. She started to walk well, and went home to live with her elderly brother. Gradually her progress came to a halt. Instead she became overactive, stressed, and complained of pain and the inability to cope at home.

She was referred to the occupational therapist to see if any aids were required. She was seen at home and the first session was spent getting to know Joan's world, and her problem. The ABC technique was used to understand the implications of being overactive. Joan described this as running around in ever decreasing circles, getting nothing done, but always feeling exhausted, on edge, and guilty.

Joan's construct was *overactive* v. *passive*, and her preferred pole was *passive* (see Figure 9.4).

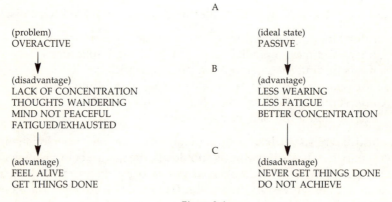

A

(problem)
OVERACTIVE

B

(disadvantage)
LACK OF CONCENTRATION
THOUGHTS WANDERING
MIND NOT PEACEFUL
FATIGUED/EXHAUSTED

(advantage)
FEEL ALIVE
GET THINGS DONE

C

(ideal state)
PASSIVE

(advantage)
LESS WEARING
LESS FATIGUE
BETTER CONCENTRATION

(disadvantage)
NEVER GET THINGS DONE
DO NOT ACHIEVE

Figure 9.4

The therapist discussed the implications of the ABC information, and what other possible alternative pole could be found instead of *passive*. Joan suggested perhaps being *a normal sort of person* v. *overactive*. The implication of this construct was explored (Figure 9.5).

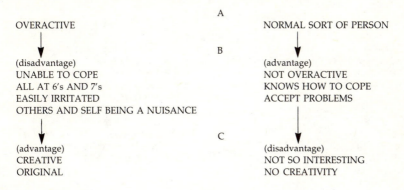

Figure 9.5

Joan and the therapist further discussed the idea of taking things in her stride, considering self as much as others, planning activities, but being flexible and creative. This was the alternative area of experimentation.

Joan did not need any aids or adaptations. Instead she and the occupational therapist planned ways of simplifying the housework, and cooking, so that it would fit in with the activities Joan wished to do 'but had not the time'. She divided up the tasks into manageable chunks, so that she could see the results of her new found way of behaving.

Interestingly, her Kellian aggression had an effect on her relative, who started doing some of the housework, cooking, gardening, and began to treat Joan more as an equal than an unpaid housekeeper.

Case 2

Jane was in her mid-thirties when admitted to a psychiatric hospital. She was diagnosed as a depressive, inadequate alcoholic. Her life before she was admitted had been very traumatic.

She had been in hospital about a year. There had been various attempts at getting her settled into the community, all of which had failed, inexplicably.

Whilst in hospital she had been assessed, and found totally able to live outside. She could look after herself, manage her own affairs, keep down a full-time job, develop her social life. But she was unable to live in the community for long before she had to return to hospital.

The therapist took a closer look at how she saw herself, and her world. This revealed a bipolar construct which had no positive pole.

This was *bad* v. *mad*. The ABC revealed the implications of this (Figure 9.6).

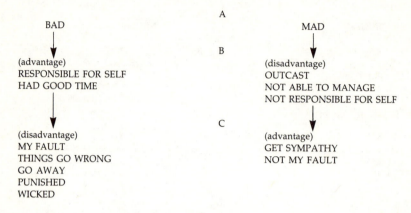

A

BAD   MAD

B

(advantage)   (disadvantage)
RESPONSIBLE FOR SELF   OUTCAST
HAD GOOD TIME   NOT ABLE TO MANAGE
            NOT RESPONSIBLE FOR SELF

C

(disadvantage)   (advantage)
MY FAULT   GET SYMPATHY
THINGS GO WRONG   NOT MY FAULT
GO AWAY
PUNISHED
WICKED

Figure 9.6

If Jane chose the *bad* pole she was responsible for her husband's suicide, and everything bad that had happened to her. She could have a good time, drinking and going out with men, but by doing this she considered herself bad. Being *mad* in some ways was easier as it was not her fault, but she was rejected even though she was not responsible for her actions.

The therapist worked with her to explore other possible alternative dimensions. One probable area was to do with being creative (this was discovered after looking at her repertory grid). The therapist used loosening techniques including art and drama which encouraged her to explore new possibilities. Creative writing was another area which Jane enjoyed and was successful in (an article of hers had been published). The therapist validated these experiments. They also worked on the underdeveloped area of self esteem/confidence. She gradually developed new useful constructs which hopefully would take the place of her old system.

The therapeutic partnership

The occupational therapist and the patient share the job of devising the therapy programme, using the information that has been gained as a basis for negotiation. The therapist should be aware that behaviour is a way of testing out the construing process, and the prediction of events. The work done with the patient is part theory – looking at alternative ways of construing events – and part practical – testing out the theory. The therapist should pay attention to the area of the person which is most likely to produce good results in the future. This may not necessarily be to do with the cause of the complaint. Getting the person to re-construe is the most useful way of preventing him making the same mistake again (getting out of the rut).

People do not have to have insight to change. If a different way of behaving 'pays off' for a person, he does not have to know why it is better than the old way, he just gets on with his life. After all if you have a puncture is it not more important to mend it and carry on with the journey than find out what actually caused the flat tyre if it is not immediately obvious?

In what way does the patient reconstrue

When designing 'the self' the person will only change in a way which is meaningful to his life. So the therapist should design the programme with the person to enable him to carve out and build the future, without knocking down the present or dredging up the past.

The patient should look at areas which are acceptable to him (e.g. a farmer would not be happy or comfortable in a high-rise flat in a city). The person is free within his boundaries to build the self he can accept.

The therapist should remember that the patient may have a lot invested in his problem. The self without the problem is often difficult to envisage. He has a well developed idea of himself with the problem. The patient has come to see self plus problem – be it depression, obesity, arthritis. He may not be able to foresee what he would be like without it (so make haste slowly).

One possibility is that he has developed the notion that without the problem he would be the 'Ideal Self' (not usually possible). As he gradually relinquishes the problem he may realise that he is still no nearer to his ideal self. In fact as this different (new) self he may not be able to predict how he is likely to behave in most situations, so instead of losing the problem, he has gained another. He may well prefer to return to the old self with the problem (in therapist terms, relapse). This behaviour may be seen by the occupational therapist as failure, but to the client he would see it as going back to familiar ground. Possibly he moved too fast, and did not have enough bridges or scaffolding around to prevent him from falling.

The patient should be encouraged to see the problem in as many different ways as is possible (using loosening techniques – art, drama, discussing his dreams, and so forth) so that alternative solutions may be considered.

When planning a treatment programme, consider the progress carefully, as it is bad enough for the patient not to understand the therapy, but it would be terrible if he were unable to predict himself and his future. It would provoke intolerable anxiety. Anxiety is a constant part of day-to-day living. After all we all get anxious if we are faced with the unknown, be it the bus being late, or what will the boss say if we were late. Anxiety 'cannot be observed directly'. The occupational therapist has to discover how the patient appears to manage and control anxiety. Part of therapy is to help the patient cope with and manage anxiety more usefully for him.

A person who looks into the future and sees nothing but confusion and chaos becomes naturally worried. Although Kelly suggests that the logical construct may be *worry* v. *no worry*, it is impossible to do, as he has to do something. The occupational therapist should help him find positive and active alternatives.

For example:

1 Divide the future into manageable chunks.
2 Get the patient to think of day-to-day living, what to have for supper, make a list of what is needed at the shops.
3 Plan for the near future and leave on one side the unpredictable.
4 Try out the practical experiments, think of something pleasant to do so life is not all horrible – e.g. have a long soak in a bubble bath, go for a walk.
5 Learn alternative ways of coping with the constant threat of anxiety.

As an occupational therapist it is important to remember that everyone experiences anxiety. Therefore the treatment programme should be planned with the patient to keep it to a minimum. Always discuss what the treatment entails, and if he agrees with it, how he may carry out the experiment.

The occupational therapist has no right to either accept or take on the patient's responsibility. Among other things it indicates what little faith he has in the patient's ability. It is an insult to the patient's capability, and potential. Also it is a full time life's work to take on the responsibility of someone else, reassuring continually. It is like looking after a full grown baby for life.

We have agreed that it is an important aim for the occupational therapist to ensure that the patient keeps charge of his own life; but having said that it is also the occupational therapist's job to:

1 Design a programme especially for the patient.
2 Devise experiments which are – appropriate to the patient
                                   – in manageable chunks
                                   – safe, do not expose the patient to unnecessary risks.
3 Keep in mind the aims and objectives of self and patient.

The objective is to reduce the possibilities of failure while increasing success, and confidence, and reducing risks of danger to a minimum.

The programme should be taken one step at a time, so the patient can see that he can succeed.

Always work with the patient as a team, sharing the effort and success. In this way you help him achieve his goal. His solution may not be ideal for the occupational therapist but it is *his* life. Therapy is like a chess board being able to move in various ways and having a composite approach to its objective. The therapist should be able to know the objective and be several moves ahead to predict the next step, but be flexible enough to change it if necessary.

The body and mind are a whole, not like a Lego man where one part can function independently from another. Patients are complex animals. It is impossible for the occupational therapist to treat one part of the person alone. The patient does not deliver a leg to the department for a treatment session, and collect it after the allocated time. He has to live with it, cope it twenty-four hours a day, plus all the possible misery, discomfort, and problems for the family. When he comes to occupational therapy he needs comprehensive not modular treatment. Often there are psychological and family implications of which the occupational therapist should be aware.

Does Personal Construct Theory also help the occupational therapist in the field of psychiatry

The occupational therapist understands the definition of psychiatric terms, illnesses, and the diagnosis that labels patients, particularly their behaviour, and the interpersonal interaction of the mentally disturbed patients.

Is the medical model the most useful way of understanding the patient? Is it helpful to the patient? Perhaps we should see the patient differently, not as a psychiatrically ill patient; *but* as a person who is doing the best he can at that time to make sense of his world and to cope with his increasing anxiety. A patient is a person with a hypothesis (albeit a miserable one), who is testing it out. This person is asking for help to improve his life, and to find alternative solutions to his problems. It is important to see patients as people in their own right (just like us) struggling to regain some sort of order and responsibility for themselves.

Instead of sticking to the 'medical model' – the pill-pushing, the well-defined way of looking at this different being, the patient, and treating him by blotting out his symptoms and so getting him to fit into our institution's boundaries – perhaps we could try to understand his inner conflict, and his method of dealing with it, his symptoms?

We may offer pills to alleviate the painful symptoms on a short term basis; but also offer a treatment programme which is designed to help the person reconstrue, and thus find better ways of coping with his life. We should help him seek other ways of defining the problem and working with him on finding more useful (for him) solutions. The skills of the occupational therapists are ideal in assisting the patient to do this.

If the occupational therapist does not adhere to the well-defined medical diagnosis, particularly in psychiatry, how does he understand the process going on in the patient? What is the disorder? This is where Personal Construct Theory is beneficial. Kelly suggests a disorder is 'any personal construction which is used repeatedly in spite of constant invalidation' (Kelly, 1955). So why does not the person just change the disordered constructs? Well, it depends how well a person's construct system is organised. For instance, if one part of the system does not work well, the person may not be able to tear it out and build again to replace it, as the rest of the structure may not be able to hold up without it. You cannot pull out the dry rot on the ground floor of a building without constructing strong supportive scaffolding around it. Some buildings (construct systems) do not have enough scaffolding erected and so the diseased part is considered better than no part at all, or the complete collapse of the system.

The occupational therapist's job is to work with the patient to shore up the system and gradually, very carefully (with the co-operation of the patient) replace the dry rot parts with sound timbers, whilst the person continues to exist in the house. Too much change at once will cause the building to collapse. To the patient this is disaster – so to prevent it he guards his building very carefully.

All people have erected construct systems to make sense of their world. People who have psychological disorders do not exist differently from the others of us, but they have got stuck. Kelly suggested that 'the goal of therapy may be very simply to alleviate complaints – complaints of the person about himself and others and complaints of others about him' (Kelly, 1955).

The occupational therapist should listen to what the patient is telling him, sensitively, and using the credulous approach, suspending all judgment, accept that what the patient says is 'true'. He must endeavour to construe the patient's instructions, develop the ability to subsume (take on) the patient's constructions. He must also remember that the information being used is very personal and private, so it must remain confidential.

The treatment programme must be designed for the patient, not the medical diagnosis. Understanding how the patient sees his world is the main aspect on which to plan the therapy, but the medical and social issues relating to this person must also be borne in mind.

The therapist 'should formulate an adequate hypothesis, keep experiments within conceptual framework, design his procedure so that not too many factors will become variables at once, and prepare himself to construe the outcomes'.

The person: the patient

When people are ill they often choose to adopt the role of the patient, different from 'well' people. They hang a label around their own necks, which says 'I am dependent, and am leaving the thinking and decision making to the hospital staff'.

When treating patients in hospital remember that they are likely to feel vulnerable. The person can only cope with so much at once, and already he is probably experiencing anxiety, and anger (why should this happen to me?). So make sure when explaining or giving instructions that they are clear and precise, and always check that the patient has understood what has been said.

A research project revealed that patients who can directly express their anxiety and anger will fare better, and are likely to have good rehabilitational prospects later; unlike the patients who express their anger indirectly or passively.

Time

Time is a very important aspect of life; time heals, but not alone. It is uni-dimensional. Based on now, we can look back and remember the past and change our opinion of it; we can hope for the future; but we behave and live now. There is no mileage in 'if only' or 'yes but'. 'If only' is a U-turn back to misery and hostility. So let us act 'as if' . . . is possible. Let us try it out. 'Nature abhors a vacuum' and so do therapists. Nothing is worse than being fatalistic if the problem does not resolve itself. One feels better if one tries to do something new about sorting it out. Time plus effort – the effort of designing a programme from which to start trying for new horizons – might produce the desired effect.

People can only work at their own speed (not yours) and with the material they bring. Build on this material, changing, developing, creating where possible, but 'cut your garment according to the cloth' and do not expect to change the person totally.

Role play

One important way of offering the possibility of change is variations on the theme of fixed role play/enactment. It may not be possible to develop a complete fixed role enactment; but the occupational therapist could use role play in various forms to encourage change and improve the patient's life.

Role play is used in social skills, drama, discussion, etc. It is important to realise when offering someone a role however small it can permeate throughout their system, like throwing a pebble into a pond – the ripples travel across the whole pond. Many occupational therapists use role play but many do not think of the implications of it. They know it works but perhaps not why.

Points worth remembering about role play

It should be played as make-believe. In this way it is less threatening, one step away from reality. It must not depict a perfect person, and should have spontaneous touches to make it more interesting. It takes the patient off the spot and puts the task on the spot. It encourages the idea of change. It mobilises the patient's resources, without directly correcting faults. It should be done in a playful atmosphere, not with a feeling that this is something that has to be done. The occupational therapist should be willing to role play as well as the patients. It is something the patient can continue to practise outside the department. It is a way for a patient to take responsibility; a way of experimenting for himself.

In role play the patient should become excited about the things he is able to do, discover what happens when he changes certain behaviour. What is the 'knock on' effect? What if he should try a different way of behaving? He learns to translate the different and new messages from other people. What happens to his construing processes? These are important parts of the role play. If the new role is useful to the patient, he can take it on board and practise it until it becomes part of his system.

Kelly suggested that occupational therapy had many aspects. It could be used diagnostically, for instance 'if the activity was freely chosen by the patient or carefully assigned by the occupational therapist and carefully observed, a lot of the person's construct system can be discovered'.

Words are not the only or indeed the primary means of communication, and so it is important to study the other means of communication which patients use. If the patient is unable or unwilling to use words, the occupational therapy activities may be the central approach. 'The occupational therapist can observe new constructs emerging, and can introduce new elements which, if embraced, will give new constructs appropriate range and permeability and provide the client with facilities for validating them' (Kelly, 1955).

Constructs are not divided into ones relating to 'physical things' and those which are to do with 'mental or social things', e.g. 'a client who loves to pound nails, dig holes, or grease machinery is likely to be using constructs which govern his relations with people as well as his relations with things. As the client's activity and modes of approach to these tasks change, his relations with other people are almost certain to change perceptively. This important fact can be used as a basis for bringing about genuine therapeutic changes in the client's interpersonal relations' (Kelly, 1955).

Occupational therapy can be educative. The patient may learn new skills to aid him socially, vocationally, and recreationally, and thus aid the development and understanding of people. Occupational therapy may be used in any form which will aid the patient reconstrue. The whole aim is to offer the patient a different and exciting way of coping with life. The whole point of occupational therapy is to offer an activity which will enable the patient to use it in his process of rehabilitation. This is not a way of keeping him busy simply to help him pass the time.

Personal Construct Theory offers a resource which can be used in all aspects of the profession, be it clinical, managerial, administrative, research, teaching, and of course personal understanding.

In my view it changes a fuzzy ad hoc set of pointers into a revolutionary, scientific, precise, understandable hypothesis, which can be universally used.

10 · Changing conversations: a constructivist model of training for psychotherapists

VINCENT KENNY

Introduction

Live and learn

This chapter introduces a radical constructivist (Kenny, 1985a) model of training for psychotherapists based upon the writings of George Kelly and Humberto Maturana. The work of both authors emphasises a view of living systems which provides a model of personal change which is applicable to the formal contexts of training, teaching, therapy or indeed to any context where the processes of what we call 'learning' are central. Kelly and Maturana construe 'learning' as synonymous with 'living' and hence a somewhat superfluous notion as Kelly (1969) illustrates in the following quote:

> Man lives best when he commits himself to getting on with his life. Since I see the concept of learning as nothing less than this, the term seems redundant when applied to a living creature.

For Maturana (1985) learning involves undergoing structural changes while conserving our organisation (identity) intact. To lose our biological organisation (autopoiesis) is to die. Hence learning *is* living. In living-learning we continuously re-invent ourselves as autonomous personal systems, our organisational identities being reaffirmed or reformed by flowing along the path of our actions. We become what we do. In this regard von Foerster (1986) points out that we should not construe ourselves as 'human beings' but rather as 'human becomings'.

The nature of our self-invention and the issue of system change has occupied many authors (Kelly, 1955; Bateson, 1972; Maturana and Varela, 1980; von Foerster, 1981) especially in regard to psychotherapeutic change. Kelly (1969) outlines eight strategies for triggering psychotherapeutic changes many of which involve enabling the client to become an observer of himself, his complaint and his medium of existence. The complaint may be construed as the optimal way in which the client may relate or connect himself to his world. From the constructivist point of view the complaint illustrates both where the person's construct system breaks down (Kelly, 1955) and where the 'real' world exclusively manifests itself (von Glasersfeld, 1984) in its unknowability. What we 'know' as 'reality' is what we bring forth through our operations of distinction (Maturana, 1986). Ultimately, therefore, all we can come to know is the organisation and structure of our own system, i.e. the manner in which we organise ourselves. Any training course must therefore create the maximum context for becoming an observer of one's own self-organisation, how we invent, maintain and propagate our construct system. Each trainee must become responsible for his own self-invention, become aware of the organisational processes whereby his system conserves and modulates itself, and take the personal risks involved in accelerated change.

Learning to learn

Developing awareness of self-organisation (your own or that of another) is different from 'knowing about' yourself (factually) or from 'knowing how' to (skilfully) control or manipulate your system. Mair (1980) points out that personal knowing is not attained by a purely cognitive analysis of a living system.

> If we are to come to know ourselves or others more intimately we need to feel for and inhabit aspects of ourselves rather than merely identify and manipulate from the outside. . . . To be met and recognized in this way can be deeply reassuring but it can also be alarming and threatening. This is not merely because the other may be sensed as penetrating your disguises and defences, but because you also may come to know yourself in ways you had previously managed to avoid (p. 114).

One of the avoided or invisible aspects of our system tends to be our 'deutero-learning' (Bateson, 1972) or how we learn to learn. If we do not alter our habits of punctuating the stream of experiential events then we will conserve the existing construct system structure which creates our personal meaning space. Thus the 'meaning of life' remains unaltered. Bateson states that:

> . . . 'learning to learn' is a synonym for the acquisition of that class of abstract habits of thought with which this paper is concerned; that the states of mind which we call 'free will', instrumental thinking, dominance, passivity, etc., are acquired by a process which we may equate with 'learning to learn' (1972, p. 166).

In psychotherapy deutero-learning is well exemplified in the phenomenon of 'transference' where the patient transfers onto the therapist a number of personal constructs which have been previously developed to punctuate and construe earlier relationships. Much of psychotherapy may involve the therapist attempting to extricate himself from such transferences and to enable the patient to observe these aspects of how he learns to learn. Since our self-organisation intrinsically involves our 'learning to learn' style, any attempts to change our style implies a change of self-organisation, often manifested initially in varying degrees of self-disorganisation.

Talking to yourself

Maturana and Varela (1980) have experimentally demonstrated the organisational closure of the autopoietic system. Kelly (1955) also found it necessary to 'close' the construct system in order to make sense of our experience from the 'inside' (Kenny, 1985b).

> Within the realm of relevance his personal construct system defines for him, each man initiates what he says and does. Thus his words and acts are not mere events consequent upon previous occurrences, but are expressions of what is relevantly affirmed and denied within his system (Kelly, 1969, p. 35).

Maturana and Varela (1980) point out that because the system is organisationally closed we cannot, at the moment of experiencing, distinguish between a hallucination and a perception. That is, we cannot distinguish an 'inner' signal from an 'outer' signal because the system is essentially relating to (talking to) itself. Some of Kelly's eight strategies for change focus on enabling the client to 'tune in' to his inner invisible conversations and begin to bring hitherto invisible processes to a higher level of awareness. The psychotherapeutic conversations for change initially concentrate on making the 'inner' construct system conversations more explicit. Maturana (1985), following Searle and Austin, outlines several different classes of conversation, and other authors have found the notion of conversation to be a very powerful framework for dealing with the wholeness, autonomy, recursiveness and closure of self-organisation (Mair, 1970; Pask, 1975, 1976, 1981; Varela, 1979; Thomas and Harri-Augstein, 1985; Braten, 1986).

Varela's (1979) view of the conversation paradigm is this:

> In fact, a *conversation* has been a basic image . . . as a paradigm for interactions among autonomous systems. It is a paradigm as well as a particular instance of an autonomous system, and these two sides of it go together. Its role as exemplary case of autonomous interaction comes from the fact that a conversation is *direct* experience, the human experience *par excellence* – we live and breathe in dialogue and language. And from this direct experience we know that one cannot find a firm reference point for the content of a dialogue. There is no methodological escape from dealing with the elusiveness of understanding, and this makes it very evident that whatever is

informative in a conversation is intrinsically codependent and interpretational. Whatever is said in order to fix and objectify the nature of a conversation's content is said from a perspective, from a tradition, and is always open to question, to revision, to disagreement. This is not failure or weakness, but the heart of the process.

In-forming v. information

Varela's comments on the interpretational and codependent nature of conversation necessarily leads us to abandon the old notion of 'transmitting information'. To illustrate this Maturana and Guiloff (1980) use the tale of King Midas who wanted the power to be able to transform the structures of any system into gold. The resulting nightmare of the 'Midas Touch' underlines the necessity for living systems to be organisationally closed and determined by their own structures. This structure-determinism is at the core of the radical constructivist approach to learning. Constructivist conversations (whether in therapy or in training) therefore focus primarily on the organisational closure and structure-determinism of the construct system.

Within the constructivist framework 'information' can no longer be seen as an 'input' but only as a perturbation which may or may not trigger a compensation within the construct system. Varela (1979) uses the word 'in-formation' in its original etymological sense of *in-formare*, to form within. Within the training or therapy context we hope to enable the trainee/client to come to in-form themselves in a different manner, i.e. to re-invent their self-organisation. In discussing Kelly's (1955) view of the person as 'a form of motion', in a continual Heraclitean flux, Mair (1980) makes the following observations:

> At all times we are silently and invisibly engaged in moving and forming and reforming and approaching and withdrawing and transforming and holding and releasing and making and breaking and composing and decomposing our ways of being in relationship within our worlds. In each and all of our multiple and subtly changing relationships we are orchestrations of in-forming motion (1980, p. 126).

Perturbations and compensations

Instead of trainers making 'inputs' of knowledge, skills or attitudes to their trainees we must refer to our interactions as 'perturbations' (which the trainee may ignore or disallow as triggers to his system) emphasising that we cannot force our way *into* the trainee's autonomous system but are restricted to interacting (from the outside) with the whole system. Kelly's definition of threat includes the idea that all our constructs are (ultimately or distantly) interconnected (in internal dialogue) and when we perturb any one construct we necessarily set off a chain reaction, just as touching one strand of a spider's web sets up interactions throughout the whole web.

Many of the existing models of training can be seen to depend on the assumption that the direct instructions of the trainer act as controlling 'inputs' to the system of the trainee who will 'output' the appropriate response or 'skill'. Pereira Gray (1982) lists the following analogies of the trainer-trainee relationship: (1) the animal trainer, (2) the puppet on a string, (3) the driving instructor, (4) the military model, (5) the producer/actor, (6) the parent/child, (7) the older sibling, (8) the doctor/patient. Most of these are based on the fallacy of 'instructive interactions' (Varela, 1979) and attempt to ignore the organisational closure and structure determinism of the autonomous person. For Varela (1979) communication and linguistic interactions are *intrinsicially non-informative*. The trainee must be continually re-focused upon his own learning to learn processes in order to be able to 'in-form' himself. Thomas and Harri-Augstein (1983) distinguish between 'dependent learning' and 'self-organised learning', the latter individuals being defined as:

> . . . effective personal scientists – scientists dealing in the art of the soluble, constructing viable models of both their learning opportunities and of their own learning experience and acting on the basis of these personally relevant and viable models to optimize their learning performances (1983, p. 334).

The central effort is directed towards facilitating conversations which increase the trainees' effectiveness as personal scientists and hence to become more self-organised in their learning. Thus, we may see the different models of training as different forms of conversational organisations. Those premised on the authoritarian 'transmission of information' we may see as 'conversations for conversion, conservation and conformity', and those at the opposite end of the scale based on organisational closure we may see as 'conversations for codependent core-construction'. It is to the latter we now turn by outlining Kelly's (1955) approach to training.

A constructivist training model for psychotherapy: the ontology of the observer

The main aim of training, according to Kelly, ' . . . should be to help the therapist develop a professional construction system which is printable, psychologically informed, systematically intact, scientifically supported, amenable to searching inquiry, and in process of continuing revision' (1955, p. 1180). Given the uniqueness of each person's construing system, the therapist's construct system must be a 'system of approach' with which he can understand and subsume the great range of systems which he will encounter in his practice. The primary concern is in regard to the adequacy and articulation of the therapist's own subsuming construct system which needs to be elaborated at two levels in order for him to be able to understand the construct system of others. The two levels to be elaborated are: (a) the verbal construct system (the therapist's 'intellectual insight'), and (b) the preverbal construct system (his 'emotional insight').

The client's interests are best protected when the therapist's training focuses primarily on the 'formation of systematically sound professional constructs'. This implies, among other things, an apprehension of the principles of scientific methodology, what constitutes scientific evidence, the capacity to tolerate the uncertainty of maintaining one's system open to investigation and continuous revision, and an intimate familiarity with the nature of the 'knowledge' one applies and the processes which transform it. This delineates Kelly's notion of the professional scientist who is also a humanistic scientist.

> Humanistic science is science in the grasp of men, not men in the grasp of science . . . In pursuing its course it makes the most of man's range of experiential capacities, even those that are inarticulate (1969, p. 145).

Kelly sees all persons as scientists and all scientists as persons. He regards 'man as an experimenting creature, of which a scientist is an example'. His humanistic scientist is therefore a subject in his own research. He designs his personal experiments 'to make his experience an optimal one. Thus he can not lose sight of the fact that he is himself the principal subject of his own experimental intervention' (1969, p. 139). This applies equally to the client-as-scientist and to the trainee psychotherapist-as-scientist. It is his ontology as observer that is at the centre of Kelly's theory. The role relationship between the trainer and the trainee parallels that of the research supervisor with his research student. The supervisor is an expert in framing fertile questions and the student is an expert in his subject matter – in this case in his own ontology. The flexibility of role relationships needed is illustrated by the following quote:

> Personal construct psychotherapy is a way of getting on with the human enterprise and it may embody and mobilize all of the techniques for doing this that man has yet devised. Certainly there is no one psychotherapeutic technique and certainly no one kind of interpersonal compatibility between psychotherapist and client. The techniques employed are the techniques for living . . . (1969, p. 221).

Kelly emphasises a view of psychotherapy in terms of a way of life, i.e. as a *role* as opposed to seeing it in terms of 'insights'. He preferred to see psychotherapy as dealing with the ways in which the individual 'fits' (von Glasersfeld, 1984) with his 'reality'.

Much of this 'fitting' takes place at the level of preverbal construing.

This is a major part of the focus of Kelly's training considerations, namely:

> . . . the therapist's construct system as a whole, and especially those preverbal substructures which need to be approached through psychotherapeutic channels. Just as a good deal of the client's behaviour is organized under constructs which are not symbolized by him on a verbal level, so the psychotherapist, being a person too, also lives under the aegis of a personal construct system not always clearly marked by names and guideposts (1955, p. 1180).

To be able to unpack the preverbal levels it is necessary to work with trainees in very small groups or on a one-to-one basis. Sometimes it requires the trainee to enter psychotherapy.

Psychotherapy for trainees

Kelly sees it as often appropriate that trainees should have some experience of personal therapy, working on their own complaints particularly in pre-verbal areas. He sees several functions that this might serve:
(a) Illustration of technique: by undertaking a personal psychotherapy the trainee will directly experience the use of certain psychotherapeutic approaches to change. Experiencing therapeutic perturbations as a participant gives a different understanding to that of observing them as a bystander.
(b) Grounds for role relationships: experiencing therapy creates a strong foundation upon which to base his later role relationships with his own clients.

> Since a role relationship requires the subsuming of some part of the construct system of the person with whom the role is played, the more the therapist can understand about how it feels to sit at the other side of the table, the more appreciative of his own client's position he is likely to be. Even experienced therapists are likely to be surprised at how different the therapeutic situation looks when one is in the role of a client' (1955, p. 1181).

Similar perspectives may be gained by the use of psychodrama, role-play, video-tape feedback and so forth.
(c) Discovering parallel processes: there are many parallels in the relationship of therapist-client and trainer-trainee relationship, and in terms of the radical constructivist view, the change processes are identical. Since all change is dictated by the structures of the individual system, the notion of 'pathology' must disappear from our lexicon since it is a value-judgment based on the idea that the system 'ought to' have behaved differently to the way its structures determined. Kelly emphasises the 'psychology of acceptance', i.e. taking the system where it is and understanding how its actions are the only choices extant within the construct system. Equally, Maturana (1985) emphasises that 'the system can only do what it does'. Dell points out that

> . . . we think that instructive interactions should have taken place but that the organism failed to be correctly instructed because it is defective . . . A person who does not see the world 'correctly' (one who fails to be 'correctly' instructed by 'reality') is considered to be defective or pathological. Reality, however, is not objective. Reality is consensual (1986, p. 232).

Kelly (1955) raises the question as to whether a 'therapist will do a better job if he does see the client as resembling himself?' In answering his own question Kelly draws a distinction between construing the client as similar in identity to oneself or seeing the similarity in terms of both having the same unsolved problems. The radical constructivist position defines the similarity in the more abstract terms of structural transformation. To see oneself and the client as organisationally closed self-referential systems liberates the therapist from much confusion and unrealisable responsibilities. It is each system which changes itself, the most a therapist can attempt is to design orthogonal perturbations (Kenny, 1987) which may trigger structural changes in the client's system. Where the trainee therapist has experienced the threat of such transformations in his personal therapy he is more likely to abandon the notion of 'resistance'. Experiencing radical change within oneself is also a direct encouragement to the therapist who then knows what is possible in attempting to trigger changes in his clients.

(d) Discovery of self-appearance: the therapist must have the capacity of entering into a variety of role relationships (Kelly outlines twelve common construals of the therapist's role pp. 575–81, 1955), and of extricating himself from certain roles which the complainant will transfer onto him. An important aspect of therapy is to facilitate a fluidity of role relationships for both the therapist and the complainant. The processes of self-revelation and feedback experienced in therapy will begin to give the trainee some idea of how he is perceived by others and what type of roles they tend to expect him to play. Participation with fellow trainees in an ongoing experiential group greatly enhances this process.

(e) Self-improvement: experiencing psychotherapy may also precipitate significant structural changes in the trainee's system, triggering what Balint (1977) referred to as the 'limited, though considerable, change in his personality' necessary to become a therapist. Kelly reminds us that the problem of deciding whether psychotherapy should begin at all is matched by the problem of deciding when it should end.

> No matter how deeply he explores himself in the course of therapy, there are always unknown impressions lying just below the last layer he has uncovered (1955, p. 1184).

Since much therapy involves a necessary phase of transition and dis-organisation, one point at which to choose termination is where the trainee's system has reached another level of reorganisation or coherence. This applies both to the level of constructs dealing with experiential intimacies and also to those constructs relating to professional practice. Obviously personal problems and professional problems cannot be arbitrarily separated, but it is often the case that trainee's therapeutic activities deteriorate markedly at certain junctures where they experience a form of 'stage-fright' (Polanyi, 1973) or paralysis from becoming self-observers in a particular manner. That is, by becoming aware of personal action which would normally be 'invisible' to them they can no longer act spontaneously. It is better not to terminate personal therapy during one of these incoherent phases of practice. As a caveat on trainees being asked to participate in a personal therapy ('purification') Kelly notes that he has seen 'some instances in which it appeared that psychotherapy, while of real personal help, made a bad therapist out of a mediocre one' (1955, p. 1184).

Thomas and Harri-Augstein (1983) emphasise that 'achieving new levels in learning performance usually involves serious personal change. It involves the disruption and breaking of existing poorly organised skills and the establishment of new attitudes and personally strange ways of thinking, feeling, and behaving' (p. 349). Changes in self-organisation always involve a 'learning trough' during which the learner needs to be supported both in and outside of the personal therapy context.

Transference

For the radical constructivist all constructions are transferences of the structure-determined system. Thus the trainee and trainer are no different to their clients in that all their constructions are transferences. Kelly (1969a) points out that ' . . . constructs must be employed which were originally devised for dealing with others, and it is to be anticipated that they will, at best, be an imperfect fit' (p. 222). The question of 'fit' is asked through our interactions with the person we are construing and the answer we get may lead us to reconstruct this person. Transference only becomes a problem in psychotherapy, training or whatever when a person recurrently imposes the same transferred construction on another person (e.g. the trainee onto the trainer) and, equally recurrently, is not capable of making sense of the disconfirming evidence which results from his actions. In short, the transference becomes a problem only when the person seems unable to fully complete the experiential cycle and invent new anticipations with which to relate himself to his therapist/trainer/spouse etc. Here we see the importance of the therapist's flexibility in extricating himself from transferences in such a way that the disconfirming evidence *invites* the client/ trainee to complete the cycle and invent new alternative constructions.

The experiential cycle

Kelly points out that an individual's construct system varies as he successively construes the repeated patterns whereby he punctuates events. Within PCP human experience is constituted by continuously involving ourselves in actions which may lead to unanticipated outcomes (i.e. those which differ from or elaborate our predictions) which in turn dislodges our constructions of ourselves. Kelly describes the unit of experience as a five-phase cycle beginning with Anticipation and following with Investment, Encounter Confirmation or Disconfirmation and Constructive Revision leading to new Anticipations.

> Stated simply, the amount of a man's experience is not measured by the number of events with which he collides, but by the investments he has made in his anticipations and the revisions of his constructions that have followed upon his facing up to consequences (1970, p. 19).

Prevision, intervision and revision

The experiential cycle can be of very short or long duration. A short cycle is illustrated by the action of biting into an apple which we anticipate will be sweet. Having encountered the apple we may experience a disconfirmation when we taste sourness which might lead us to revise certain predictions based on the colour of an apple. A longer cycle is the time of postgraduate training that trainee therapists must undergo. We may view it as follows:

(1) Anticipation: as in psychotherapy this is the planning stage where an assessment of the trainee's needs, aims or complaints are elaborated. Reflexively, this also applies to the trainer or 'supervisor' who anticipates achieving certain aims within the course curriculum. These aims depend very much on the particular philosophy of psychotherapy and model of training employed.

(2) Investment: the second stage is where the trainer and trainee begin to involve themselves in the training process and agree to engage in certain actions which they trust will lead them to the desired anticipated outcome.

(3) Encounter: this is the action phase of the experiential cycle where the participants will experiment with training methods in attempts to actively elaborate the trainee's construct system. For example, the analysis of videotaped consultations is a common experimental format.

(4) Dis/Confirmation: throughout the experiments the participants will experience a variety of results attendant upon the twin processes of feedback (confrontation) and self-disclosure, i.e. telling the other something about himself or telling the other something about yourself. The manner in which these conversations are dealt with are crucial to the

overall outcome. As Kelly notes 'Confirmation may lead to reconstruing quite as much as disconfirmation – perhaps even more' (1970, p. 18).
(5) Constructive Revision: in terms of a two-year course there are many methods of assessing the overall enterprise in terms of the outcome. For the trainee he must construe what revisions have taken place in his construct system. For the course staff they will be interested in what the trainee's performance could imply for future courses, perhaps altering their aims and methods for the next intake of trainees.

The task of 'supervision' therefore can be broken down into the threefold task of prevision (Anticipation-Investment), intervision (Encounter-Dis/Confirmation), and revision (Constructive Revision) within the experiential cycle.

The anxiety of uncertainty

For Kelly it is important to develop the capacity to live in a world of uncertainty as opposed to a world without doubts. Consequently, he framed his experiential cycle as one which ends with a new question (anticipation) which necessarily triggers the cycle again and again.

> But, still, if I had to end my life on some final note I think I would like it to be a question, preferably a basic one, well posed and challenging, and beckoning me on to where only others after me may go, rather than a terminal conclusion – no matter how well documented (1969, pp. 51–2).

Living with uncertainty is a necessary ability for the psychotherapist. This is made easier for him by using the philosophy of constructive alternativism which defines psychotherapy as a creative enterprise, where neither the therapist nor the complainant can know the final outcome because there is no such thing. The human enterprise is an open-ended one, and, as Kelly remarks, 'I am not sure most of us would care to be dragged, kicking and screaming, through life by its certainties, or to have our burning curiosities extinguished by being doused with a bucketful of truth' (1969, p. 43).

Kelly warns us to beware of the obvious and remarks that 'those things I once thought I knew for sure, those are what get me into hot water, time after time' (1969, p. 51).

Perturbations and pearls

However, trainees shift continuously between living in a world of uncertainty on the one hand, and a world without doubts on the other. Sometimes when they try to occupy the doubt-less world they become hostile and substitute 'extortion for problem-solving', i.e. mistakes are not acknowledged and disconfirming evidence is distorted to fit their anticipations. In the language of radical constructivism (Maturana, 1986), a mistake is a 'miss-take' where we bring forth a reality for which we can find no consensus. The hostile person remains within his idiosyncratic closure and disavows the consensus languaging necessary to distinguish hallucinations from perceptions. There are several other ways of dealing with disconfirmatory evidence. For example, the trainee may simply alter his specific prediction without altering other constructions of the system. He may base his next anticipations on some other construct structure within the going system, and so on.

To add further to our world of uncertainty, there is an asymmetry between experimental results which are either confirmatory or disconfirmatory of our predictions. While the failure of a prediction invites us to reconstrue, the ostensible success of a prediction still allows much doubt to remain in the situation. For example, successful outcome may only superficially appear to look like what we had predicted, or the confirming result may not have depended on what we had imagined it to do.

> At best, the confirmation of a prediction is no more than tentative evidence that one may be on the track of something. The psychology of living in a world that is largely unknown – and in rapid transition, besides – leads us to hope for little more than ad interim support for our beliefs (1969, p. 39).

For Kelly, what is more important is:

> . . . our ability, while alive, to pose further questions by our invested behaviour, and thus to enter the stream of nature's fluid enterprises as an entity in our own right (1969, p. 39).

Elsewhere he states that: 'what man knows best is established by what he fully experiences, not exclusively by what he is compelled to concede' (1969, p. 140). This is important for the trainee in that he must be supported and encouraged to complete his experiential cycles in as full a manner as possible. If the trainer becomes hostile and attempts to extort admissions regarding disconfirmatory evidence the trainee may well immunise himself against such 'truths' and remain inaccessible to this midas manoeuvre.

Bateson discusses the manner in which humans are self-corrective against disturbances like this:

> . . . if the obvious is not of a kind that they can easily assimilate without internal disturbance, their self-corrective mechanisms work to side-track it, to hide it, even to the extent of shutting the eyes if necessary, or shutting off various parts of the process of perception. Disturbing information can be framed like a pearl so that it doesn't make a nuisance of itself; and this will be done, according to the understanding of the system itself of what would be a nuisance. This too – the premise regarding what would cause disturbance – is something which is learned and then becomes perpetuated or conserved (1972, p. 429).

Questions of ontology

All of the above help to remind us that the primary task is the unpacking and explication of the trainee's ontology of observing. The exploration is best kept underway by the creation of good questions through which the burning issues of the observer can be constructively pursued. Trainers are not in the business of 'producing' certain 'skilled behaviours' in their trainees but rather are facilitating the trainee to put himself in the way of asking some important questions through experiential experiments.

Kelly comments that, 'Behaviour is not *the answer* to the psychologist's question – it *is* the question. And, just as all questions are anticipatory, behaviour is anticipatory too' (1969, p. 21).

The personal construct therapist is not attempting to produce certain types of behaviour or personality:

> He is concerned, rather, with the constructions that man, including himself and his patient, places upon the world and how these constructions are tested out. For him, behaviour is not the answer, it is the principal way in which man may inquire into the validity of his constructions (1969, p. 220).

Equally, it should be apparent that a constructivist trainee-therapist does not participate in a personal therapy in order to be inducted into the received body of truth of the group, as occurs within the 'successionist' schools, but rather, as was outlined above, as an exploration of his own ontology of observing. It should be equally apparent that the conversations for self-reorganisation are not merely cognitive exercises but involve the whole embodiment of the individual in a series of experiential experiments. Smail comments:

> In order to change, the person has to do something. Change does not take place through somehow juggling the contents of one's head, but through placing oneself bodily in a new relationship with the world (1980, p. 178).

Psychotherapeutic procedures with trainees

Kelly outlines a number of procedures in psychotherapy which are particularly relevant to the trainee in personal therapy.
(a) Use of summaries: the trainee-client is asked to write a summary of each session shortly after it ends. This account should include not only a description of the session but also of his own feelings during the session and between sessions. A variation of this is for the trainee, having done the written summary, to then review the videotape of the session and to write a commentary on his summary in the light of his analysis of the tape. This helps to illustrate many facets of the experience, including the selectivity of construing, the blind-spots in the

construct system, issues of threat, and mechanisms for disallowing therapeutic perturbations in order to conserve one's own organisation. I often ask trainees/complainants to keep (as part of their summaries) a list of experiences/constructions which they feel reluctant to discuss in the session. This helps the trainee to recognise the importance of non self-revelation at certain times as a mechanism of self-conservation.

(b) Judging (reflexive observer role): this involves both the therapist and the trainee-client stepping out of their dyadic therapeutic role relationship and taking up an observer position to review the session just completed, developing a conversation on the content and process of the consultation. Both observers are free to comment on the approaches of the therapist, what was selected for therapeutic conversation, what was not said, what issues were not pursued etc.

(c) Aggressiveness: sometimes trainee-clients will feel unable to deal spontaneously with their 'real problems' and will appear to be only 'going through the motions'. When this occurs the therapist is sometimes tempted to confront the trainee more aggressively but it is often more fitting to ask the question as to whether the trainee should continue his personal explorations at all in this form since the trainee is not there primarily to focus on his personal life but rather to learn how to practise psychotherapy. He engages in a personal therapy only to the degree that it ultimately helps him to constructively create perturbations likely to trigger structural changes in his clients. Put another way, within a thoroughgoing personal therapy the constructs that are developed are *core constructs*, i.e. those vital to one's self-maintenance processes, whereas the new constructs developed within a training course are usually experienced as *peripheral constructs*, i.e. those which are used more impersonally or objectively. However, many trainees may experience core construct changes during their training and will show concomitant interference with their practice. At certain times trainees should temporarily cease practice in order to protect their clients from psychonoxious effects. Kelly notes that:

> The course of psychotherapy is likely to be rocky . . . characterized by impulsive decisions, inconsistencies of judgement, guilt, great feelings of need for quick success, or for the warm approval of one's associates, alternating with insularity, loose thinking alternating with literalism, and the sudden opening of large areas to the confusion of anxiety. A person who is undergoing these experiences is bound to work out his problems with his own clients as experimental subjects . . . his professional outlook is likely to continue to be unstable (1955, p. 1187).

There is often a natural limitation to the personal exploration insofar as the trainee may choose not to reveal some of his more unsavoury aspects to the therapist if the therapist is also involved in the training, especially in the area of assessing the trainee's ability, suitability and fitness to practise as a professional psychotherapist. For this reason it is preferable for any personal therapy to occur with therapists not intimately involved in the rest of the training course.

(d) Dependency: Kelly points out that the trainee-client is more stuck with the therapist than the ordinary client who leaves the therapist behind when he has changed himself. The student in contrast anticipates a longer term relationship, depending on the therapist not only for 'purification' but also for support and approval in being admitted to the profession.

> The kind of professional person produced under these conditions is likely to be narrowly dependent upon authoritative figures within his own profession, covertly resentful of administrative organisation, and ambivalently militant in his doctrinal position (1955, p. 1187).

The central problem here is for the trainee to disperse his dependencies. One way of reducing the trainee's dependency is to not encourage him to 'confess' his more intimate issues especially if these involve guilt. In the context of therapy Kelly warns strongly against this and adds that 'It is almost inevitable that it will be impossible for him ever again to deal as an adult with the listener or with him in a detached fashion' (1955, p. 640). A further aid in dependency dispersal is the training of students in a group context where they can disperse the dependencies among the group members who can act to provide consensual validational evidence to each individual so that it is not expected directly from the trainer. This also tends to broaden the range or experimentation that each trainee undertakes.

Training conversations

Before the trainee gets involved with his first psychotherapeutic client he will already have spent a lot of time assisting other therapists in dealing with their clients, done many preparatory interviews, participated in staff conferences evaluating treatment progress and so forth. His first venture should be undertaken only within the most competent training context. It need hardly be said that excellent therapists do not necessarily make good trainers. The capacities to be a good trainer must be developed in the same way that one must learn to become a good therapist.

Kelly preferred to work in close supervision with three or four trainee therapists who would be paired off, with one member of each dyad monitoring all the other's interviews. When training meetings occur the trainer asks for verbal accounts of the sessions from both the interviewer and the monitor. A third perspective is provided where the trainer himself has observed some of the sessions taking place (either 'live' or on videotape afterwards). Kelly required his students to report the session in detail using the following four categories:

(a) Anticipation I – what was the trainee's plan for the session. This anticipated mapping should have incorporated elements of the previous staff training conversations about this case.

(b) Observation I – this is a concrete account of what the trainee selects as his more important observations which allows one to gauge how well he was able to anticipate the client's actions together with providing some new elements for consideration. This material is presented by the trainee in a chronological form, having prepared this section of his report by reviewing his videotapes and discussing the session with his monitor. Also the report should indicate in the margin the time of occurrence of each event noted. This further facilitates the supervisory staff when they wish to replay any particular passage from the tape.

(c) Observation II – the third part requires the trainee to reframe the session at a 'professional level of abstraction' – in contrast to the second which is at a low level of abstraction. This encourages the development of the trainee's ability to use the professional construct system, not least to generate new clinical predictions which may be incorporated into the plan for the next session.

(d) Anticipation II – the trainee must predict what the client is likely to do between sessions. This generates a range of specific hypotheses which may be tested during the next session with the client. An important result here is being able to gauge just how well the trainee has subsumed the client's construct system in that he is successful at anticipating the client's movements within the channels of his system.

> . . . one of the contributions of the psychology of personal constructs is the development of a way of predicting how a person will behave if he suddenly throws his present pattern of behaviour overboard. By seeing a client's constructs and their opposites as channels of potential movement for him, the clinician has some basis for forecasting what adjustments will appear to the client to be available when he finds himself up to his ears in people (Kelly, 1955, p. 237).

This scheme outlined above contains two forms of anticipation and two forms of observation: the plan for the next session, what the client is likely to do before the next session, what concrete events can be described from the previous session and how to reframe these at a high level of abstraction. In term of the Cycle of Experience, Anticipation I incorporates the anticipations that the trainee has made from the previous training conversation together with the investment he wagers on his planning and predictions. Observation I encompasses the actual encounter of the consultation together with the evidence the client produces which confirms or disconfirms the trainee's predictions. Observation II includes the type of reconstruing the trainee does about the complaint, the client's construct system and about his own subsuming system. Anticipation II represents the new anticipations at the beginning of the next cycle of experience where the trainee invests in a new set of predictions which will be cycled through in the next period. As always, the customer (client) cannot be wrong. He provides endless perturbations to the trainee's development of a viable subsuming professional construct system. The training conversations are a crucial context within which the trainer enables the trainee to undergo structural transformations and develop sufficient system plasticity to be able to continue a life-long process of inner conversations for core reconstructions.

Summary

In this chapter I have outlined a radical constructivist approach to training for psychotherapists. In this approach the trainer abandons the myth of instructional interactions and rather creates a perturbing context which aims to trigger and elaborate the trainee's recursive self-organisation. Within this pattern of conversations the trainee is encouraged to make his tacit theories, assumptions and values more explicit, especially those aspects of his system which govern his 'learning to learn' styles. Overall the aim is to articulate and elaborate the trainee's construct system to the point where he may effectively and professionally subsume other construct systems and know how to trigger structural movement within systems manifesting 'complaints'. A large part of the training process focuses on facilitating the trainee to arrive at a different embodied relationship with the world. To achieve this it is necessary for the trainee to embark on many experiential experiments.

In psychotherapy what is emphasised is getting the client into risking experimental actions. The purpose of therapeutic conversations is not to produce 'insights' but rather to trigger movement along construct dimensions which will lead the client into committed actions. The emphasis for trainees is also to get them into action with their own clients. Just as we want to witness the client-family's complaint 'live', i.e. we get them to *do* their complaint in the consultation and not merely *talk* about doing their complaint, equally the trainee must be witnessed engaged in therapy with his clients in a 'live' manner (i.e. 'sitting in', one-way mirror etc). This allows the trainer to intervene where necessary both for training purposes and also to protect clients from trainee incompetence. Since we become what we do, the only way for a trainee to become a therapist is by *doing* it. Acting *as if* he were a therapist is part of the optimal learning context where the trainee generates a powerful self-referential dialogue within his organisational closure leading to structural questioning (often in the form of explicit actions) in the flow of clinical events that comprise his reality. The answering perturbations are likely to trigger widespread structural changes throughout his systems. The conversations between trainer and trainee are seen as part of the cycle of experience where, at the prevision or revision stages, they attempt to construe anticipatorially or retrospectively the experience of the intervision where in a face-to-face personal encounter the trainee tests his understanding of the client's understanding. Since there is no knowledge (or understanding) without the knower (or the one who understands) then the trainee becomes fully responsible for the clinical 'realities' he brings forth. Since we may invent many different realities we are constrained to continually examine the manner in which we make such inventions and take the responsibility for our creations. These ethical and aesthetical construc-tivist considerations are best summed up by von Foerster's (1984) twin imperatives as follows:

1 'Act always so as to increase the number of choices.'
2 'If you desire to see, learn how to act.'

11 · Personal Construct Psychology and counselling: a personal view

HELEN JONES

Foreword

' "What is truth" said jesting Pilate, and would not stay for an answer.'

I have never been quite sure what he did next, but one thing, I think, was certain, and that was that he did not listen to the truth presented to him by a rather famous man, whose death has been one of the major guilts experienced by the human race ever since. 'If only', we say, 'if only we *had* listened!'

I use this fairly major example of the danger of believing that your own truth is the *real* truth as my way into exploring the advantage that there may be in using Kelly's view of truth as an acceptance of the multi-truths of other human beings. Kelly does not reify truth, he simply, good scientist that he is, sets up a hypothesis that there may really *be* a truth 'out there' and that being so we can get on with the business of discovering how our own truths fit in with it. What is exceptional about Kelly is that he offers no secrets, only questions. Your truth is as good as my truth, both real enough, but we are never allowed to forget that our regnant beliefs may be lurking in the shadows to trap us into believing that we *really* know, and, like jesting Pilate, don't bother to wait for an answer to our questions.

Counselling provokes the questions that lead both counsellor and client into a more invitational mood. Indeed Kelly would have liked the noun dropped from the English language in favour of a more mobile verbal style of communicating.

Our concern in counselling is to get at 'truth' in our client's terms, and to help him or her to move towards the consideration of other possible truths which he has, as yet, not thought of, and to amalgamate them in some form which may be helpful to him. Then we are really in the business of transformation, transcending the obvious, inventing the world we inhabit and making it one where we can develop and grow. We do not need Kelly's truth – he was very willing to share it with us in order to help us do the same with our own.

So the view of counselling in this chapter is my own view, stemming from my understanding of Kelly's theory of Personal Construct Psychology, and yours to read, discard, borrow or ignore as you choose. We need not be 'victims of our autobiographies', we need not 'obey our destinies', we can be fully autonomous human beings responsible for ourselves in a world where we feel at one, and responsible for our place in it *with* others.

We *do* inhabit a world of real, living, pulsating others, and to have *them* out of our experiments when we are sitting quietly with our clients in a counselling 'laboratory' or going out to 'change the world of others' by our interventions can give us the sense all too easily that yes, indeed, there *is* a truth 'out there' and that we have all too little to do with it as we explore, in fantasy, the possible worlds we may invent for ourselves, or impose on others.

The main skill of the counsellor, then, is to sustain the delicate balance between the awareness that change is possible and to help the client design personal blueprints which he can then live out in his own world of real people. It is to help a person become aware of the constraints which confine him to the extent that he can choose how much they constrain him. This is perhaps the main threat in the whole process. To loosen the delicate threads which hold us together in the world of real people is a powerful thing to instigate. It is so important to have an opportunity to share a fantasy world with someone who is close enough to your own belief system not to disbelieve it. I always liked the theatrical tradition of suspension of disbelief, and this is at the heart of counselling from a personal construct perspective. Anything is possible, for the limited time you have together.

Just before writing this chapter I was relistening to a tape I made of a short workshop presentation made by Don Bannister in 1984, where there were only two or three participants, and it was therefore more of a conversation than a workshop. He was talking about the way he wrote his novels. He was talking about the novel being the legitimate form of fantasising – an occupation he conjectured as occupying the major part of most people's lives, but one which most regarded as secret and even time wasting. We discussed the attitudes some of us had towards watching *Dallas* or *Dynasty*, for example, instead of doing something 'really important'.

I suppose counselling is seen in this way too by society – as something 'remedial' or for other people, not you yourself, and not really important. I think it is a pity that we currently live in a world where to take time out for personal fantasy is often seen as luxuriant time wasting.

I hope my account of 'time wasting' with my client Michael will contribute towards changing such a point of view.

Introduction

I regard Personal Construct Theory with respect. It is an elegant theory applicable to counselling which both allows and forces its practitioners to stand back and monitor rigorously the methods and approaches they are using. It is hard work. And for me, whose general style is to clutter myself with memorabilia and the past, it has become invaluable.

I am approaching the writing of this chapter with the same kind of diffidence that I feel when I meet a new client, whether the client is a person with problems relating to personal difficulties (psychotherapy) or issues relating to their work (coaching, training or counselling) or, perhaps, a manager trying to make better sense of the systems he feels locked into. In my approach there is initially little difference.

I am faced with an unknown person, a complex structure of beliefs and values who has asked me to help him make better use of the world he or she inhabits.

It is a daunting prospect and also a very exciting one. I try to suspend the fear and awesome nature of the task and to behave in a *credulous* way. I believe what I see, hear, and feel emanating from my client. I listen.

Just now I am listening to myself. I am recalling the same sense of doubt which assailed me when I was asked, in the course of studying a modern language degree, to approach a piece of literature, a fragment only, as if that were all the information I had, and to *analyse* it.

I rebelled. Surely, this was to do a disservice to the magnitude of the work? It would debase it to take the fragment in isolation? I was wrong.

In fact to approach it as I would have liked, in great readable chunks, would have made me interpret it in my own terms and to make it my own. I had always enjoyed literature in this way and this was *not* the intention of the exercise. I was supposed to look at the essence of the piece, to explore its shape, to look at its antecedents and style, to suggest some patterns based on my *observations* and *research*. To be scientific about it in fact. This was extremely hard for me, but I ended by valuing the approach and respecting the structure it gave me when I looked at a piece of old or modern French – a student of each and certainly no mistress of either.

Development

I came across Personal Construct Theory in much the same way twenty years later when I had recently begun to practise as a counsellor with a generally humanistic style. The shock I experienced when I recognised the similarity of structure to what I had been doing with French literature was refreshing and I decided as far as possible to get involved with the theory. Some eight years later I am attempting to describe to you its importance for me as a counsellor.

One client

I have suggested that a 'client' can be anyone. I think counselling is a valuable experience for anyone to have, whether or not they have 'problems'. It is a privilege for both counsellor and client to have the opportunity to explore in depth a personal world with a partner who is essentially non-judgmental and there only to help the formulation of hypotheses about behaviour and ideas and monitor their outcomes in a creative way. It is a loving relationship.

I want to use as my referral point for this chapter the work I did several years ago with a client who allowed me to 'practise' my developing understanding of Personal Construct Psychology with him. So I do not apologise for what were often errors in my style. Personal Construct Psychology allows for them by suggesting a clear theoretical framework within which to work, and the client allows for them too if he and the counsellor reach an agreement together about checking things out.

Kelly points out that:

> The client needs to assume that something can be created that is not already known, or is not already there. The fortunate client has a partner, the counsellor. He does not know the answer either, they face the problem together. They formulate hypotheses jointly and upon each other, take stock of outcomes and common hunches. Neither is the boss. The counselling room is a protected laboratory where hypotheses can be formulated, test-tube-sized experiments can be performed, field trials planned and outcomes evaluated. The interview is an experiment in behaviour (1955).

This seemed to me a pretty good place to start when I first met Michael about six years ago.

He wrote, before our first meeting, a character-sketch for me. Kelly's first rule was simple: 'If you want to know about someone ask them, they may well tell you.' I add to this that the trouble is often that you may not hear their reply.

So he suggested a form of asking which might be a helpful place to begin, and that was to ask the client to write a character-sketch of himself in the third person, just as if he were a character in a play. He was to write it sympathetically and intimately, as if by someone who knew him extremely well, better than anyone else could ever really know him.

Not all clients want to write like this, but Michael did, and this is what he said:

> *Michael* is a balding, overweight, middle-aged American. Surprisingly, I don't think that bothers him at all.
>
> He has the typical anxieties that people get about their job: 'Do I do a good job? Will my contract be renewed?' He needs a bit of reassurance from time to time, but in spite of all, he doesn't really believe he'll lose his job. On the other hand, he really doesn't believe he'll make VP or even director.
>
> The past year has been a particularly bad one for him. George, with whom he had lived for five years, suddenly died after a six-month, paralysing illness in hospital. This causes him to question everything in his life. What should he value in life, etc.
>
> He is homosexual, and so was George, but they were not lovers, rather like brothers. They depended on each other very much. Michael, perhaps, gave some stability to George's life. George, on the other hand, gave Michael's life a vitality that seems to be missing in him.
>
> That, maybe, is the real nub of his problems. He likes people very much, but has difficulty touching them, both literally and figuratively. He seems friendly enough to meet and chat with (about most things), but after a while, if discussion seems to be drying up, he'll look for any excuse to get away.
>
> His friends in London he met mostly through George, and they have been very good about having him to dinners, but he only feels totally relaxed with a few of them, and is worried about losing contact with the majority.
>
> He's a very giving person, but maybe he gives too much. Is he trying to buy affection?
>
> I don't think he's ever properly accepted being homosexual, and therefore not to be discussed in family and some other circles.
>
> He's probably afraid of the prospect of growing old alone.

Creativity and core constructs

Kelly describes counselling as a 'situation in which one person helps another achieve a psychological reconstruction of life. Thus, the aim of counselling is to open up the personal world of experience in which the person feels stuck so they may find alternative ways of coping with the world of events which confronts them.'

If we were to open up the personal world of experience in which Michael felt stuck we had the complete story in this first statement about himself. My aim was to begin to understand better the *creative movement* which helped Michael to function currently in his world, his style of loosening and tightening, and the core beliefs and values which lay behind his statements. I could not make any assumptions but I could work with his own view of himself.

Kelly's analysis of the self characterisation which he describes at length in Volume 1 of *The Psychology of Personal Constructs* is very helpful in considering the material in a person's character sketch.

What I in fact usually do is to include my client at this point at the beginning of our conversations together. It is helpful to ask him to monitor his own sketch, and together to look at the introductory statement, the question marks which may be implicitly there in the face of the future at the end of the piece. We can look at the development of themes; the personalities mentioned; the contrasts in terms of ideas; the unstated opposites; the 'mistakes' in punctuation and grammar; the pauses and so on.

The aim of this exploration is to begin to open up the personal world of the client. We can become aware of the areas of structure which can *easily* be elaborated and of those, often as yet unverbalised, areas which may *not* easily be touched on yet. There is an indication of how propositional and open to alternatives the client may be, and where he is tightly closed or loosely able to look at options.

Creativity in Kelly's terms is the constant weaving between loosening and tightening. The tragedy, he suggests, of so many human beings is that they only live half the cycle.

Reconstruction, which is what counselling contributes to, is essentially to open up the flow of creativity in the client and to help him to tap into the personal power he intrinsically possesses to look constructively at the alternatives in his world. The counsellor *cannot* invent the alternatives, but he *can* invent the opportunities in which they may be explored in relative safety. He cannot do this without a fairly accurate understanding of the core world of the client. Such diagnostic work is essential before any real 'therapy' can begin. Much counselling may consist only of good joint diagnostic work, since the creative nature of the human being usually produces its own healing. This view would accord with that of Maturana's theory of autopoiesis, the self-regenerating system which is available to us if only we can relearn the process of activating it by listening more closely to all aspects of our selves.

In terms of exploring core constructs in the early stages of work, I am also looking, through the character-sketch, and in the course of conversation, at the dimensions of constriction and dilation and the fears, anxieties, threats, guilts and hostilities which the client is revealing and how aggressive, in Kelly's terms, he is capable of being.

Since these are moving, transitional states I can of course only have an impression of how they work at this stage for the client, but they are valuable categories of information to bear in mind and need careful consideration all the time we are working together. When, for example, will it be too much to make a suggestion about something at present not considered by the client? Will the threat of the as yet unknown possibilities be too much for him or her to consider or for the counsellor to consider either – the joint levels of threat and anxiety may just be too high for them to deal with yet.

I mention this problem now relating to Michael since it links particularly closely with the problem we were jointly facing right at the start of our work together. Michael's last statement in his character sketch was:

'He's probably afraid of the prospect of growing old alone.'

This was indeed a core construct. What we both 'knew' at another level of awareness, a submerged one for me and possibly a suspended one for Michael, was that his life would not be a long one, and that the issue of 'aloneness' was therefore one to be addressed with some immediacy.

To make the statement I have just done is to speak not with hindsight but conviction. I am writing about counselling, now, with reference to someone I worked with some time ago, particularly to emphasise that PCP is not 'just a cognitive approach'. It does allow the client and counsellor the freedom to work with the deeper levels of awareness often called the unconscious to try eventually to find the 'verbal hooks to fish for the non verbal constructs' which Don Bannister describes.

To work in a PCP way with these levels is difficult since the commitment by the counsellor is to be *fully* part of the enterprise he is asking his client to undertake. He accepts the level of dependency required by the joint exercise in a committed way for the time it takes, and to use such deep levels of commitment where both partners are faced with anxiety and threat about 'not knowing' is very hard to do.

Michael and I 'knew' from the start that we were working with some very core constructs. This was clear from the character-sketch and we therefore also 'knew' that it was not yet the time to look at the fear expressed in that last sentence. It was an indication of where we might *not yet* go.

Other methods and techniques used

Where we started was with the structure Michael offered in his character-sketch. He described himself as someone who had difficulty touching others, both figuratively and literally. He also indicated that the friends he had were through his dead friend and partner George. George had been an extravagant character living a publicly stylish life in which Michael often felt alien. He had been able to cope with and relish this in the comfort of George's charisma. Now that his friend had died he was threatened with exposing the self who had yet to emerge in a still alien world, alone. We agreed to work on this theme in a very structured way and he felt safe with the ideas we discussed, stemming from techniques associated with Personal Construct Theory.

Because he and I had contracted to test out the specific approach together and he knew I was only just becoming familiar with it myself, I was able to present all these techniques to him as *experiments* on my part as well as his.

From the earliest meeting he agreed that for him to make *case notes* as well as me was a very good idea. He liked the idea of sharing in this way our comparative experiences of the interviews we had together. He was truly able to see himself as the student, expert in his own life but less expert in applying his theory to living it, being supervised by someone more experienced in the understanding of the psychological model we were using.

For me the structures stemming from PCP were an enormous help in these early stages when we were establishing between us an *empathic* and *credulous* relationship. At first he was a very silent person, shy and anxious, and I remember thinking how helpful it was to have 'something to do together'. I was not, and am not, averse to silences in counselling. I am more confident now than I was then to its presence in the early stages in counselling. But nevertheless it really does help to get started if you and the client share a task. Michael and I shared the task of a repertory grid to begin with. We took our time over this and the grid was used to elaborate our conversations over about three sessions.

He liked doing it. He invented one or two characters in addition to the 'real' people in his list of role titles. One of them was the Tubeman. This character allowed Michael to be angry and even violent. This was a very different Michael from the one presented in the character-sketch and in our general conversation. I mention it particularly because it helps to demonstrate one of the advantages of taking a repertory grid as a starting place in therapy. Even the task of deciding who might be used as elements in a grid allows reconstruction to be contemplated. Michael himself was surprised by the Tubeman and to find how much his temper was aroused by people who 'shove you around' on the Tube. He began to talk more after that, he began to be 'aggressive'.

The elicitation of constructs which followed this role selection also appealed to Michael. He spent a long time reflecting on the choices he made and the similarities he found between some of the characters. I included myself in the list since it seems generally sensible to me that the counsellor's involvement in what is actually going on is crucial. It gives immediate indications of the transferences and counter-transferences which are around for the two of you and this is very helpful information. Including myself in the grid was an acceptable thing for Michael too. He found it interesting to discover that he found me similar to a woman teacher in his life, from his primary school days, whom he had trusted. Other women later in his experience were not yet to be trusted. He discussed with me at this point that his 'homosexuality was not quite real to him'. He had not had a similar close relationship to a woman other than in what had felt debasing ways when he had 'looked for any excuse to get away'.

Including me in the grid allowed him to talk about this major core area of sexuality which we would address later, in a fairly dispassionate way at this early stage of counselling. For me it was valuable since one of my anxieties while becoming a therapist was the danger of getting hooked in to one area of a person's construing too soon and too quickly and becoming blind to other issues. This would have been an obvious error with Michael who came to see me after the death of his homo-sexual partner with concerns about his sexual nature. I do not suggest that these were not of great importance to him, nor that we did not work with them later in some depth, but the *immediate* issue, which was in the character-sketch, was the nature of being alone and Michael's need to understand this before the early death which he suspected awaited him. I and Michael, as I said before, 'knew' about this in some non-verbal way.

The repertory grid gave me the stepping stones in to the way things fell into clusters in Michael's world. It raised questions for him and we spent a considerable time exploring these questions and possible alternatives to them.

What soon became the important activity was role-playing. This emerged from Michael's memory of George's dramatic style. Reenact-ment of scenes with Michael and myself inventing and reversing roles, helped his grieving for George and allowed him to begin to discover the community of his own selves which were emerging. He very much admired with me Miller Mair's ideas about such a community and its therapeutic possibilities. We equally shared a delight in the *Logic of Passion* by Don Bannister which for Michael offered a commonsense which had been lacking in him. He had spent many years in the company of people who 'accused' him of being too much in his head, and the debunking at last of that notion was very releasing to him. *Fun* began to enter our originally very sad and reflective sessions as Michael began to glimpse the possibility of change in himself.

We decided to look at the issue of dependency. I had personally found that Kelly's Situational Resources Grid was useful to me. We were about to have a summer break from each other. Michael was to go back to the United States to attempt to talk once more to his family. This was the first time he had seen them for some years and he wanted to try to relate to them in a different way. The previous meeting had been when he had 'come out' as a homosexual, and the timing and approach he took had not worked and he had been rejected and humili-ated by their response. He felt ready to make another attempt to meet them in the role now of a human being whose sexuality was essentially his 'private affair and not to be shared with his family'. In any case he was now developing a close relationship with a woman he trusted and although this was in its early stages Michael felt very protective of it and did not want to share it with his family until it had grown more firm. He was going home as a 'friendly but private' man. We were also aware that he was unwell. We did not yet know how unwell.

The Situational Resources Grid was a piece of homework I gave him to work on while we were not meeting for about six weeks. I based the homework on Kelly's view of how to deal with people who have to wait a while for an appointment ('Autobiography of a Theory') – that if you give people something to do for themselves it may help them to do just that.

My plan turned out to be both an error and a success. I think it demonstrated for me particularly the strength of using a counselling model which regards *all* experiments in behaviour as useful even if the outcome is invalidating. It just depends on how sensitively you work together on the invalidation.

There was in fact too much powerful material emerging from the grid for Michael to absorb during a long interval in our therapeutic work together. Kelly said that most people like to talk about their difficulties and as a way of gathering information it is most useful to ask them to do so. My timing was in some ways wrong. Michael had too many memories and painful family experiences already to deal with on his journey back to the States without my asking him to look at an A to Z of problems in addition. It was a rather clumsy error.

Proper supervision of counselling is essential in my view, and I was fortunate to be sharing the work I was doing with Michael with a supervision group who offered me great support. They helped me to cope with what I directly experienced as my failure in the episode I have just described. They helped me understand better the way I could as a therapist deal with invalidation as constructively as with validation in *my* behavioural experiments as a therapist. In this instance they gave me the courage to move into loosening work with my client, to use his dreams at last and the anger which expressed itself towards me very directly after his return from the family visit. It was time for movement and perhaps I had hoped that we had done enough? I don't know.

Summary and review

I have tried, in the section above, to give a sense of the way in which with Michael some specific techniques offered a valuable starting place for many of our interesting conversations. Counselling *is* interesting. In the example of the use of the Situational Resources Grid I have illustrated also a way in which techniques can intrude in a negative way into the process of counselling – if the immature counsellor (as I certainly was) gets a bit too keen on them. I am in no way disparaging the technique – simply my own introduction of it. Since this episode I think I have made enormously extensive use of the ideas behind the situational resources grid. I use parts of the whole and aspects of it much more frequently than the whole thing just as with fixed role therapy I use parts of the model as appropriate for my client. The whole thing seems rarely to be called for.

I have not mentioned, since they seem to be permanent tools of my trade, the use of laddering, pyramiding and the ABC technique (described more fully in Chapter 1). They are all a part of the conversational, checking out style I like to adopt.

Personal style

There is no such thing as a 'PCP counsellor'. I like to keep with me constantly Kelly's idea about the danger of 'hardening of the categories' and to be as propositional as possible about my style of working.

PCP helps me as a counsellor in many many ways. As I have described briefly above, my work with Michael was particularly helped by the structure of many of the techniques I used.

I wonder, looking back, if I could have disposed of all of them, I would perhaps have done a better job without such direct use of them, but they were for me personally extremely valuable in learning to look at the process of counselling through a number of theoretical perspectives which from my previous stance, an eclectic one, might have been unavailable to me. It is also easy to say with hindsight that 'techniques' as such were not useful. I am being doubtful – as perhaps Kelly himself was when he referred to 'insight' as being what you 'are left with when you are stripped of imagination'. It was a powerful statement which has stayed with me.

Perhaps my personal style as a counsellor has emerged very much through the fragments, or 'insights', which have stayed with me as I have studied and taught the work of Kelly during the last five years. I am very familiar with many aspects of his work (though many others are still very foggy for me) and I have gradually evolved a style of working which uses those parts of the theory which blend well with my personal view of the world, and also those parts which I am well aware represent very different perspectives.

What seems to be possible for me, which was not so before, is that I have developed some confidence to work with people from enormously different backgrounds.

As a member of the 'helping professions' for most of my career, I had a stance stemming from that position. I saw myself as being able to make a contribution to the improved welfare of people who had 'problems'. I don't think I *ever* saw myself as being able to *solve* people's problems, but I did have some sense of my worth as a counsellor for the depressed, worried, anxious and despairing students who would come to see me in my welfare capacity as student counsellor. I also saw myself as having some skills in vocational guidance, and for the purposes of the job I tried to separate the style of my work according to the 'title' it was given, by the client or referral agency.

Becoming involved with PCP has changed all that. I had to make a major shift in my own construing in order even to begin. It was facing the repertory grid which made that begin to happen. I felt so alienated by all those numbers and statistics and unsure how they could really relate to the complexities and magnitude of the human psyche. As I have indicated earlier, I liked a good story. I remember well the rigour with which my teacher at that time, Fay Fransella, would emphasise constantly that it was *process* that we were concerned with as therapists and psychologists, not *content*. This view is ingrained in me now and as a teacher and supervisor myself, I try to exact something of the same discipline from my own students.

But, of course, it is more than that. Through the awareness of the client's and my own processes it becomes possible to relate to a wide selection of content. This, I think, is one of the major advantages of using a PCP approach to counselling. We all, still, have our stories to tell.

I do not have to confine my work to that of counsellor working with people in distress. PCP allows me to make sense of all kinds of situations.

As Gavin Dunnett has described elsewhere in this volume, self reflexivity is the essential starting place for anyone working in a PCP mode. It is really necessary to practise on oneself.

For example, what I am doing now is an experiment in behaviour.

My theory this morning, is that if I write this section of the chapter, at this time of day (early morning) after I've been out for a brisk walk in cool, fresh, air, I shall do a better job than to write it at the end of the day when I shall have had various hassles to contend with – relating to buying and selling property; a personal meeting which may not be easy to manage; some telephone calls relating to my future work; and the fact that I have a slight cold which will no doubt be more obvious this evening than it is this morning.

Anyway, I have a perhaps regnant view about life that 'it is important to get going early in the morning otherwise you lose the best of the day'.

I have just told you quite a lot about myself.

If I were to read those statements from a client I would have enough material to keep me busy for quite some time. I may of course be right to hold such a theory about 'early starts'. But then early starts in one respect can make me late in others and I may become 'in a hurry'. I have another core construct about 'wasting valuable time' and being 'in a hurry' is very stressful and very definitely time wasting. So conflict arises for me – some implicative dilemmas and so on.

I am explaining this particular dilemma to demonstrate just how easy it is to get locked into the content of what is going on in oneself. The kind of self-reflexivity I have begun to describe is really important for any counsellor. It is really important to check out my own prejudices, guilts, threats, anxieties and hostility so that they do not intrude on the work I am doing with my client. This is part of being *credulous*.

I am trying to explain now that I feel that the techniques associated with PCP are very valuable for me as a counsellor, especially in terms of application to myself. The lucky counsellor will have some clients who are willing to share in those experiments, especially in the early days, when techniques, like learning to ride a bicycle or changing an electric plug, seem so dominant and difficult. Once they are learned, they can become part of the kitbag the counsellor normally carries around and picked out for use only when appropriate.

My work with Michael sounds on reflection to be very stumbling and slow. In fact, I *was* lucky and he really did enjoy learning some techniques with me and the slowness was right for him. There was, however, a rebellion and this relates very much to my personal style and the development of my confidence as a counsellor.

The story continues – a hitch, the counsellor's threats and fears

After the long summer break, when he had taken away the Situational Resources Grid, Michael returned for therapy. There was a difference in him. Far from being ready to terminate our work together, there was a sense of the *real* business now beginning. The *real* business was powerful and Michael was asking me to enter into a large undeveloped area of *threat* being expressed in powerful dreams and anxieties about the nature of his core being.

Did he fear the woman he was becoming involved with? Or could he forget the 45 years of rejection he had experienced at the hands and hearts of women, and make a truly loving relationship before he died, which he was now aware would happen before too much longer?

I was afraid and rather ashamed to begin with that I thought I might have been responsible for keeping him away from these big issues because I had not trusted enough what I can only still describe as my intuition in the early days of our work. I was trying not to overtrust my intuition at that time in order to be more scientific in my approach.

Kelly helped here too. He tells us that a good counsellor will do anything to help his client get better, and that means being inventive, and committed and going in feet or head first if that is appropriate. You can't stay on the sidelines. I am continuing to emphasise this commitment, since so often PCP is seen as 'cold'. It is only cold if its practitioners (clients and counsellors) make it so. Kelly's clear, practical, workable theory is so valuable particularly because it is left stark enough for the practitioner, or reader, to make the humanity exist through his own understanding of the theory. It allows for a total personal interpretation and Kelly suggests that if it does not work in that way it is time to move on and write another theory. So far I have neither wanted nor needed to do that.

Working at other levels of awareness

What Michael and I moved into together was working at a very deep level with the dreams and anxieties and fears that were besetting him after his return from the States. I had no way to 'plan' techniques, so of course my skills developed rapidly. I understood my client well, in his terms (the grids and data collection had ensured that), and my conversations with him stemmed from a deep subsuming of his world. So I was no longer afraid to develop *loosening* techniques, to use dreams, to free associate, to move into the darkest, lightest and deepest areas of his core being. It was perhaps the most important thing I had ever done – to get off the fence and remove the technical barriers I had been imposing and to feel for the first time truly professional in the work I did with Michael.

Psychologists are human too!

I *think* he valued our work. I *know* I did.

What I valued especially was that in this relationship I had been able to contain the implications of all that we did together within a structure which was compatible with Michael's. I was able to remain 'objective' with the help of a lot of PCP ways of doing things. I was able to be 'involved' as a partner in the experiments. I was able to take risks which were within my understanding of the boundaries around us and best of all my confidence in my own sense of inner 'knowing' was able to be brought into play in the more creative final stages of our counselling time together. We were both being human and engaged in a joint creativity.

Miller Mair says that 'Psychologists are human too' – I am glad to agree with him. The danger can be when they behave as if they are not.

The most important thing for me about PCP is that it allows for the infinite variety of human ways of behaving without imposing a good or bad opinion of any of them. To be non-judgmental in the way I *have* to be when counselling actually gives me the opportunity to enlarge my *own* vision. It is very creative.

The outcome

Michael took the risk of trusting the woman he loved. He moved in with her, became a part of her large family, he was accepted and loved and sexually fulfilled. He married her.

She was with him when he died two years later. He was not alone.

Implications

The last section of this chapter has the formidable title of implications.

It was hard how to decide to write it as a personal essay on the practical applications of PCP. It seemed to me that I was engaged in Miller Mair's personal venture of 'knowing' and 'being known'.

It is for this reason that I chose to write in relation to one of the more powerful experiences I have been involved in as a counsellor, where often I felt vulnerable; often unsure of myself as I tried to apply a new style to my counselling approach; and aware of the great risks we all take when we begin to 'interfere' in the personal worlds of others. I was aware of the risks of loving, since that is an essential part of counselling. Loving, in the sense that Maturana uses the word, is 'being stuck' into another person's system and knowing that is the case.

A counsellor has to create the climate for love, he has to be 'stuck' into his client's system. He also has to be able to get 'unstuck' at frequent intervals and the strain of this is considerable. It is like being a foster mother or father for a while. The commitment has to be very great, but the awareness that the contract is limited must always be there.

The implications of this involvement, which is part of working from a Kellyan stance, are that the counsellor will need enormous personal awareness and much support from others who understand the strain and style of such work. Supervision is essential and I personally feel that individual supervision about the huge personal investment of energy in the task is just as important as the strength, support and alternatives offered by a supervision group.

I feel that PCP counselling can be effective for everyone and the more that occurs, the less need, potentially, there will be in the future since an alternativist viewpoint should become the norm. The world should benefit.

12 · Facilitating individual change in Personal Construct Therapy

ROBERT A. NEIMEYER AND STEPHANIE HARTER

The objectives of psychotherapy must include the skilful facilitation of those human processes upon which all of us, scientist and client alike, depend . . . Indeed, the initiation and continuation of a lifetime effort to conjure up ever-fresh visions of what is worthwhile is itself a goal of therapy (Kelly, 1966/1980, p. 21).

It has been estimated that 250 to 400 forms of psychotherapy are currently being practised (Kazdin, 1986). With this profusion of approaches available, it is legitimate to ask what a discussion of personal construct therapy has to offer to either the committed practitioner of one of these models, or to the bewildered clinician who has given up trying to choose among them! In writing this chapter, we will try to convey our belief that Personal Construct Theory has something important to say to both of these readers. In particular, we believe that it provides a clinically rich perspective on the processes that both impede and promote personal change, whether undertaken in the specialised context of psychotherapy or in the course of daily life. Our goal here is to illustrate a few orientating concepts that help sensitise the clinician to these processes – whatever his or her preferred theoretical approach. Interested readers are encouraged to consult other sources for a more detailed discussion of personal construct techniques (Epting, 1984; Landfield and Epting, 1986; Neimeyer, 1986; Neimeyer and Neimeyer, 1981) and clinical research (Beail, 1985; Button, 1985; Neimeyer, 1985a).

Social hypotheses

Unlike many contemporary schools of therapy that derive their distinctiveness primarily from the techniques they employ, personal construct therapy can be distinguished on the basis of its underlying theory of human personality (Kelly, 1955). As detailed in the opening chapters of this volume, construct theory conceptualises human beings as *makers of meaning*, functioning as personal scientists who construct theories to adequately interpret, anticipate, and guide their behaviour in relation to their social and physical environments. The usefulness of this system does not depend upon its correspondence with an objective reality, but upon its ability to allow the person to transcend passive submission to external circumstances by creating imaginative alternatives.

Viable personal science depends on the individual's ability to continually revise her construct system in response to the outcomes of her personal ventures. Psychological disorder can be said to occur whenever this personal construing process becomes stagnant, arrested, or chaotic, so that meaningful elaboration, testing, and revision of the individual's system is rendered impossible (Neimeyer, 1985a). For instance, like professional scientists, clients often forget the subjective origins of their own systems, and mistake them for statements about an objective reality. This inadvertent dogmatism blocks effective revision of the system in response to disconfirming information. The person may hostilely continue to repeat the same unsuccessful behavioural experiment, or distort the feedback she receives to support her personal theory. An example of this process is provided by the case of Joan, a severely depressed woman in her thirties who had been sexually abused as a child.

In spite of her success in her profession, Joan perpetuated her childish, helpless role in relationship to her mother. As if to justify her position, she spent the first several therapy sessions providing evidence for her construal of her mother as domineering. According to Joan, her mother would enter Joan's house when she was away at work, wash her dishes, keep track of her social and sexual relationships, call her several times a day – the list was endless. The therapist's straightforward response to this complaint was to suggest various ways for Joan to exercise more assertiveness in dealing with her mother, a strategy that met with limited success. Instead, Joan 'dug in her heels', justifying her inability to take any action on the basis of her mother's relentless control and her own inability to 'hurt' her mother by limiting her involvement in Joan's life. As a result, her mother's 'intrusions' continued, Joan became more disorganised and desperate, and the mother's phone calls began to be met by screaming and profanity.

Ironically, Joan's behaviour effectively prevented any disconfirmation of her predictions regarding her mother's behaviour, continuing the stalemate between them. Even her eventual response of screaming 'Get the fuck out of my life!' carried the implicit message to the mother that she was simply a rebellious child who needed parental help. Similarly, the mother's continuing intervention, while expressing legitimate parental concern in her own eyes, was construed by Joan as evidence of her need to dominate and control her life. Although Joan's construction of her mother's behaviour as relentlessly intrusive may have been quite accurate, it allowed her no viable alternatives within her present system. She had the choice of either maintaining a stance of helpless dependency, or rebelling and being a 'bad daughter'. These alternatives, of course, offered her little real freedom of movement, since they represented simply contrasting ends of the same fundamental construct of herself as an immature child relating to her mother.

As in Joan's case, many of the failures of construction that become apparent in treating individuals relate to their difficulty in formulating, testing, and revising hypotheses within social and family relationships. The therapist's role is then to help the client generate alternative approaches to the 'facts' that to her seem so obvious (Kelly, 1969a), in order to create new pathways of movement.

When dealing with such rigid constructions, the therapist's reframing of the situation may be more effective if it is presented tentatively or even humorously. The only requirement is that the reconstrual effectively cover the facts as the client sees them and provide a viewpoint that offers fresh behavioural alternatives. The use of humour may reduce the threat of comprehensive change and allow the client to suspend her constructions enough to entertain an alternative hypothesis (Viney, 1985).

In an attempt to loosen Joan's construction of her relationship with her mother, the therapist began a session by asking her to assume that her mother regretted not being able to protect her when she was a child, and was attempting to make up for it, by being extremely solicitous of her in the present. In light of this, she asked Joan to help think of ways to give her mother plenty of opportunity to be a 'mother' by asking for her help as often as possible. Several examples were playfully suggested, such as seeing how many dishes she could dirty in one day and leaving the mother a note asking her to do the laundry as well. Joan dropped her usual tearful demeanour and began to laugh as she enjoyed brainstorming alternative experiments to see just how much mothering her mother needed to do, such as calling her to pick her up at a singles' bar in the middle of the night. Apparently these experiments were never implemented, but Joan ceased complaining about her mother in therapy and increased attempts to form new friendships. Upon the therapist's inquiry, she reported that her mother was not calling her as much and was no longer a major problem in her life.

Although our use of a paradoxical construction in this case resembles interventions in family therapy (Watzlawick, Weakland and Fisch, 1974), its application was consistent with a personal construct perspective. For instance, rather than being presented as an authoritative prescription, it was presented as a collaborative hypothetical experiment. Also, since other family members were unavailable, the therapist was primarily interested in increasing the flexibility and elaboration of Joan's construction of her family relationships, rather than changing the family system, per se. Other techniques from family systems therapy have been adapted for use by construct therapists in both family and individual contexts (Alexander, 1987; Kenny, 1987; Procter, 1985, 1987).

The ecology of self

Eschewing the traditional division of thinking, feeling and behaviour, Kelly saw the construct system not as a logic-tight set of cognitions, but as an integral, evolving whole, inseparable from the individual experiencing his life. The component constructs are not necessarily verbal or intellectual, but may be emotional, behavioural, or even physiological. Emotional experiences are particularly vital, as they indicate how well the construct system is functioning and signal when our system is in need of revision (Bannister, 1977). Furthermore, new behaviours, even symptomatic behaviours, may represent emerging fringes of the system that are not yet fully elaborated or articulate.

As the term construct *system* implies, personal constructs are interdependent, as are life forms in a complex ecology. The therapist cannot arbitrarily add a construct and expect it to thrive unless it is compatible with the current system. Removal of a construct that appears 'irrational' or 'distorted' to the clinician may likewise upset this delicate ecological balance, with unexpected results. Seen in this light, what might be labelled as resistance on the part of the client becomes an adaptive mechanism for maintaining the integrity of the construct system and of the person himself. Effective psychotherapy requires a subtle appreciation of the nature of a client's personal system, both because its content determines the locus of intervention, and because its structure imposes constraints on the kinds of change strategies to which the client is likely to be most responsive.

The systemic interdependence of constructs in a system has become particularly evident to us in our therapeutic work with women who were sexually abused as children. Early in our experience with these women, we were frequently frustrated by our inability to remove the self-blame that they often expressed regarding the incest experience. Typically, even our most skilful efforts to invalidate the victim's construction of herself as culpable were strongly resisted. Worse, we sometimes discovered to our chagrin that 'successful' invalidation of this distorted self-image could produce even more damaging consequences. Following one such intervention, the invalidated client expressed even greater pain over a lifetime of unnecessary self punishment. Moreover, straightforward confrontation of the client's self-blame in therapy can result in extreme anxiety, since it can threaten the stability of an identity that the woman has spent a lifetime elaborating. When we conceptualised the reactions of these women to our interventions in terms of Kelly's (1955) writings on core role structure, we began to respond differently. For several abused women, their blaming of themselves for the incest, even if unjustified from a moral standpoint, had become a central construct in their explanation for their past and present experiences. When this core construct was removed it demanded massive reconstruction of their life history, central figures in that history, and their identity.

When we encounter resistance in our attempts to absolve these women's self-blame, we have found techniques derived from Kelly's (1969b) approach to dealing with guilt to be more effective than simple 'rational' disputation. In brief, we: (1) speculate with the client on what she did and whether it might be judged as morally reprehensible from a variety of perspectives; (2) assuming that she is convinced that she did do something to encourage the abuse, or could have done something to prevent it, accept this as a *hypothesis*, rather than continue to dispute it; (3) examine current incidents to see if there are ways in which she is continuing to invite or allow abuse; (4) formulate experiments in which she behaves 'as if' she no longer deserves to be abused. Stated differently, this hypothetical, action-oriented approach represents an attempt to encourage the client to broaden her perceptual field, and in so doing deepen her sense of control in her life, by actually doing things differently (Dunnett, 1985). We have found that as clients adopt this experimental approach, they begin to develop less evaluative constructs for acting in relationships, such as 'trusting/not trusting', 'self-protective/vulnerable', or 'supportive/confrontive'. Interestingly, as these new and more differentiated constructions of relationships begin to be elaborated, the original construct of 'blameworthy/innocent' often appears to be a less compelling way of explaining and anticipating relationships, and is frequently spontaneously suspended.

Kelly's description of core role structures and the guilt resulting from their disruption is broadly applicable to addressing issues of guilt in therapy. Because core role constructs are essential in maintaining a person's sense of herself as a social being, a therapist will rarely be successful in attempts to change those structures directly. However, guilt does provide an important signal of the need to revise the implicative links of core structures to resolve inconsistencies in the system and to allow the person to deal elaboratively with new experiences.

As an example of guilt resulting from disruption of core role structures, Harriet expressed extreme distress due to her conviction that she must have somehow distorted her daughter's outlook on sex as a child, or the daughter would not have become a lesbian. Recognising the central role of conservative values in her system, the therapist realised that arguments that homosexuality was normal would have been quickly rejected and would have endangered the therapy relationship. However, she also hypothesised from Harriet's often painful attempts to maintain contact with her daughter that her role as a mother was an even more central identity construct. Ignoring the more problematic implications of 'good moral training' for her core role as a mother, the therapist attempted to strengthen the alternative implications of this role by citing Harriet's efforts to be open and supportive even when she didn't agree with her daughter's choices. Acknowledging Harriet's pain at her daughter's choice, the therapist praised her reported attempts to be caring and accepting as evidence that she was a remarkably good mother. Harriet participated in this elaborative process by suggesting additional ways in which she had been supportive or could be more supportive in the future. The therapist also suggested that sharing feelings could provide a valuable part of a strong mother–daughter relationship, and encouraged her to consider how she could be a better mother by more openly sharing her own feelings and problems with her daughter. As Harriet elaborated her mother role to include the more developmentally appropriate subordinate constructions of 'being supportive' and 'sharing feelings', she became less concerned about her moral responsibility for her daughter's choices. Her behavioural experiments with these new constructions yielded a closer relationship with her daughter and her daughter's partner, and she reported less distress and more satisfaction in that relationship.

The case examples in this section illustrate that disrupted evolution of the construct system by traumatic life experiences, changes in social relationships, or even well-intentioned but poorly conceptualised therapeutic interventions can result in negative emotions, such as guilt, depression or anxiety. Although some therapeutic orientations may regard these emotions as pathological symptoms to be eliminated, personal construct therapists regard them as vital 'impact statements' reflecting disruptions in the delicate ecology of self. Careful attention to these signals can help the therapist identify sources of systemic stagnation or imbalance, and plan ecologically sound interventions that promote further evolution of the system.

On growth and regression

Whether examined over the course of a lifetime or a successful therapy, one of the most striking features of our construct systems is their capacity to change. Yet as the preceding sections imply, changes in our construction of self and others do not occur haphazardly. Instead, the evolution of personal meaning systems results from a complex dialectic between the 'external' challenges with which life confronts us and the 'internal' regulative principles of our construing process. On the external side of this dialectic, experiences that are optimally discrepant with our current constructions serve as an impetus to extend our personal theories in order to anticipate and interpret new domains (Mancuso, 1977). But if the experiences encountered are too discrepant with existing constructs, then they are likely to provoke considerable *anxiety* on the part of the construing person. On the internal side of this dialectic, the development of new structures typically takes the form of a progressive elaboration of the old. Thus, as we grow, we typically do so in ways compatible with our core identity constructs (Neimeyer, 1987a). To become aware of impending changes in our sense of self that are inconsistent with this core role structure can occasion the experience of *threat* (Kelly, 1955). These two conditions – the anxiety of stark unpredictability and the threat of radical inconsistency – represent important constraints on human change processes, constraints that both lead people to seek therapy and to limit the kinds of change they can tolerate in it.

These considerations carry at least two important implications for the practising psychotherapist. First, while useful psychotherapy usually requires that the client tolerate a modicum of anxiety, the therapist should be careful to avoid precipitating a client into decisions that confront him or her with too much unpredictability too quickly. An example of this principle was provided in the course of therapy with a gay client named Ken. Ken had been involved in a long, if unsatisfying and distancing relationship with James, who at forty-two was a few years his senior. Although James had given no real indication of commitment to Ken, the two men had been engaged in an intermittent social and sexual relationship for nearly ten years, during which Ken had refused to pursue relationships with anyone else. Therapy was precipitated when James became involved with another man – the first such relationship that James did not deny when Ken confronted him about it.

Over the course of several months of therapy, Ken provided seemingly endless documentation of James' tendency to use him as a convenient shoulder to cry on during rocky periods in his relationship with his new lover. But their frequent telephone contacts – always initiated by James – gave no hint that even if the new relationship were to fail, James would be willing to return to Ken. In spite of this, Ken continued to wait (angrily but passively) in the wings, hoping against hope that James would return and they would at long last form a truly reciprocal and mutually satisfying relationship. As this waiting period stretched into its second year, the therapist became impatient with Ken's willingness to continue the relationship, with James at any emotional cost. Gradually, the therapist became more insistent that Ken de-escalate what both recognised to be a painful and destructive involvement. During this period, Ken became visibly anxious in the therapy room, and needless to say, made little headway toward emancipating himself from his ambivalent relationship with James. Although his inability to do so was the result of several factors, one of the most significant in retrospect was his almost total inability to anticipate what his life would be like without James at its focus. Stated differently, the relationship with James may have been unsatisfying and painful, but it was also predictable and intensely meaningful. As such, it represented a more tangible and less anxiety-provoking alternative than the abstract possibilities of happier, but entirely hypothetical relationships that he might form. Reformulating his 'resistance' in these terms, the therapist reversed directions and started encouraging Ken to cultivate a range of casual and intimate relationships with friends, co-workers and relatives. Therapeutic movement resumed as he gradually extended his constructions of alternative relationships on the basis of these experiments, and (almost spontaneously) began to become more assertive in his relationship with James.

The second, more internal constraint on possible change arises from the requirement that it be consistent with, or at least orthogonal to, the client's existing core role structure. This principle was illustrated by the treatment of Tally, a case study of whom has been provided elsewhere (Neimeyer, 1987b). As a deeply religious woman, Tally found that her Christianity provided her with the central meaning of her existence, guiding her decision making in nearly every important area of her life. But a repertory grid analysis suggested that her faith was a two-edged sword, insofar as 'religious' people were viewed as experiencing a 'lot of problems', while people who were 'not religious' were viewed as 'free of concerns'. This signalled one possible obstacle to therapeutic progress, namely, that to overcome her familial and relational problems would be at odds with her core identity as a devout Christian. In discussing these grid results with her therapist, Tally affirmed her belief that 'the devil gets to God's people and gives them a hard time', whereas 'people who don't care about the Lord seem to prosper'. With this limit on feasible change clearly in mind, the therapist was able to help Tally retain her cherished religious identity, but gradually loosen its implications for a deeply problematic existence. As a result, Tally began to experiment successfully with a less constricted, more socially integrated identity that was broadly compatible with, rather than antagonistic to, her core values.

These reflections on the nature of personal evolution should temper our audacity as therapists to press for change in our clients, without first developing a delicate understanding of the features of their construct systems that limit such change. Too often, in our eagerness to help clients lead more satisfying lives, we fail to respect the constraints imposed by the structures in which they currently live. As a consequence, we may waste effort or even jeopardise the therapy relationship in misdirected attempts to 'force them out of their shells' to engage in new, apparently more adaptive behaviour. But human beings do not function like hermit crabs, who jettison their shells to look for new structures when they outgrow the old. Instead, their growth process resembles more closely that of the chambered nautilus, which rather than rejecting its original shell gradually extends its structure, all the while preserving the symmetry of the new with the old. Also like the nautilus, humans have a tendency to retreat more deeply into their old structures when they face too great a threat – even the threat of therapy. For this reason, construct theorists often rely on less threatening, invitational strategies of change in therapy, some of which are described in the next section.

The uses of enactment

Wilma was a middle-aged woman whose marriage of twenty years had become increasingly unsatisfying, to the point that her relationship to her husband resembled a business relationship more than a marriage. The collaboration and mutual validation that characterises 'healthy' couples (Neimeyer and Hudson, 1985) had long since disappeared. In personal construct terms, Wilma's marital role had become severely constricted (permitting only a narrow range of behaviours in relation to her husband) and tight (stereotyped and unchanging over time). Both of these tendencies were reinforced by her superordinate religious beliefs, which carried fixed implications for most facets of her behaviour, ranging from prohibitions on the wearing of jewellery to acceptable definitions of a wife's 'duties' to her husband and family.

Interestingly, Wilma also loved the theatre. She frequently went to plays sponsored by the local university or community repertory companies. Moreover, her enthusiasm for drama was not restricted to passive appreciation – she also enrolled in theatre classes in order to experiment with enacting different parts in class productions and dramatic readings. These alternative roles were frequently at some variance with the meekness and inhibition of her 'real personality'. In fact, while she enjoyed enactments of characters from musicals, she was even able to partially identify with the role of Virginia Woolf! As the importance of these enactments unfolded over the course of therapy, it became clear they functioned as far more than simple diversions from her otherwise mundane life.

It was observations like these that led Kelly (1955) to place such emphasis on the use of enactment techniques in therapy. Kelly recognised that individuals attempt to behave in ways consistent with existing core role structures, and for this reason, are more capable of exploring the implications of new outlooks under the protective mask of make-believe. In his own therapy with a rigid client, for example, he frequently would spontaneously cast the client in the role of a friend, another family member, or even in Kelly's role as therapist (Neimeyer, 1980). All of these 'casual enactments' were ways of prodding the client to view the world, if only temporarily, through different eyes, as a means of helping him realise that life could be construed – and lived – differently. The more formal technique of fixed role therapy, in which the client is coached in enacting an imaginary role in his current life for a specified period of time (Adams-Webber, 1981; Kelly, 1973), is essentially an extension of this strategy.

Considered more broadly, therapy can be conceived as a kind of *creative play* in which imaginary roles are constructed and then tried on for size. Like the play of children, this therapeutic role playing should not be prescriptive so much as experimental. This emphasis on imaginary role construction and enactment is illustrated by the case of Sheri, a graduate student in her late twenties majoring in communication. Although she performed well in most aspects of her classwork, she experienced paralysing anxiety at the prospect of presenting in class – obviously a skill she was expected to develop in her chosen major! In particular, she was distressed by vivid images of people in her audience smirking and furrowing their brows whenever she would fumble a point or mumble a word or phrase. As a result, she began to skip classes that required oral presentation, and to despair over ever obtaining her degree or functioning in her profession.

Sheri came to therapy after her own attempts to 'talk herself out of her irrational fears' had failed. Like many psychotherapists, Sheri had focused on trying to eliminate her anxious behaviour and thinking patterns, but without having any viable alternative role to fall back on. As a consequence, she made little headway, and simply compounded her problem by adding to her public speaking anxiety a substantial dose of self-criticism for her inability to overcome it! As a step around this impasse, the therapist requested that they take the focus off of Sheri for the moment, and instead observe other speakers in as many situations as possible. Jointly, they brainstormed a heterogeneous list of instructors, campus visitors, ministers, student presenters and even political figures, each of whom modelled a different kind of enactment of the speaking role. As homework, Sheri was to carefully monitor the performance of each of them, taking notes on how each captured the audience's attention, handled eye-contact, paced the presentation, and particularly, how each recovered from any minor false steps that he or she might take. Sheri carried out the assignment over a two-week period with genuine relish, since in her preoccupation with her own performance, she had never really slowed down to observe the speaking behaviour of others. She returned to therapy with copious notes on the performance of the various models, especially one male teacher who effectively used humour to recover from occasional errors in the content or style of his lecture. From these data, the therapist helped Sheri fashion an imaginary speaker's role that included aspects of the behaviour and the inferred outlooks of the various models. They then discussed and enacted the role in therapy, with each playing the part of speaker and observer in turn. Finally, Sheri carried out the experiment in the crucible of the classroom itself, and was subsequently praised by the instructor and several students for her smooth and 'natural' performance. As she began to actively seek out opportunities to practise the new role (e.g. by asking discussion questions in social studies classes), she gradually began to modify aspects of the role to accommodate it to her own style. Thus, the value of the imaginary role was not in providing a 'correct' model of how to behave in speaking situations, but in helping Sheri 'get outside herself' long enough to experiment with behaving differently. After she had experienced the freedom of 'trying on' a new perspective, she was able to elaborate her core identity to encompass aspects of the new role, and eventually, to accommodate it to the demands of different speaking contexts. This outcome illustrates construct theory's focus on therapy as a form of *self-creation* rather than *self-correction*. In this view, therapy should add to the person's constructive competencies, rather than simply excise some dysfunctional behaviour or irrational belief. The uses of enactment promote this growth by first cultivating the cuttings of new behaviour in the protective greenhouse of make-believe, before grafting them onto the roots of the client's original identity.

Conclusions

In this chapter we have tried to convey some of the spirit, rather than the detail, of Personal Construct Therapy. Specifically, we have tried to elaborate a few of the implicit themes in Kelly's theory that have most engaged our own attention: its view of individuals as theorists in their own right, who cannot easily assimilate negative evidence until they glimpse an alternative theory that accommodates it; the image of the self as a delicately balanced ecology that both enables and constrains personal development; the person's need for a modicum of consistency and predictability, which lays the groundwork for a more empathic understanding of resistance; and the approach to therapy as creative play that seeks to augment rather than reduce the client's identity and behavioural options. Too often, in their eagerness to be technically effective, therapists blindly intervene without a subtle appreciation of the resources and limitations embodied in their client's system. In our view, Personal Construct Theory provides a clinically sensitive framework for surveying these resources and limitations, and hence for more skilfully facilitating the human process of change.

Acknowledgments

Preparation of this manuscript was assisted by a grant made to the department of psychology, Memphis State University Center for Applied Psychological Research, through the State of Tennessee's Centers of Excellence Program.

13 · *Elaborating Personal Construct Theory in a group setting*

GAVIN DUNNETT AND SUE LLEWELYN

This chapter describes some parts of an experiment carried out by the authors in the first half of 1984. Coming from overlapping backgrounds – one with more experience of running small groups (S.L.), the other with more experience in using PCT (G.D.) – we felt that combining both skills might prove effective in a small group setting. As both of us were at that time working in the British National Health Service, the prospect of a highly reflexive, experiment-encouraging method, with a focus on the day to day problems of participants inside and outside the group setting, was particularly attractive. Furthermore G.D. felt strongly that the possibilities for group therapy as outlined by Kelly (1955, pp. 1155–79) had been neglected and needed to be tried in the context of a proper working group. We decided, therefore, to set up a small psychotherapy group for ourselves to see whether it was possible to run it on PCT lines, what the problems would be from the perspective of both patient-participant and leader-participant, and whether it seemed a fruitful line to explore further.

Background

Kelly's original work (1955) is strongly orientated towards working with the individual. It is after all *Personal* Construct Psychology, and the bulk of the second volume is devoted to the processes that occur within the range of convenience of individual therapy. However, at the end of his book, in the chapter on special forms of psychotherapy, he lays down his views on group therapy. It is significant that these follow his discussion on enactment, as this technique clearly has a major role for him in a group setting. He notes seven reasons why group therapy may have advantages over individual therapy – as a base for experimentation, to learn about discrimination between different people, to challenge pre-emptive construing, to confront constellatory or stereotypic constructs, to provide a variety of validational evidence, to encourage the dispersion of dependency, and to be economically viable (pp. 1156–8). From these points he enumerates six phases in the development of therapy in a group:

1 Initiation of mutual support
2 Initiation of primary role relationships
3 Initiation of mutual primary enterprises
4 Exploration of personal problems
5 Exploration of secondary roles
6 Exploration of secondary enterprises

With typical thoroughness he then discusses these one by one elaborating both how the process develops and some of the pitfalls that may occur. It is very clear that enactment is used frequently to encourage interaction and experiment, but also, that no specific rules for the running of the group are laid down. Indeed, compared with the descriptions of individual therapy, group therapy is minimally elaborated, and as such, leaves an enormous number of questions unanswered.

Having decided to set up this group our next step was to attempt to survey the literature on groups run along personal construct psychology lines. We wanted to benefit from others' previous experience where possible. We were startled to find a complete dearth of information about how to run a group in this way. Subsequently, Koch (1985) has written about what personal construct theory, research and practice has to contribute to the understanding and running of therapeutic small groups. In his chapter, many circumstances are described in which elements of PCT have been used to review or explain small group activity, although the use of PCT as a measure of change is more thoroughly examined than its use as a therapeutic strategy in its own right. Much of this useful research has been repertory grid based, and has indeed found a practical role for this methodology in small groups. Towards the end of his chapter, Koch examines three ways of interpreting groups along PCT lines, but in his conclusion he writes:

It can be seen by the discussion of these three types of group approach that the personal construct approach has great applicability. Although many would go further and elaborate it into a form of therapy in its own right, this does not appear to have as great an advantage as suggesting it as an approach which could be used to encompass and understand many therapeutic approaches. It offers an approach with which to understand at a greater and more personal depth the way in which members of therapeutic groups construe, function and change as a result of their group experience (p. 26).

While this certainly gives PCT a valuable role, it seems a limiting conclusion bearing in mind the lack of any systematic attempts to 'elaborate it into a form of therapy in its own right'.

Llewelyn and Dunnett (1987) have elsewhere argued the case for considering PCT as a valuable underlying methodology for running small therapeutic groups. It seemed to us that to elaborate the theory further required a practical experiment.

The Plan

A number of decisions about how to set about this project were taken fairly easily, while others developed as we went along. The group was to be of fixed time and length, with a closed membership of a maximum of ten including two leaders/facilitators. For practical reasons it was decided to run the group for sixteen weeks, one session per week, in one and a half hour slots. We saw ourselves as participant/facilitators – participant because we too were experimenting albeit at a different personal level; and facilitatory because it seemed the best word to describe the kind of 'encouragement to elaborate and experiment approach' that we wanted to foster. We accepted referrals from all colleagues – medical, psychology, and social work – and assessed them all ourselves. Our criteria for acceptance were deliberately broad and our main exclusion was frank psychosis. Each referral was asked to discuss how they hoped a group might help them with their difficulties, and were encouraged to ask us about the group and how it would function. In fact, despite working in a district reputedly short of psychotherapeutic facilities, we received far fewer referrals than expected, possibly due to its being an experimental methodology not understood by many of them. Eventually, we achieved a group of eight people; six women and two men. With ourselves, this made seven women and three men, an imbalance which worried us a little.

Having offered them the group, and their having accepted, we then arranged for a colleague to see them individually to ask them to write a self-characterisation, carry out a standard repertory grid, and to fill in a hostility questionnaire. This was done primarily for the research aspect of the group: the intention being to repeat all these again at the end of the sixteen weeks. A separate colleague was felt to be important, both to reduce bias during the evaluation at the end of the group, and to avoid the initiation of therapy individually before the group started. We hoped to use the grid within the context of the group, while using all three measures to assess a before/after effect. In addition to these, the prospective group members were each asked to list their problems in order of importance as they saw them, and rate their severity. Again, participants would be asked to do this again at the end of the sessions.

While this was going on, we ourselves were deciding what we should do both before and during the group meetings. We decided to write a note of our anticipations and intentions for the experiments as a whole separately; and after each group, write a résumé of the group, and our plans and anticipations for the group members at the next meeting. Thus for each meeting, each of us would have predictions and plans, a note of the outcome, and an overall review. We could then check these with each other, as well as providing a record of the process and progress of the group. Finally two other decisions were made. First that we would be supervised by someone throughout the course of the group. Our choice was Professor David Smail from Nottingham who agreed, provided that we were prepared to tape record the groups and let him have them weekly. This became the second decision which could only be implemented at the first session of the group, with the agreement of all group members. As it happened both these decisions became extremely valuable and helpful as the group progressed.

Initial Anticipations

One of us (S.L.) wrote as follows:

1 Expectations

(a) Group expectations: my expectation and hope for the group is that it will allow group members to develop through experimentation with their construct system, more flexibility and less hostility in their construing of self and others.
(b) My expectations: I expect to find this group anxiety provoking because I don't as yet have the appropriate constructs for dealing with the situation. Hence I am planning at the moment to use a lot of structure which will, I think, reduce my anxiety. I am also intending the group to be reflexive in that I would want to experiment with some of my constructs simultaneously, although I would see this as secondary to group experimentation.

2 Methods

As stated above, I would hope to use a number of different methods in the duration of the group. If we want to achieve a lot of progress in a short time, I would want each individual to work hard at understanding their own system, but not at the expense of group cohesion. Hence I would want to introduce each session with some group based exercise, both to serve as a warm-up and to serve as a reinforcer for the group's sense of belonging. I think that role play will play quite a part in the group, as we encourage people to look at the implications of the constructs they are unearthing. Hence I would want to have a rough structure for each session worked out beforehand, so that we know what we are aiming for, although of course allowing for changes dependent on the material brought by the group.

3 Structures

The following would be my plan for the development of the group, although I am not certain of the order in which such structures could take place.

(a) Derivation of core role constructs, probably by laddering.

(b) An exercise to discover the first origins of core role constructs, i.e. to see when such constructs became salient, and the issues around them.

(c) Uncovering of non-verbal constructs operating in present life which may be handicapping to present functioning.

(d) Role play of conflict situations in the present, to discover the operation of core role constructs and how they may present difficulties.

(e) Experimentation in changes in construing ourselves and others which may be suggested by other group members.

(f) Discussion of the concept of hostility and seeing how this operates to prevent people developing fuller repertoires and behaviour. Encouraging people to behave in an aggressive rather than hostile way through exercises.

The above structures to be planned in some sequence, probably following that laid down by Kelly in volume 2.

4 Problems

I expect that our main problem will be the maintenance of cohesion in the face of considerable personal experimentation. The idea of group work to start each session and finish each session should try to militate against this. Another problem may be transferring any gain from the therapy sessions to the outside, I therefore think we must encourage individuals to practise their newly acquired skills by means of homework. I am also a little concerned about how we manage to control and develop the sessions so that all members have an equal chance to benefit. I am concerned that the more articulate clients may dominate the sessions, and that we will have drop-outs from the less confident. However I am also anxious about drop-outs from those who become very intellectually critical of the theory, so that we may have to spend time convincing them of our belief in the theory.

Throughout all this must run the dual thread of the technique we are using and our personal support for the individual member. We must maintain a balance between the two so that we are perceived by the group members to be both caring and competent. I also think I shall get very fed up with the technique before very long, and wish that I had never embarked on trying to use construct theory approach.

Upon reflection, G.D.'s anticipations must have been written in a haze of optimism. In many practical respects they mirror what was written above, but included such statements as 'I anticipate that members of the group will stay throughout the group, and find the approach refreshing and stimulating' and 'opportunities will exist for carrying out a group repertory grid, and discussing and reviewing the grids completed before the group began'. But broadly, and with some relief, there was agreement between us about what was likely to happen.

The participants

1 Wendy: Wendy was twenty-three years old. She had been seen by a psychiatric colleague with a history of a weight loss of around 10lbs, which made her feel nauseated and concerned. She had some extra stress having recently started to study 'A' levels with the hope of going on to university. There were problems at home where she did not get on well with her mother and was frightened of father's rages. She had virtually no personal relationships and her only boyfriend was someone she had a drink with about once a month. Assessment had shown no evidence for true anorexia nervosa, nor a clinical depression, although she was clearly unhappy. A group was thought to be helpful for 'generalised relationship difficulties'. She described her own problems as (a) not liking self – fighting self; (b) inability to make relationships; (c) eating problems; (d) lack of self-confidence; and (e) sleeping problems. In addition, Wendy informed us at the point of assessment that she was going to have to miss a certain number of group sessions because of a pre-arranged trip abroad. With some reluctance, we agreed to this.

2 Diane: Diane was a thirty-three-year-old married woman who had previously been treated for periodic panic attacks, sleep disturbance, occasional thoughts of overdose, a general feeling of low self-esteem characterised by poor self-confidence and lack of assertion. In addition she had an overriding feeling of being not good enough for her husband and feeling insignificant in the relationship. She had received medication but this had not helped very much. She described her problems as (a) depression; (b) anxiety; (c) low self-esteem and persecution feelings; (d) feeling that she can't cope/self consciousness; (e) feeling that everyone else is talented and herself not; (f) fear of losing husband. Although keen to attend the group, she had a long distance to travel which meant that she might occasionally be late arriving.

3 Marge: Marge was twenty-eight, and was having therapy with an individual counsellor before being referred. Unfortunately she decided

after the initial tests, and just before the first session, not to join the group.

4 Wilhelmina: Wilhelmina was a married lady in her early forties originally referred to G.D. for investigation of unremitting back pain for which a myriad of other agencies had failed to account. Although clearly desperate for help, she found psychological explanations very difficult to accept and work with despite being intelligent and well-read. Individual work with G.D. prior to referral to the group had suggested some marital problems and difficulties in coping with two teenage children, as well as an almost total void of personal activities. Individual work had proved frustrating and fruitless and referral to the group was in the hope that a variety of evidence might be more persuasive than the one viewpoint of a single therapist in encouraging her to review the psychological issues. Her own assessment of her problems was of (a) depression because of pain; (b) panic about pain (lack of control); (c) pain itself; (d) loneliness; (e) social problems (mixing with others); (f) problems with daughter – no patience; (g) feelings of rejection when husband sustains arguments; (h) worry about loss of parent.

5 Ethel: Ethel was an attractive woman in her mid to late thirties. She had been an inpatient with depression and suicidal threats, but had also had symptoms of panic, anxiety and obsessionality. While in hospital she seemed to make a rapid recovery becoming the life and soul of the unit, as well as being assertive and demanding. By contrast, approach of discharge would inevitably bring on more symptoms, and return home, a deluge. Despite this pattern, she resolutely denied any difficulties at home as did her husband. She saw herself as being 'mentally ill' – a label she fought to retain. Referral to the group was in the hope that she might be able to examine why she needed this label so badly, and thus give herself some room to consider alternatives. Her list of problems included (a) no confidence; (b) anxiety; (c) feelings about being different from others; (d) inability to relax; (e) inability to control feelings of being 'mental'; (f) inability to express feelings; (g) feels not being appreciated by others; (h) anxious when alone.

6 Richard: Richard was a previous individual therapy client of S.L. who had recently been re-referred. A young man (thirties) he had had a number of psychiatric referrals including possibly psychotic depression, and suicidal attempts. He had had a difficult childhood and there remained large problems in both intra-family relationships and general relationships, especially with women. He was very artistic with a volatile temperament, very direct and assertive. His problems he defined as (a) lack of self-confidence; (b) perfectionism; (c) fear of losing self-control; (d) feelings of aloneness/isolation; (e) relations with family; (f) frustrations about career and resentment against family; (g) damage through relationship in the past; (h) difficulty about relating to other people (especially men); (i) problems in writing.

7 Roger was a man in his early thirties who presented himself as a 'man of the world', cocksure and assertive. He also was extremely depressed with problems relating to his marriage and to his view of life. He had been adopted shortly after birth and had never traced his biological parents. In assessing him, it was clear that he was both tempted by the idea of some emotional help and also very unsure of the risk he must take. We wrote after the assessment: 'Both . . . feel that it will be difficult to work with Roger but that it is worth the attempt.'

8 Holly: Holly was twenty-three and worked in the health service. She was referred complaining of lack of confidence, insecurity and worrying about what people thought of her, especially at work. The psychiatrist who referred her thought she was 'rather immature, intelligent . . . climbed out of the family social class, feels very belligerent about her mother . . . supports feminism but at the same time would like the security of marriage. I would describe her as having a rather late adolescent crisis.' We found her a warm and pleasant person, very confused about her life and relationships and very isolated. She had become depressed and had taken an overdose largely because she couldn't think of anything else to do. She was very keen to join the group and listed her problems as (a) depression; (b) suicidal tendencies; (c) insecurity; (d) anxiety about guilt; (e) perfectionism in job.

The action

In the presentation which follows a number of points need to be made clear. With pre-group anticipations and post-group analyses from both facilitators, tape recordings of every group, and comments from our supervisor, the amount of material to draw upon is enormous. In order to try to present some consistency, we have made an arbitrary decision only to use our own anticipations and analyses. These are often quoted verbatim, and the authorship is signified by initials at the beginning of the quote. Second, we have chosen not to present the material provided by the participants directly: for example the self-characterisations or repertory grids. Our intention is to try to provide a view of the process of a PCT group, rather than the outcome or change in specific individual members. Further work remains to be done on the outcome material.

Session one

G.D. 'Predictions: that there would be initial awkwardness at getting to know people but that this would improve. Most people would be prepared to talk (except Wilhelmina). There would be some discussion about the taping but they would agree. Plans: Introducing game (name for yourself e.g. garrulous Gavin). Introduction of ground rules by Sue. Introduction of taping. Start of interaction on backgrounds. Bakan introspection on self-characterisations. Homework on results of introspection.'

This first session proved to us immediately that we were not going to predict accurately all of the time! Although we proceeded as planned, the session felt awful. To add to our uncertainty, Diane arrived very late. G.D. 'Awful session. We didn't predict that seven people with relationship problems would be unable to deal with social problems of the first meeting! Worst first session of a group ever.' S.L. 'I was a little angry with Gavin because he talked too much and was also anxious. I left the group feeling perturbed and somewhat ashamed of my inability to handle the group effectively. But I somehow felt that the group would all attend next week.' At the time, that seemed very optimistic. Although we had explained the rules, and attempted to encourage an initial discussion of all our expectations of the group, we felt inadequate and rejected. G.D.'s only accurate prediction was of being 'garrulous Gavin'. With hindsight, both of us were working outside our usual range of convenience; G.D. with groups, and S.L. with PCT. One incident only had allowed us to begin exploring constructs. G.D. 'Roger offered Holly a cigarette but she refused. Later looked at incident. Holly had none to offer back: would have felt guilty accepting. Roger just felt snubbed. Ethel wondered why he hadn't offered them around. Tried to use the situation to explore predictions and experiments. Fell on stony ground.'

Session two

At the end of the first session, Ethel had offered to bring tea and make it at the beginning of this one. Although we weren't sure that it wouldn't take up time or avoid other issues, the first session had felt so awful we had agreed. S.L. 'All the group were present. The atmosphere was immediately more friendly as we shared a cup of tea . . . We started by playing the cushion game, which included all the group commenting on the appearance of others and their feelings concerned with last week. This allowed some exploration of feelings such as anxiety and anger. The group said they were sorry for us after last week.' We then divided the group into pairs, asking them to describe an aspect or incident of their life to the other – the aim being to subsume the other's construct system. Individuals then role played what they had heard to the whole group. G.D. 'All mentioned current problems with a lot of self-disclosure (method clearly reduced threat very considerably). Roger talked of first marriage and current girlfriend (unmarried mum); Wilhelmina talked of pains and frustration at not being believed; Wendy and Holly were opposites – Wendy wants to be outgoing and alive and acts the opposite, Holly vice versa (Wendy really blossomed during this); Diane talked of second marriage and jealousy of husband; Ethel couldn't relay much of Richard (which made him cross but he said so at the end). Ethel's story was of breakdowns and whether she was going mad. In the discussion, much agreement that facts were reported but the emotions weren't (especially Wilhelmina's desperation, Roger's sadness and Richard's intensity). Used this to suggest group's function. Opportunity to evaluate what one thinks one has said against what people hear (Roger's cigarette incident came up again).' This all seemed much more hopeful and G.D. felt PCT was proving a useful model! S.L. (with commendable caution) 'The group ended with optimism and some sense of determination. I was anxious that members may have revealed too much too soon.' Just before the session ended, Wendy, as pre-arranged, told the group that she had to go abroad for a month. More positively, we set Wilhelmina some homework to try out at home and let the group know how she fared next week. The group had enabled her to loosen her construing of her husband's behaviour, and then tighten on an alternative stratagem for dealing with it.

Session three

G.D. predicted Wilhelmina would not have done the homework; S.L. that she would have! S.L. 'We planned to find out about Wilhelmina's homework and then to spend time with Holly and her reported distress. Lastly we would give the resistance to change grids and develop some of the homework from that.' In the event Wilhelmina had done her homework but had concluded it had been a failure. Ethel sympathised that she too had to put up with a difficult husband and children. G.D. dealt with this as hostility, and encouraged her to try again over the next week and review the outcome. Holly's distress over her boyfriend was role played, initially with Roger and Holly, and then with Wendy (as boyfriend) and S.L. as Holly. Used this discussion to raise issues of dependency, and members' constructs of it. The group ended with Richard expressing considerable discomfort at being in the group. In reflection on the group, G.D. wrote 'we got some role play going which seemed useful and instructive. The main problems were having to pass by Richard's discomfort until so near the end that we could not deal with it, and what I see as Ethel's hostility – determination to extort from the group validation that there is nothing she can do that she has not already tried.' S.L. added, at the end of her reflections, ' . . . there is so much going on we miss a lot using this method.'

Session four

This followed our first supervision session. Our aims were similar. G.D. 'Holly and Wilhelmina have homework to discuss, and Richard needs time. So I will introduce those three areas at the beginning, get Holly and Wilhelmina to report, and then lead into Richard's "not being a group person". I might try to get him to ladder this construct (what is the contrast pole?) and compare this with other people's construing. To some extent this will have to be played by ear to see where it leads, but if possible we would like to do a resistance to change grid (prior to either dependency grid or a rerun of the repertory grids next week).' G.D. had again predicted that Wilhelmina would not do her homework, and was again wrong. (Therapist hostility?) Again we did not get to the resistance to change grid, but a lot of risks were being taken, and all the group members had contributed and shared. G.D. 'People are doing things outside the group which was one of the intentions, and there is a very good group feeling developing. There also seems to be an amazing amount of change happening very fast – too fast?'

At this point, a number of comments can be made. First, we had moved much faster through Kelly's phases of group development than we had anticipated having easily reached the exploration of personal problems. Second, despite our avowed aim to structure the sessions and be practical (with construct elicitations, laddering, resistance to change grids and so forth), the group members were bringing such important material so quickly that we were having to devise the structure as we went along. Third, everyone was still there despite the emotional intensity, and what we construed as discomfort. It seemed that the PCT approach made the members feel less threatened and more valued, and despite the serious subjects, appeared to enjoy the sessions.

Session five

Holly arrived drunk. We attempted to get each of the group members to do a 'resistance to change' grid which either we could not explain adequately, or they could not understand, or should not be attempted in a group setting. Some useful information did come from them – Roger was surprised by his refusal to give up the construct of physical attractiveness. G.D. 'Ethel annoyed me because I could not make sense of what she was trying to say and eventually said so, and her response was sort of triumphant, "it's what I do to everybody".' S.L. 'Somebody mentioned that we might be sad that people hadn't really co-operated with the exercise, and we commented that it was an experiment which had not succeeded very well.'

Session six

Totally dominated by Roger. None of our aims or predictions came about. G.D. 'My predominating memory is of Roger's long exposé of himself, his apparent determination to say he wasn't seeking help, and his difficulty listening to other people's attempts to communicate with him. . . . He was sitting between Sue and I and yet neither of us felt we could touch him even though that was what we both felt we wanted to do. His hurt about not belonging, his adoption, his inability to see how good his adoptive parents had been, his need to compensate to others to make up for his own rejection, and the disastrous series of relationships that this has caused: all these vie in my mind for priority. And over all this was the unspoken yet hinted at dread that it was all futile, and circumstances would go on repeating themselves. . . . Somehow he needs to reconstrue his adoption, and the superordinate constructs that exist around it, but I suspect that this is very threatening to his core role constructs. Roger is who he is by virtue of being adopted, and reconstruing that event more positively challenges his view of himself and what's important to him now.'

Session seven

By this time we were faced with major issues from almost all members of the group. The plans included feedback to Roger, telling him of our own response to his outpouring of last week; dealing with Richard's attempts to structure; considering Ethel's feelings about her husband and holiday; and an attempt to draw out some of Diane's feelings about herself now, especially relating them to those of Roger's as revealed last week. Fortunately, other group members also seemed aware of the range of problems, and we managed to look at everything as intended. Richard managed to talk very frankly and very personally and seemed to learn from his surprise about his reception. G.D. had given up any idea of discussing the already completed repertory grids – there was just too much to do. Both our reports were running to more than two sides of typewritten foolscap paper, and we were wondering how to finish in sixteen sessions!

Session eight

S.L. 'We started the group by following Richard's suggestion of five minutes each to outline current feelings and indicate whether time was wanted. . . . Roger expanded on his sexual infidelities, wondering why he had done this. . . . We talked a bit more about sex and marriage. At one point Gavin discussed his own marital breakdown which appeared to surprise the group.' G.D. saw this as an opportunity to invalidate some constructs appearing that the therapists were perfect and had the solutions to everything. We were fallible too. S.L. continued 'On the whole we found this a very exhausting and emotion- ally difficult group', which seemed to sum up the whole experiment.

At this point we broke for a week as it was Easter. There was some sign that we had moved on to exploration of secondary roles within the group, but it was not really developing as predicted. An enormous amount of material had been raised, and the group was becoming much more verbal in content with less role play or physical activity. Attempts to explain the group activity in PCT terms did not seem constructive; individually, however, it was very helpful. We agreed to proceed on the basis of subsuming the individual's construct systems within the group setting, and trying to encourage loosening of tight construing, and more circumspection in the CPC cycle. However it didn't seem to us, or our supervisor, that in essence we were doing anything markedly different to any other kind of group.

Sessions nine to eleven

These were mainly consolidation, with continued discussion and explor- ation of constructs in areas already raised in the group. Various members failed to attend, and three members were absent for session eleven. A recurring problem was hostility which we attempted to explain and explore differently in each case. In one session G.D. had a long dialogue with Ethel who was repeatedly saying her husband was useless and unloving, but despite all kinds of encouragement would not explore alternatives open to her. Totally frustrated, G.D. eventually asked 'Why did you get married then?' to which immediately came the answer 'I had to'. It was clear that she had felt trapped in a loveless marriage, but when later asked directly why she did not leave, she astonished herself by instantly replying 'But I would lose my home'. No one had ever asked her directly before, and she had never realised the reason. From then on her hostility decreased dramatically and she became able to be much more constructive.

Session twelve

Everyone came. G.D. 'Somehow it felt significant – especially since Sue kept saying at the beginning that there were *always* drop-outs.' It was becoming evident that some of the movement at the beginning of the group was not being maintained. S.L. 'I . . . felt that there is a lot of pain here which we are going to have to accept, given that the group is going to terminate fairly soon.' Wilhelmina was very upset with the return of pain and husband problems and Wendy looked dreadful. The tone of the group was very emotional.

Session thirteen

S.L. 'We aim to calm the group down a bit, following the emotional exposure of last week. In the meantime we want to direct the group attentions more to problem solving work, especially given the impending break for four weeks.' With holidays and other commit- ments, one of us would be away and neither of us felt we wanted to run the group on our own! We put this to the members who fortunately supported us and agreed to the break. Our attempts to calm down and be practical seemed successful. Partly this was done by asking for practical examples of change outside the group, and partly by the use of humour. S.L. 'The session ended with everybody in quite cheerful mood and Gavin and I definitely feeling that we are getting somewhere with this group. Everybody seems to be progressing, even Wilhelmina.'

Session fourteen and fifteen

These were before and after the four-week break. Session fourteen was a wind-down before the break, and session fifteen a recapitulation of the many events that had occurred to all in the intervening period. We were all conscious of the proximity to the end of the group, and the emphasis remained on the achievement of individual members and the possibilities for further experiments after the group had finished. We made clear that anyone who felt they needed further help after the group was over could approach one of us to discuss what might be available. We also noticed that most of the group arranged to meet together afterwards for a drink, and it transpired this had been happening for some time. We both felt miffed at not being invited!

Session sixteen

Final session and minor disaster – G.D. had been involved in an accident and could not come. As a result it rather fizzled out with no one wanting to delve deeply into any subject including G.D.'s absence. Only Wendy asked for further help at the end, while Wilhelmina only wanted an assurance that she could contact G.D. should the need arise.

Discussion

There are a number of questions to which answers are required. Does PCT provide a group methodology? Does PCT provide an individual methodology in a group setting? Did Kelly's description of group process accord with our experience? How did the functioning of the group differ from our expectations and why? What went wrong, if anything? Finally, was the experiment successful in validating or invalidating any of the constructs tested, and should it be repeated?

In our view, based upon this one experience, PCT does not specifically provide a group methodology. This ties in with the second question in that it does seem to provide an individual methodology in a group setting. We found it practical and helpful to use PCT in understanding and working with the individual problems, and the group provided a useful social context in which reconstruing and experiment could take place. When looking at the group process, however, PCT seemed less helpful than more traditional approaches, and hard though we tried to remain within our construction of a PCT model, both we and our supervisor repeatedly saw in our group processes common to most small psychotherapy groups. While PCT may be easier/more acceptable to the clients in the group, its use does not seem to change how the group as a whole works. This begs a discussion about the relation of social psychology to PCT which is a matter of some debate, although Jahoda (1985) for one states definitely that social issues are outside the range of convenience of PCT.

Following on from these points is the question of whether Kelly's description of group process accords with our experience. This is more difficult to answer categorically. Certainly the first few sessions appeared to move through the first four phases as he described. But they did not feel like separate stages, and the speed with which the group passed through them suggests they are in themselves less important than his writing accords. The exploration of secondary roles and then secondary enterprises was also less well defined than anticipated although this may have reflected our own lack of experience in the group endeavour. But on the basis of this group, these phases also seem inadequate to explain the processes occurring and further elaboration and/or experimentation is called for.

There is no doubt that the group did not function as we had anticipated. All the members who started remained, and there was a strong sense of group cohesion despite much hostility within it. An enormous amount of very personal and emotive material was presented very quickly which undermined our plans at group assessment procedures and enactment of problem areas. Although some structured elicitation and laddering of constructs took place throughout the sessions, this tended latterly not to lead to the enactments envisaged in Kelly's own proposals. This may, in part, have been due to the relatively short fixed length of the group, and a longer more open-ended group may have been able to proceed more slowly and with a greater sense of control by the facilitators. Conversely, had the time span been longer or open-ended, at least two of the members might well have left.

The introduction of grid techniques into the group was not successful. The use of the resistance to change grid (Fransella and Bannister, 1977) was misjudged and felt destructive rather than elaborative. Our intention to use the previously obtained repertory grids foundered due to the excessive amount of material provided, and the lack of any obvious introduction or need for them. While with individual therapy a structured assessment period is fairly easily defined and explained, within a group the same type of process feels constricting and authoritarian. One further point to note was that our construction that proceeding with a PCT philosophy would give the group members an active say in how the group developed and what it did, meant that our control of the structure was less than we had anticipated. Despite careful plans we often found ourselves being led rather than leading! But although this was not our intention, it did not feel therapeutically incorrect: more that the results of the experiment were different but not less appropriate.

Did the experiment validate or invalidate our construing? Running the group was certainly worthwhile both therapeutically and as a PCT experiment. Although matters did not develop as anticipated, it did provide valuable information about both the benefits and pitfalls of PCT in a group setting. While it would be too generous to say that it validated *all* our hypotheses about the use of PCT in a small group setting, it did validate enough to make a follow-up group by ourselves or others a reasonable and potentially elaborative exercise.

Postscript

An informal review of the participants one year after the end of the group revealed that five out of the seven had had no further contact with the psychiatric service (Ethel, Wilhemina, Roger, Diane and Holly). Ethel and Wilhelmina verbally, and Holly by letter had thanked us for the group and said that they had enjoyed it in parts and that it had helped. Wendy had continued in individual therapy with a new therapist, and a chance meeting with G.D. indicated that she felt she had received some benefit although had needed much more help subsequently. Richard had not enjoyed the group, did not feel he had received any benefit, did not like the methodology, and had been re-referred to the psychiatric service.

Acknowledgments

Our thanks are due to David Kellett for his assistance with the research parts of the experiment, and to David Smail for his support, encouragement and invaluable comments throughout the group.

Glossary

(All items in quotations are from Kelly, 1955)

ABC technique was developed by Tschudi (1977) in order to look at the implications of desired change (see p. 10).

Aggressiveness 'is the active elaboration of one's perceptual field.' This is the way we broaden our horizons and find out about things. It is a positive activity despite its linguistic links with 'aggression', and indeed some aggression can be seen as aggressiveness!

Anxiety 'is the awareness that the events with which one is confronted lie outside the range of convenience of one's construct system.' No particular change in one's system is anticipated: it is simply that no constructs currently are available to predict what is going to happen.

Constellatory constructs. These are constructs that when used also bring into action a group of other constructs willy nilly. If one construct applies, then they all apply.

Constriction 'occurs when a person narrows his perceptual field in order to minimize apparent incompatibilities.' Effectively, he chooses to close his eyes to a group of people, events or things in order to avoid having to face up to a dilemma which recognition of their existence would cause.

Constructs are the fundamental tools with which a person discriminates between what he perceives (elements) in order to make sense of his world by being able to predict what will happen next time he is presented with the same type of perception. Each construct is bipolar, i.e. one pole is defined by being contrasted with the other. The two poles are known as the 'emergent' pole, which is the one presented first in the circumstances, and the other is the 'contrast' pole for obvious reasons.

CPC cycle 'is a sequence of construction which involves in succession, circumspection, pre-emption and control, and leads to a choice precipitating the person into a particular situation.' This is really about how people go about making choices which lead to action: initially they consider all the options (circumspection), then give themselves one pair of alternatives (pre-emption), from which they then decide to act upon one of these (control). For a broad discussion, see Dunnett (1985) or Boxer (1982).

Creativity Cycle. 'The Creativity Cycle is one which starts with loosened construction and terminates with tightened and validated construction.' It is a continuous process, allowing the person to develop new ways of dealing with events using their current construct system, and incorporating these new uses of constructs once experiments based on them have been validated.

Credulous approach. This is taking the attitude that whatever your client or patient tells you is true within their construct system. The fact that they are telling you something means that it has some meaning for them, even though it may not be clear to you, or may be different from the meaning you would normally ascribe to such a statement.

Dilation 'occurs when a person broadens his perceptual field in order to re-organise it on a more comprehensive level. It does not, in itself, include the comprehensive reconstruction of those elements.' A person in the business of being prepared to consider a greater range of elements (people, activities, whatever) than hitherto in order to use his system more comprehensively (c.f. *constriction*).

Enactment is the process of encouraging a person to act out a particular role or event in order to promote reconstruction and change (see chapter 1).

Fixed role therapy is a specific type of enactment suggested by Kelly and described in chapter 1.

Grids (including Implications, Resistance to Change, Situational Resources). A system originally described by Kelly as the Role Construct Repertory Grid, and now widely developed in an array of different contexts and formats. In its simplest form it is a method of examining how a collection of constructs are used individually in relation to a specific group of elements. The examination can be mathematically and statistically analysed to give a range of information for therapeutic, research or comparison purposes. Further information can be obtained from Fransella and Bannister (1977), Beail (1985) and Stewart and Stewart (1981) amongst many others.

Guilt 'is the awareness of dislodgement of the self from one's core role structure', i.e. you act in a way which is not the way you would normally expect yourself to act.

Hostility 'is the continued effort to extort validational evidence in favour of a type of social prediction which has already been recognised as a failure.' Here, a person tries to force the people round about, or the circumstances to fit in with a view of the circumstances despite already having received ample evidence that the view is wrong. The view held is often seen to be too important to change, and so the person tries to alter the evidence instead.

Laddering is a process of exploring the hierarchy of part of a construct system starting from a relatively concrete construct (subordinate) to a relatively abstract construct (superordinate) one (c.f. pyramiding, Landfield, 1971).

Loose constructs 'A loose construct is one which leads to varying predictions but retains its identity' (c.f. tight constructs).

Loosening is the process in which a person is encouraged, using their current constructs, to make different or alternative predictions based upon them.

Pyramiding is a process of exploring the hierarchy of part of a construct system starting from a relatively abstract (superordinate) construct to a relatively concrete (subordinate) one (c.f. laddering, Hinkle, 1965).

Reflexivity is the process of using the theory to understand the processes going on in both client and therapist.

Role-relationship is the process that occurs when one person begins the attempt to subsume the construct system of another person. He tries to see the world through the other person's eyes, and so develops a relationship.

Self-characterisation is a technique to help client and therapist understand the client better by encouraging a written statement of the client's view of himself (see chapter 1).

Slot-movement (slot-rattling). The process that occurs when a person who has behaved in a way described by one pole of a construct changes and starts behaving in the way described by the contrast pole of the same construct. No new construing occurs despite apparent major change in the person.

Submergence. 'The submerged pole of a construct is one which is less available for application to events.' Sometimes, a person will only effectively use one pole of a construct, the contrast being effectively forgotten about.

Subsume. This is the process by which one person attempts to look at the construct system of another, without losing his own. A therapist subsumes his client's system in order to understand it both in terms of the client's use and view of the world, and in terms of what may be a problem within his professional understanding of the processes of Personal Construct Psychology.

Suspension. 'A suspended element is one which is omitted from the context of a construct as a result of revision of the person's construct system.' As the person's system is revised, not only are new constructs created to deal with events, but old ones may be altered thus reducing the number or range of elements to which they can be applied. Such an element is suspended in relation to a particular construct.

Threat 'is the awareness of an imminent comprehensive change in one's core structures.' Something is happening which is going to force you to review the important *central* constructs you have about yourself, and you do not relish the prospect!

Tight constructs. A tight construct is one which leads to unvarying predictions.

Tightening is the process in which a person is encouraged, using their current constructs, to make defined predictions upon which experiments can be based.

Bibliography

Adams-Webber, J. (1981), 'Fixed role therapy', in Corsini, R. J. (ed.), *Handbook of Innovative Psychotherapies*, New York, Wiley.

Alexander, P. C. (1987), 'The therapeutic implications of family cognitions', *Journal of Cognitive Psychotherapy*, in press.

Balint, M. (1977), *The Doctor, his Patient and the Illness*, London, Pitman Medical.

Bannister, D. (1960), 'Conceptual structure in thought disordered schizophrenics', *Journal of Mental Science*, 106, pp. 1230–49.

Bannister, D. (1962), 'The nature and measurement of schizophrenic thought disorder', *Journal of Mental Science*, 108, pp. 825–42.

Bannister, D. (1963), 'The genesis of schizophrenic thought disorder: a serial invalidation hypothesis', *British Journal of Psychiatry*, 109, pp. 680–6.

Bannister, D. (1977), 'The logic of passion', in Bannister, D. (ed.), *New Perspectives in Personal Construct Theory*, London and New York, Academic Press.

Bannister, D. (1985), 'The patient's point of view', in Bannister, D. (ed.), *Issues and Approaches in Personal Construct Theory*, London and New York, Academic Press.

Bannister, D. and Agnew, J. (1977), 'The child's construing of self', in Landfield, A. W. (ed.), *Nebraska Symposium on Motivation*, Lincoln, University of Nebraska Press.

Bannister, D. and Fransella, F. (1966), 'A grid test of schizophrenic thought disorder', *British Journal of Social and Clinical Psychology*, 5, pp. 95–102.

Bannister, D. and Fransella, F. (1971), *Inquiring Man*, London, Penguin Education.

Bannister, D., Adams-Webber, J. R., Penn, W. I., and Radley, A. R (1975), 'Reversing the process of thought disorder: a serial invalidation experiment', *British Journal of Social and Clinical Psychology*, 14, pp. 169–80.

Barclay, P. (1982), *Social Workers and Their Tasks*, NISW.

Bateson, G. (1972), *Steps to an Ecology of Mind*, New York, Ballantine Books.

Beail, N. (ed.) (1985), *Repertory Grid Technique and Personal Constructs*, London, Croom Helm.

Bergin, A. E. and Lambert, M. J. (1978), 'The evaluation of therapeutic outcomes', in Garfield, S. L. and Bergin, A. E. (eds), *Handbook of Psychotherapy and Behaviour Change: An Empirical Analysis*, New York, Wiley.

Bexley Hospital Psychology Department (1980), 'The evolution of democracy in an NHS psychology department: Bexley Hospital Psychology Department', *Newsletter of the British Psychological Society Division of Clinical Psychology*, 28, pp. 24–30.

Boberg, E. (ed.) (1981), *Maintenance of Fluency*, Amsterdam, Elsevier.

Boxer, P. J. (1982), 'The flow of choice: the choice corollary', in Mancuso, J. C. and Adams-Webber, J. R. (eds), *The Construing Person*, New York, Praeger.

Braten, S. (1986), 'The third position: beyond artificial and autopoietic reduction', in Geyer, F. and van der Zouwen, J. (eds), *Sociocybernetic Paradoxes*, London, Sage Publications.

British Association of Social Workers (1975), *Code of Ethics*.

Brumfitt, S. M. (1984), 'A personal construct investigation into loss of communicative ability in the aphasic person', M Phil Dissertation, University of Sheffield.

Brumfitt, S. M. and Clarke, P. (1983), 'An application of psychotherapeutic techniques to the management of aphasia', in Code, C. and Muller, D. J. (eds), *Aphasia Therapy*, London, Edward Arnold.

Button, E. J. (1983), 'Personal construct theory and psychological well-being', *British Journal of Medical Psychology*, 56, pp. 313–21.

Button, E. J. (ed.) (1985), *Personal Construct Theory and Mental Health*, London, Croom Helm.

Caine, T. M., Foulds, G. A. and Hope, K. (1967), *The Manual of the Hostility and Direction of Hostility Questionnaire (HDHQ)*, London, University of London Press.

Caine, T. M., Wijesinghe, O.B.A. and Winter, D. A. (1981), *Personal Styles in Neurosis: Implications for Small Group Psychotherapy and Behaviour Therapy*, London, Routledge & Kegan Paul.

Cullen, C. (1985), 'Chairperson's letter', *Newsletter of the British Psychological Society Division of Clinical Psychology*, 49, pp. 4–5.

Cutting, J. (1985), *The Psychology of Schizophrenia*, Edinburgh, Churchill Livingstone.

Dalton, P. (1986), 'A personal construct approach to therapy with children', in Edwards, G. (ed.), *Current Issues in Clinical Psychology*, vol. 4, London and New York, Plenum Press.

Dalton, P. (1987), 'Some developments in individual personal construct therapy with adults who stutter', in Levy, C. (ed.), *Stuttering Therapies: Practical Approaches*, London, Croom Helm.

De Bono, E. (1967), *The Use of Lateral Thinking*, Harmondsworth, Penguin Books.

Dell, P. (1986), 'Why do we still call them "paradoxes"?', *Family Process*, vol. 25, no. 2, p. 223–34.

Dunnett, G. (1981), 'Personal construct theory and psychiatry: a consumer approach?', paper delivered to the 4th International Congress on Personal Construct Psychology, Canada.

Dunnett, G. (1982), 'What PCP can offer psychiatry', *Constructs*, vol. 1, no. 5.

Dunnett, G. (1985), 'Construing control in theory and therapy', in Bannister, D. (ed.), *Issues and Approaches in Personal Construct Theory*, London and New York, Academic Press.

Dunnett, G. (1987), 'Phobias: a journey beyond neurosis', in Fransella, F. and Thomas, L. (eds), *Experimenting with Personal Construct Psychology*, London, Routledge & Kegan Paul.

Epting, F. R. (1984), *Personal Construct Counseling and Psychotherapy*, New York, Wiley.

Fransella, F. (1972), *Personal Change and Reconstruction*, London and New York, Academic Press.

Fransella, F. (1985), 'Individual psychotherapy', in Button, E. (ed.), *Personal Construct Theory and Mental Health*, London, Croom Helm.

Fransella, F. and Bannister, D. (1977), *A Manual for Repertory Grid Technique*, London, Academic Press.

Green, D. (1986), 'Impact on the self: head injury in adolescence', *Constructs*, 4, no. 1.

Higginbotham, P. G. and Bannister, D. (1983), *The GAB computer programme for the analysis of repertory grid data*, Second edition.

Hinkle, D. (1965), *The Change of Personal Constructs from the View Point of a Theory of Construct Implications*, unpublished PhD Thesis, Ohio State University.

Hinkle, D. (1970), 'The game of personal constructs', in Bannister, D. (ed.), *Perspectives in Personal Construct Theory*, London and New York, Academic Press.

Hollis, F. (1966), *Casework: a psycho-social therapy*, New York, Random House.

Jahoda, M. (1985), 'The range of convenience of personal construct psychology', invited address to the sixth International Congress on Personal Construct Psychology, Cambridge, England.

Jourard, S. M. (1971), *The Transparent Self*, New York and London, Van Nostrand Company.

Karst, T. O. (1980), 'The relationship between personal construct theory and psychotherapeutic techniques', in Landfield, A. W. and Leitner, L. M. (eds), *Personal Construct Psychology: Psychotherapy and Personality*, New York, Wiley.

Kazdin, A. E. (1986), 'The evaluation of psychotherapy: research design and methodology', in Garfield, S. L. and Bergin, A. E. (eds), *Handbook of Psychotherapy and Behaviour Change*, New York, Wiley.

Kelly, G. A. (1955), *The Psychology of Personal Constructs*, vols 1 and 2, New York, Norton.

Kelly, G. A. (1960), 'Epilogue: Don Juan', in Maher, B. (ed.), *Clinical Psychology and Personality*, New York, Krieger.

Kelly, G. A. (1963), 'The autobiography of a theory', in Maher, B. (ed.), *Clinical Psychology and Personality*, New York, Krieger.

Kelly, G. A. (1966/1980), 'A psychology of the optimal man', in Landfield, A. W. and Leitner, L. M. (eds), *Personal Construct Psychology: Psychotherapy and Personality*, New York, Wiley.

Kelly, G. A. (1969a), 'Man's construction of his alternatives', in Maher, B. (ed.), *Clinical Psychology and Personality: The Selected Writings of George Kelly*, New York, Wiley.

Kelly, G. A. (1969b), 'Sin and psychotherapy', in Maher, B. (ed.), *Clinical Psychology and Personality: The Selected Writings of George Kelly*, New York, Wiley.

Kelly, G. A. (1970a), 'Behaviour is an experiment', in Bannister, D. (ed.), *Perspectives in Personal Construct Theory*, London and New York, Academic Press.

Kelly, G. A. (1970b), 'A brief introduction to personal construct theory', in

Bannister, D. (ed.) *Perspectives in Personal Construct Theory*, London and New York, Academic Press.

Kelly, G. A. (1973), 'Fixed role therapy', in Jurjevich, R. M. (ed.), *Direct Psychotherapy*, Coral Gables, University of Miami Press.

Kenny, V. (1985a), 'An introduction to the ideas of Humberto Maturana: Life, the Multiverse and Everything', invited paper presented at the Instituto de Psicologia, Rome, Università Cattolica del Sacro Cuore.

Kenny, V. (1985b), 'Autopoiesis and alternativism in psychotherapy: fluctuations and reconstructions', paper presented at the sixth International Congress on Personal Construct Psychology, Cambridge, England.

Kenny, V. (1987), 'Family somatics: a personal construct approach to cancer'. In Neimeyer, R. and Neimeyer, G. (eds), *Casebook in Personal Construct Therapy*, New York, Springer.

Koch, H. (1985), 'Group psychotherapy', in Button, E. (ed.) *Personal Construct Theory and Mental Health*, Kent, Croom Helm.

Landfield, A. W. (1971), *Personal Construct Systems in Psychotherapy*, Chicago, Rand McNally.

Landfield, A. W. (1980), 'Personal construct psychotherapy: a personal construction', in Landfield, A. W. and Leitner, L. M. (eds), *Personal Construct Psychology: Psychotherapy and Personality*, New York, Wiley.

Landfield, A. W. and Epting, F. R. (1986), *Personal Construct Psychology: Clinical and Personality Assessment*, New York, Human Sciences.

Lawlor, M. and Cochran, L. (1981), 'Does invalidation produce loose construing?' *British Journal of Medical Psychology*, 54, pp. 41–50.

Lidz, T. (1968), 'The family, language and the transmission of schizophrenia', in Rosenthal, D. and Kety, S. S. (eds), *The Transmission of Schizophrenia*, Oxford, Pergamon.

Llewelyn, S. and Dunnett, G. (1987), 'The use of personal construct theory in groups', in Neimeyer, R. & Neimeyer, G. (eds), *A Casebook in Personal Construct Therapy*, New York, Springer.

Luria, A. R. (1975), *The Man with a Shattered World*, Harmondsworth, Penguin Education.

Maher, B. (ed.) (1969), *Clinical Psychology and Personality: the Selected Papers of George Kelly*, New York and London, Wiley.

Mair, J. M. M. (1970), 'Psychologists are human too', in Bannister, D. (ed.), *Perspectives in Personal Construct Theory*, London and New York, Academic Press.

Mair, J. M. M. (1977), 'The community of self', in Bannister, D. (ed.), *New Perspectives in Personal Construct Theory*, London and New York, Academic Press.

Mair, J. M. M. (1979), 'The personal venture', in Stringer, P. and Bannister, D. (eds), *Constructs of Sociality and Individuality*, London and New York, Academic Press.

Mair, J. M. M. (1980), 'Feeling and knowing', in Salmon, P. (ed.), *Coming to Know*, London, Routledge & Kegan Paul.

Mair, J. M. M. (1985), 'The long quest to know', in Epting, F. and Landfield, A. W. (eds), *Anticipating Personal Construct Psychology*, Nebraska, University of Nebraska Press.

Malan, D. H. (1983), 'The outcome problem in psychotherapy research: a historical review', *Archives of General Psychiatry*, 29, pp. 719–29.

Mancuso, J. C. (1977), 'Current motivational models in the elaboration of personal construct theory', in Landfield, A. W. (ed.), *Nebraska Symposium on Motivation*, University of Nebraska Press.

Marks, I. M. and Mathews, A. M. (1979), 'Brief standard self-rating for phobic patients', *Behaviour Research and Therapy*, 17, 3, pp. 263–6.

Maturana, H. R. (1985), *The Maturana Dialogues*, a two-day conference on 'Man and Mind: Prowess and Perception' held at the City University, London.

Maturana, H. R. (1986), *Conversations with Humberto Maturana: Autopoiesis, Cognition and Change*, a three-day congress held at Milltown Park Institute, Dublin.

Maturana, H. R. and Guiloff, G. D. (1980), 'The quest for the intelligence of intelligence', *J. Social Biol. Struct.*, vol. 3, pp. 135–48.

Maturana, H. R. and Varela, F. (1980), *Autopoiesis and Cognition*, Boston, Reidel.

Medawar, P. (1984), *Pluto's Republic*, London, Oxford University Press.

Mowrer, O. H. (1950), *Learning Theory and Personality Dynamics*, New York, Ronald Press.

Neimeyer, R. A. (1980), 'George Kelly as therapist: a review of his tapes', in Landfield, A. W. and Leitner, L. M. (eds), *Personal Construct Psychology: Psychotherapy and Personality*, New York, Wiley.

Neimeyer, R. A. (1981), 'The structure and meaningfulness of tacit construing', in Bonarius, H., Holland, R. and Rosenberg, S. (eds), *Personal Construct Psychology: recent advances in theory and practice*, London, Macmillan.

Neimeyer, R. A. (1985a), 'Personal constructs in clinical practice', in Kendall, P. C. (ed.), *Advances in Cognitive-Behavioural Research and Therapy*, vol. IV, New York, Academic Press.

Neimeyer, R. A. (1985b), *The Development of Personal Construct Psychology*, University of Nebraska Press, Lincoln.

Neimeyer, R. A. (1986), 'Personal construct therapy', in Dryden, W. and Golden, W. (eds), *Cognitive Behavioural Approaches to Psychotherapy*, London, Harper & Row.

Neimeyer, R. A. (1987a), 'An orientation to personal construct therapy', in Neimeyer, R. A. and Neimeyer, G. J. (eds), *A Casebook in Personal Construct Therapy*, New York, Springer.

Neimeyer, R. A. (1987b), 'Core role reconstruction in personal construct therapy', in Neimeyer, R. A. and Neimeyer, G. J. (eds), *A Casebook in Personal Construct Therapy*, New York, Springer.

Neimeyer, G. J. and Neimeyer, R. A. (1981), 'Personal construct perspectives on cognitive assessment', in Merluzzi, T., Glass, C. and Genest, M. (eds.), *Cognitive Assessment*, Guildford, New York.

Neimeyer, G. J. and Hudson, J. E. (1985), 'Couples' constructs: personal systems in marital satisfaction', in Bannister, D. (ed.), *Issues and Approaches in Personal Construct Theory*, New York, Academic Press.

Pask, G. (1975), *Conversation, Cognition and Learning*, Amsterdam and New York, Elsevier.

Pask, G. (1976), *Conversation Theory: Applications in Education and Epistemology*, Amsterdam and New York, Elsevier.

Pask, G. (1981), 'Organisational closure of potentially conscious systems', in Zeleny, M. (ed.), *Autopoiesis: a Theory of Living Organization*, Holland and New York, Elsevier.

Pereira Gray, D. J. (1982), *Training for General Practice*, Plymouth, Macdonald & Evans.

Polyani, M. (1973), *Personal Knowledge*, London, Routledge & Kegan Paul.

Procter, H. G. (1981), 'Family construct psychology: an approach to understanding and treating families', in Walrond-Skinner, S. (ed.), *Developments in Family Therapy: Theories and Applications since 1948*, London, Routledge & Kegan Paul.

Procter, H. G. (1985), 'A construct approach to family therapy and systems intervention', in Button, E. (ed.), *Personal Construct Psychology and Mental Health*, London, Croom Helm.

Procter, H. G. (1987), 'Change in the family construct system: the therapy of a mute and withdrawn schizophrenic man', in Neimeyer, R. A. and Neimeyer, G. J. (eds), *A Casebook in Personal Construct Therapy*, New York, Springer.

Radley, A. R. (1974), 'Schizophrenic thought disorder and the nature of personal constructs', *British Journal of Social and Clinical Psychology*, 13, pp. 315–28.

Radley, A. R. (1977), 'Living on the horizon', in Bannister, D. (ed.), *New Perspectives in Personal Construct Theory*, London and New York, Academic Press.

Ravenette, A. T. (1977), 'Personal construct theory: an approach to the psychological investigation of children and young people', in Bannister, D. (ed.), *New Perspectives in Personal Construct Theory*, London and New York, Academic Press.

Ravenette, A. T. (1980), 'The exploration of consciousness – personal construct intervention with children', in Landfield, A. W. and Leitner, L. M. (eds), *Personal Construct Theory – Psychotherapy and Personality*, New York, Wiley.

Rogers, C. (1978), *On Personal Power*, London, Constable.

Rowe, D. (1971), 'Poor prognosis in a case of depression as predicted by the repertory grid', *British Journal of Psychiatry*, 118, pp. 297–300.

Rowe, D. (1978), *The Experience of Depression*, London, Wiley.

Rowe, D. (1983), *Depression: The Way Out of Your Prison*, London, Routledge & Kegan Paul.

Ryle, A. (1975), *Frames and Cages: The Repertory Grid Approach to Human Understanding*, London, Sussex University Press.

Sacks, O. (1986), *The Man Who Mistook His Wife for a Hat*, London, Duckworth.

Salmon, P. (1970), 'The psychology of personal growth', in Bannister, D. (ed.), *Perspectives in Personal Construct Theory*, London and New York, Academic Press.

Shotter, J. (1984), *Social Accountability and Selfhood*, Oxford, Blackwell.

Smail, D. J. (1978), *Psychotherapy: a Personal Approach*, London, Dent.

Smail, D. J. (1980), 'Learning in psychotherapy', in Salmon, P. (ed.), *Coming to Know*, London, Routledge & Kegan Paul.

Stewart, V. and Stewart, A. (1981), *Business Applications of Repertory Grid*, England, McGraw-Hill.

Sundberg, N. D., Taplin, J. R. and Tyler, L. E. (1983), *Introduction to Clinical*

Psychology: Perspectives, Issues and Contributions to Human Science, New Jersey, Prentice-Hall.

Thomas, L. and Harri-Augstein, E. S. (1983), 'The self-organised learner as personal scientist: a conversational technology for reflecting on behaviour and experience', in Adams-Webber, J. and Mancuso, J. (eds), *Applications of Personal Construct Psychology*, London, Academic Press.

Thomas, L. and Harri-Augstein, E. S. (1985), *Self-Organised Learnings: Foundations of a Conversational Science for Psychology*, London, Routledge & Kegan Paul.

Tschudi, F. (1977), 'Loaded and honest questions; a construct theory view of symptoms and therapy', in Bannister, D. (ed.), *New Perspectives on Personal Construct Theory*, London and New York, Academic Press.

Van den Bergh, O., de Boeck, P. and Claeys, W. (1985), 'Schizophrenia: what is loose in schizophrenic construing?', in Button, E. (ed.), *Personal Construct Theory and Mental Health*, London, Croom Helm.

Varela, F. J. (1979), *Principles of Biological Autonomy*, New York and Oxford, North Holland.

Viney, L. L. (1985), 'Humor as a therapeutic tool: another way to experiment with experience', in Epting, F. R. and Landfield, A. W. (eds), *Anticipating Personal Construct Psychology*, Lincoln, University of Nebraska Press.

Von Foerster, H. (1981), *Observing Systems*, California, Intersystems Publications.

Von Foerster, H. (1984), 'On constructing a reality', in Watzlawick, P. (ed.), *The Invented Reality*, New York and London, Norton.

Von Foerster, H. (1986), 'Apropos epistemologies', *Family Process*, vol. 24, pp. 517–21.

Von Glaserfeld, E. (1984), 'An introduction to radical constructivism', in Watzlawick, P. (ed.), *The Invented Reality*, New York and London, Norton.

Watts, F. N. and Sharrock, R. (1985), 'Relationships between spider constructs in phobics', *British Journal of Medical Psychology*, 58, pp. 49–54.

Watzlawick, P., Weakland, J. H. and Fisch, R. (1974), *Change; Principles of Problem Formation and Problem Resolution*, New York, Norton.

Winter, D. A. (1975), 'Some characteristics of schizophrenics and their parents', *British Journal of Social and Clinical Psychology*, 14, pp. 279–90.

Winter, D. A. (1982), 'Construct relationships, psychological disorder and therapeutic change', *British Journal of Medical Psychology*, 55, pp. 257–69.

Winter, D. A. (1983), 'Logical inconsistency in construct relationships: conflict or complexity?', *British Journal of Medical Psychology*, 56, pp. 79–87.

Winter, D. A. (1985a), 'Neurotic disorders: the curse of certainty', in Button, E. (ed.), *Personal Construct Theory and Mental Health*, London, Croom Helm.

Winter, D. A. (1985b), 'Repertory grid technique in the evaluation of therapeutic outcome', in Beail, N. (ed.), *Repertory Grid Technique and Personal Constructs: Applications in Clinical and Educational Settings*, London, Croom Helm.

Winter, D. A. (1985c), 'Personal styles, constructive alternativism, and the provision of a therapeutic service', *British Journal of Medical Psychology*, 58, pp. 129–35.

Winter, D. A. (1987), 'Personal construct psychotherapy as a radical alternative to social skills training', in Neimeyer, R. A. and Neimeyer, G. J. (eds), *A Casebook in Personal Construct Therapy*, New York, Springer.

Winter, D. A. and Gournay, K. J. M. (1987), 'Construction and constriction in agoraphobia', *British Journal of Medical Psychology*, in press.

Winter, D. A. and Trippett, C. J. (1977), 'Serial change in group psychotherapy', *British Journal of Medical Psychology*, 50, pp. 341–8.

Winter, D. A., Shivakumar, H., Brown, R., Roitt, M., Drysdale, W. J. and Jones, S. (1987), 'Explorations of a crisis intervention service', *British Journal of Psychiatry*, vol. 151, pp. 239–9.

Index